UPON THE MOUNT OF THE
CONGREGATION

UPON THE MOUNT OF THE
CONGREGATION

SAMUEL KATSARUWARE

Copyright © 2011 by Samuel Katsaruware.

Library of Congress Control Number:		2011911024
ISBN:	Hardcover	978-1-4628-9817-6
	Softcover	978-1-4628-9816-9
	Ebook	978-1-4628-9818-3

BIBLE TEXTS

All scriptures, unless otherwise stated, are quoted from the New King James Version, NKJV.

This book was printed in the United States of America.

To order additional copies of this book, contact:
Xlibris Corporation
0-800-644-6988
www.xlibrispublishing.co.uk
Orders@xlibrispublishing.co.uk
302255

CONTENTS

ACKNOWLEDGEMENTS

I salute God the Father through Jesus Christ, whose Holy Spirit made it all possible. Many thanks go to Pastor P. Motsi, whose powerful Bible based lessons triggered the idea of writing this book, and Elijah Musamba my friend and prayer partner throughout the project. I am grateful to Lloyd Taadira who read the first few chapters of the manuscript and offered useful suggestions. I would never have completed this book without the unwavering support of my wife Chipo, and children Tapuwa, Tawanda, Tanyaradzwa, Chiedza, Tatenda and Tariro. I was inwardly shocked many times by their unwavering faith that I could complete this book, even when I myself secretly felt like giving up. Finally I must thank my publisher, Xlibris, for nurturing me through the final phase of the project when I developed serious misgivings about the work.

INTRODUCTION

Do you ever wonder, when you observe the world around you, why there are so many different religions in the world? Why Christendom is so highly fragmented when all churches claim the same Christ as Saviour? Why do new Christian churches spring up daily, each departing in doctrine from the rest? Why are Christian approaches to praise and worship, baptism, the Eucharist and many other key doctrines different? Are some acceptable, and others not, before God? Why do most Christians go to Church on Sunday, yet others Saturday? Are all 'Christians' in all the different churches destined for heaven? How does God view the African traditionalist who claims to worship Him through departed ancestors? What about Christians who believe they can only reach the Most High through the Virgin Mary or the departed Saints?

When God revealed to the prophet Isaiah the reason for Lucifer's banishment from heaven, He provided the clue for answering all the questions above, and many more besides. Lucifer harbored an unholy aspiration. I am convinced that when you, dear friend, also understand what Lucifer's ambition was, you will, like me, ask yourself some hard questions, and wish for truthful answers. When we shall expose Lucifer's ambition, in chapter 2, you may agree that the devil's chief hunting ground for the souls of men is all places where people commune for worship. He waits to entrap the hearts of those responding to the natural yearning for connection to a higher power. If we have not been diligent in our search for Truth, the direct effect of Satan's ambition is to make the institutions we call our churches *potentially* the most unsafe places to be, more so because of the sense of security they impart to us.

Let the Ultimate Judge supply the statistics of candidates for heaven. In Matthew 7:13, the Lord says: "Enter by the narrow gate; for wide is the gate and broad is the way that leads to destruction, and there are many who go in by it." The theme that a minority may find eternal life runs through the Lord Jesus' entire ministry, and in Luke 13:23, a justifiably worried disciple posed the very direct question, "Lord, are there few that be saved?" The ominous reply, from He who would know was, "Strive to enter in at the narrow gate: for many I say unto you will seek to enter in, and shall not be able." Luke 13:24.

From these texts, we deduce that it is possible to live our lives fully believing in our salvation; yet while we consider ourselves worthy candidates of heaven, we may still miss eternity. The Lord reinforces this view in Luke 13:25, where he alludes to the nature of those who may not make it. "'We ate and drank in Your presence, and You taught in our streets.' But He will say, 'I tell you I do not know you, where you are from. Depart from Me, all you workers of iniquity.'" It may appear, from studying this last text as if those barred from heaven are people who hovered on the periphery of Christian life, but a study of the same sermon from the book of Matthew brings up a startling result. It becomes plain that even some who have been heavily involved in Christian activity will find the gate closed in their face. "Lord, Lord, have we not prophesied in your name? and in your name have cast out demons? And in your name done many wonderful works?" will be the pathetic plea of some deacons, pastors, bishops, preachers, healers, prophets and popes. The heartbreaking response will be: "I never knew you: depart from me, you that work iniquity". Matt. 7:22-23.

The Lord's statements quoted above may bring a sense of discouragement in our hearts, as we ponder whether the effort is worth it, if the chance of failure be so high. But other scriptures are at hand, assuring us that it is not God's desire that *any* of us should perish: "For I know the thoughts that I think toward you, says the Lord, thoughts of peace, and not of evil, to give you an expected end." Jer. 29:11. The most quoted verse in the world comes to mind: "For God so loved the world that He gave His only begotten Son, that *whosoever* believes in Him, should not perish but have eternal life." John 3:16, emphasis supplied.

Sadly, in spite of our Creator's great desire to save *all* humanity, there is cause for Him to lament, "My people are destroyed for lack of knowledge. Because you have rejected knowledge, I also will reject you from being priests for Me." Hosea 4:6. Linked with Hebrews 11:6, "But without faith it is impossible to please him," it becomes clear that God expects those who would follow Him to have faith up-front, but faith with knowledge! We are expected to diligently seek for answers from His Word. A blind faith without knowledge will generate in us an uninformed zeal to be rewarded with a heart-breaking rejection at the end of time. The following words, applied to ancient Isarel by the apostle, may well be directed at Christendom today:

> Brethren, my heart's desire and prayer to God for Israel is that they may be saved. For I bear them witness that they have a zeal for God, but not according to knowledge. For they being ignorant of God's righteousness, and seeking to establish their own righteousness, have not submitted to the righteousness of God. Rom. 10:1-3.

Naturally, this leads to the question: What is knowledge? The same Hosea text quoted above supplies the answer, in the latter part of the verse:

"Because you have forgotten the law of your God." Hosea 4:6. Knowledge, therefore, is the remembrance of God's law. King Solomon, repenting from a life of self indulgence, had this advise for posterity: "Fear God and keep His commandments, for this is the whole duty of man." Eccl. 12:13.

Organized civil disobedience undermines the law of the state, and is one of the most effective ways to bring down regimes. The devil, being the originator of this strategy, has employed it to undermine God's government since Eden. Satan has caused humans, individually or as congregations, to seek to worship God in ways that feel good to them, completely disregarding the precepts of the very One they purport to worship.

The degree to which the enemy of souls introduces error in congregations, in order to steal souls, ranges from very mild, apparently harmless deception, to flagrant disregard of prescribed precepts, even open rebellion. Whatever the degree of error, the result is nevertheless the same—loss of the right to eternal life for those accepting the lie. Once we have taken the Lord's warning in Matthew 12:13-14 seriously, we must next come to the realization that if some Christians are to be condemned, then, logically, some 'Christian' churches must be misled.

As we read on and become aware of the deceiver's aim to woo souls through the institutions you and I call "*my* church," should we not set aside our sense of human patriotism, and take a fresh look at our religion? No man has a church except it be the church of God, founded on Jesus Christ. The Lord will be returning shortly, and this may be a good time to stop defending *our* churches, simply because they are *our* churches. We must begin a thorough audit of doctrines and practices, to establish whether we *are* indeed Christians.

You may find the experience of asking yourself hard questions and challenging your long-standing position on religion strange or unsettling at first. You may admit that you have never really given deep thought to these issues. You are not alone in this neglect. Evidently, the majority of men and women in the world never seriously reflect upon these vital questions; rather, each casually presumes that the position they hold pertaining to these, and to many other key issues of life, must be the correct one.

Few of us realize how much we have simply accepted as facts, the philosophies that we picked up from around us as we grew up. Fewer still are aware that as adults we make decisions and choices based on these presuppositions, gathered since infancy. We acquired from our parents, through impressions and statements, without question, whatever they offered with respect to joys, fears, emotions, prejudices, doctrines, superstitions and 'knowledge'; storing them in our sub-conscious mind as *factual data*. This collection of data formed the basis of our earliest worldview. The process of acquisition continued over the years, with the source of 'knowledge' and 'facts' shifting from parents to peers, to teachers and 'education', to heroes, college professors, pastors, prophets, preachers, and popes! Thus gathered from external sources and internalized, the sum of our presuppositions amounts to what is generally termed *'the heart.'* The implications of this truth, though the majority in the world be unaware, are frightening!

Do you realize that you are probably a 'Christian' by mere accident of birth, rather than according to informed choice? Consider that many belong to the Buddhist, Moslem, Hindu, Catholic, Anglican, or Baptist faith simply because they were born to parents believing the same. In Africa, Japan, China, and India a great number are traditionalists simply because they grew up in societies engaging in ancestral worship. You, dear friend, may be Christian for the sole unchallenged reason that your own parents were Christian. You probably still belong to the same denomination that adopted you at birth. You could be one of those for whom choice of a church in adulthood was purely an accident of geography, your prime concern in making the selection being proximity to home. You may have chosen your church because it suited your personal taste and lifestyle; or you liked the pastor or priest.

However, the time has now come to revisit our presuppositions, with a view to remodeling our hearts with informed personal involvement. We should do this through a study of the precepts of God as revealed in the Bible, possessing always in the fore, knowledge of the devil's burning ambition to divert worship to himself. In the end, we must change and remold ourselves to suit Christ and the church, not the reverse.

This book will expose some of the errors introduced by the enemy into our churches. One of the most difficult, yet infinitely rewarding things for a human being to do is to admit being at fault, to cast away error, and embrace correction. In addressing this human trait, the first chapter will reveal the extent to which the human heart is capable of cheating itself, becoming degraded and voluntarily deceived, and remaining so in the face of solid evidence available to prove beliefs, actions, and habits, not only wrong but fatal! The propensity of the human heart to fool itself on purpose is immense, in spite of dire consequences. Little wonder the unerring discerner of hearts declares: "The heart is deceitful above all things, and desperately wicked: who can know it?" Jer. 17:9.

Pray that in studying the mental process by which many have willfully acquired a popular—but killer—habit, we may come to recognize our equal capacity to cling to error with eyes wide open. In denouncing the tenacity with which others, once addicted, have remained glued to habit, despite known deadly consequences, we must reveal our own potential for rejecting correction in the face of overwhelming plain truth. We should pray that after making this discovery, our approach to correction and to new ideas is less prejudiced than before.

The great men of God who pioneered the Reformation[1] were protesting against gross error introduced into Christendom through the Roman Catholic Church. The church, which had become almost universal through military conquest, had voted, to elevate the Tradition of the Fathers (the sayings and rulings of popes and councils) above the Scriptures, in the Council of Trent of 1546[2]. This paved the way for the introduction of human philosophy and practice into the the church. It was against the abuse of power, and the spiritual morbidity resulting from erroneous doctrines and corrupt practices, that the Reformers raised their voices. They died, most of them as martyrs, at the hands of the Roman church, before they could reverse all the errors. It was the duty of those who remained to take up the baton and continue the race. However, instead of progressing the reformation movement, followers have been content to exercise only as much truth as was revealed to the heroes of old. If there has been any change at all, it has mostly been to reverse, rather than to consolidate the gains of the initial protest.

The sectarianism that would result in the current denominationalization of Christendom began back in the days of the apostles. Read part of Paul's letter to the church at Corinth:

> For it has been declared to me concerning you, my brethren, by those of Chloe's household, that there are contentions among you. Now I say this, that each of you says, "I am of Paul," or "I am of Apollos," or "I am of Cephas," or "I am of Christ." Is Christ divided? Was Paul crucified for you? Or were you baptized in the name of Paul? 1 Cor. 1:11-13.

Here is clear evidence that professing Christians were forming camps around their various human heroes. Paul's letter obviously failed to kill the spirit of congregating around human icons, for it thrives to this day. It is even the reason for the fragmented state of Christendom today. This sad state of affairs can no better be presented than by the words of pastor John Robinson to the Pilgrims as they left Holland for the American continent in search of religious liberty. Here is part of his valedictory address as quoted in The Great Controversy:

> I charge you before God and His blessed angels to follow me no farther than I have followed Christ. If God should reveal anything to you by any other instrument of His, be as ready to receive it as you ever were to receive any truth by my ministry; for I am very confident that the Lord hath more truth and light yet to break forth out of His Holy Word. For my part, I cannot sufficiently bewail the condition of the reformed churches, who are come to a period in religion, and will go no farther than the instruments of their reformation. The Lutherans cannot be drawn to go any farther than what Luther saw, and Calvinists, you see, stick fast where they were left by that great man of God, who yet saw not all things. This is a misery much to be lamented; for though they were burning and shining lights in their time, yet they penetrated not into the whole counsel of God, but were they now living, would be as willing to embrace further light as that which they first received . . . . Remember your promise and covenant with God and with one another, to receive whatever light and truth shall be made known to you from His written Word. But, withal, take heed, I beseech you, what you receive as truth. Examine it, consider it, compare it with other scriptures of truth before you receive it; for it is not possible that the Christian world should come so lately out of such thick antichristian darkness, and that perfection of knowledge should break forth at once." (E. G. White 1911, 291-292)

Despite this clear admonition to press on in the quest for truth, few Protestants realize how much, because of stagnation, even retrogression, they exist today in the spiritual condition labeled Babylon, in prophecy. The wily enemy of souls has been at his subtle best, and many will be surprised when they fail to enter the pearly gates. A great number will regret that they neglected to study the strategy of the enemy of souls in the war. The intensity of their dissappointment when the door shall remain closed is not possible to imagine. They will have underestimated Satan's determination to achieve that for which he was prepared to abandon the glory of heaven and forego eternity—to sit *upon the mount of the congregation.*

Samuel Katsaruware

CHAPTER 1

The Smoldering Paradox

DANGER: SMOKING CAN KILL YOU

Tobacco smoke contains many harmful chemicals such as carbon monoxide, cyanide, nicotine and tar, which can cause disease and death. Non-smokers and ex-smokers, in general, live longer and are healthier than smokers. For more information, call (001)-720-3145.

PREGNANT AND BREAST-FEEDING? YOUR SMOKING CAN HARM YOUR BABY.

The babies of mothers who smoke during pregnancy are more likely to die before birth or to be born underweight. Stopping smoking before or during the first months of pregnancy reduces the risk to the baby. For more information, call (001)-720-3145.

DANGER: SMOKING CAUSES HEART DISEASE

Smoking is a major cause of heart attacks, strokes, and blood vessel diseases. Quitting smoking reduces your risk of heart diseases. For more information, call (001)-720-3145.

Unlikely source

These words have not come from the pages of a health textbook. They are not extractions from banners in an anti-tobacco rally either. These deadly warning messages appear, with variations, on many packets of cigarettes in most parts of the world today!

Health texts and journals, newspaper and magazine columns, as well as school and college textbooks describe the deadly hazards of smoking. Detailed information on the fatal consequences of the habit is readily available at the click of a computer mouse, on the world-wide-web. The warning that smoking is harmful to health clearly accompanies most advertising of tobacco in all media around the world. While the exact wording on diverse brands may vary, the central warning message always stands out clearly—*smoking kills!* Through the written word, therefore, the literate masses receive warning of the hazard—and they still smoke!

The debilitating effects of this habit are evident on the physical features of those whose vital organs have been devastated by the poisons listed on the very packet. Every morning, the eyes, the limbs, and the lungs of even the smoker who still appears healthy to the world, give a painful report of the previous day's indulgence. Through observation of wasted victims of tobacco abuse around them, as well as through signals from their own body organs, the throngs of illiterate smokers likewise receive warning—yet they puff on!

Deadly paradox

The habit of smoking is a paradox that confounds the mind of the observer. MS Word lists some synonyms of 'paradox' as 'inconsistency', 'absurdity', 'irony', 'impossibility' and 'illogicality'. Here is the absurdity: The smoker is evidently in love with himself; yet, the very means he chooses to demonstrate the fact to the world harms that very self; and he knows it! This is inexplicable irony indeed! The most learned professionals in society, priests and archbishops included, are hooked on tobacco. Indeed, the lung specialist will take a literal smoke-break from the operating table, where he is cutting away the nicotine-ravaged lung of a patient, to light up and inhale! The college professor, a sophisticated man of letters, will casually pull out his packet and share a puff with his illiterate, unrefined gardener. The habit is no respecter of class, education, race, gender, or age.

Consider now, the following baffling observation. Humanity has made tremendous achievements in technology. Just think of electricity, television, the computer, the cell phone, iPod, the internet, and much, much more. Thanks to satellite, viewers worldwide can now follow events as they unfold in the remotest hot spots, or locate any street address in the world. Imagine the level of creative genius that has gone into these inventions. Today, scientists almost casually land spacecraft on mars, with micrometer precision. There are rumors that some of the world's super-rich have already paid for their slot of a holiday on the moon. Recently I saw a picture of the world's first weightless wedding, conducted in a special craft, with the couple and guests floating happily around the cabin.

In the field of medicine, doctors routinely transplant vital organs from one person to another. They have developed mechanical and electronic gadgets to replace malfunctioning body organs and limbs. Recently, there have been press reports indicating that a team of medical researchers has discovered a possible method to cure Human Immunodeficiency Virus, HIV, and should perfect it in two years time.

Specialists are able to tell us exactly what part of our brain is responsible for what type of thought, feeling, or action. Psychologists, psychiatrists, and sociologists claim to have established the laws that govern human behavior. Not to be outdone, economists have elevated their study to a science. They can create computer models predicting how the sudden death of an American president, for example, will affect global financial markets, and how the event will influence downstream economies worldwide.

Now, comes the baffling part. The same humans, after achieving all the foregoing, will pick up a packet of cigarettes, read the warning printed in red, flick open the packet, pull one out, light up, and inhale with satisfaction! Reflect on this absurdity. Is there a way of explaining this suicidal phenomenon? In order to tackle the chapters ahead, it is important to attempt an analysis of what has actually happened in the mind of the addicted smoker, to render him oblivious to the plain and simple truths, and danger warning signs abounding in the world regarding his habit. There are as many specific reasons why people become accomplished inhalers, as there are smokers. Is there an underlying factor explaining what has really led to the virtual derailment of an otherwise intelligent mind?

The objective of this chapter

This book is not about smokers and smoking. It is about Christians and Christianity. This chapter aims to highlight some important parallels between the mindset of the smoker regarding tobacco on the one hand, and that of many Christians regarding their religion, on the other. There is nothing physiologically different between smokers and non-smokers. Mentally, there are low IQ people who smoke just as there are those who abhor tobacco. There are medical doctors, aeronautical engineers, computer geniuses, and many other high IQ people who smoke; and there are those in the same class who do not. People who smoke have simply made a choice regarding tobacco, while those who do not, have also made theirs, in that specific area of life. However, because human nature is universal, nothing will stop any person from approaching other aspects of life in the same manner the smoker has approached tobacco. In short, it is possible for any human mind to become self-deluded in adopting habits and beliefs that are as harmful to their intended cause as tobacco is to the smoker's health. The fact that a non-smoker can marvel at the lung surgeon who smokes does not eliminate the possibility of the same mental process that created the habit in the surgeon happening in the observer, in other areas of life, including religion.

If therefore, we should condemn the smoker for adopting his habit, we must have the wisdom to look at our religion, to see if we have not adopted doctrines, practices, and beliefs that cause God and the angels to marvel that we should consider ourselves worthy candidates of heaven. In reading the rest of this book, we must always revert to the case of the smoker, and ask ourselves if we are not skipping over sections of our Bibles just as smokers do the red letters on their packets. The danger of that happening is very real. The mental process that has created the smoker has probably occurred within you and me in many other areas of life. This process is termed *autosuggestion*.

The power of autosuggestion

One definition of "autosuggestion" relevant to our discussion is "The process by which a person induces self-acceptance of an opinion, belief, or plan of action." (The American Heritage Dictionary of the English Language 2009). There are as many specific reasons why people smoke, as there are smokers. One thing is clear though, when they set out to acquire the habit, they firmly believe it will add value to their lives. The first time one inhales tobacco, the body reacts as if one has swallowed an atomic bomb. This is as it should be. Smoke, nicotine, tar, and carbon monoxide come pre-programmed in our sub-conscience as poisons. However, the learner smoker, by repeatedly inhaling over a period, as well as through reminding himself constantly of the merits of the habit, causes a dramatic change in the sub-conscious database. The subliminal mind delists these toxins from "poisons," and places them on the list of "essentials foods." Now, the body must give painful warning signs whenever the level of these chemicals is running low. A habit is born.

The description in the foregoing paragraph has a parallel in peoples' religion. For many different reasons, people join a church. They approach the church fully believing in its merits. Soon, they are so immersed in its doctrines and traditions that nothing can be wrong about "their church." Autosuggestion works as perfectly in cultivating the habit of smoking as it does the belief in our chosen congregation.

However, what has stimulated the belief in the merits of tobacco in the first place? The answer is, there exists already in the mind, a favorable predisposition towards the habit. The person presupposes that smoking is good for him. What is the source of this presupposition? As we have seen in the Introduction, we gather presuppositions subconsciously from infancy through adulthood. Let us look at some scenarios that create a predisposition to smoking, and compare them to our religious experiences.

1. Born in a family of smokers, the habit comes "naturally."
   In religion, this compares to being born to Anglican, Methodist, Catholic, Adventist, or Baptist, etc. parents. Going to the same church and adopting its doctrines and teachings comes "naturally," without question.
2. The habit is trendy, and almost everyone is doing it.

The religious parallel is when people flock to a church because almost everyone they know is attending. The media is showing thousands in attendance. Numbers are more important than doctrine.

3. Many important people smoke, including national presidents, medical doctors, priests and professors.

   This mindset manifests in religion, where a person believes his church could never be wrong, not with the caliber of knowledgeable people who belong.

4. Subconscious response to advertising.

   Many people today join a church in response to the quality of its advertising on satellite television, and other media.

5. Emulation of heroes (actors, musicians, politicians etc.) who smoke.

   People flock to churches where the charisma of the pastor makes him their spiritual hero. His word becomes doctrine, and the congregation makes no attempt to measure it, independently, against the Scriptures.

Ignoring the warnings

Now we must reveal the most tragic parallel between the smoker and the 'Christian'. The smoker responds to the feelings of perceived relief offered by tobacco, and ignores the warnings of disease and death printed clearly in red on his packet of cigarettes. It feels so good it can't be wrong. Herein lies the tragedy: just as the smoker ignores the warnings on his packet, we 'Christians' ignore the warnings in the very Bible we claim as our guide. The traditions of our church in the form of the pastor's word, the church handbook, or the catechism, combined with the feelings that run through our veins, become the yardstick for measuring truth. The doctrine of the church supersedes that of the Bible, and no amount of reasoning and preaching can shake us. We will read and understand warnings in the Bible, but alas, like the smoker, will glide over them, fully believing them intended for people other than ourselves. The mental process that leads the smoker to indulge error, in the face of cancer and death-warnings, is the same that occurs in the 'Christian' when embracing error amid abounding biblical warnings of loss of eternal life.

Challenge

As we tackle the chapters ahead, it will be important for us, dear reader, to review both the content and source of our current presuppositions in matters of religion. We will need to stop and ask if those things that make us feel secure, comfortable, and good, would not prevent the acceptance of plain truth the same way they blind the smoker to the warning on his packet. There will be a need to be brutally honest with ourselves. Uninformed loyalty to our current beliefs may deny us life in eternity. For all we know, the enemy has succeeded in redirecting our institutions to his camp as he pursues the agenda to sit "upon the mount of the congregation."

CHAPTER 2

The Origin of Sin

Lucifer

Sin originated in the loftiest of places. Involving a very high profile angel of God, it fed an ego larger than heaven! Lucifer, had everything going for him. The word 'Lucifer' means 'light bearer.' (Davis 1944). He had good looks and wisdom: "You have been in Eden, the garden of God; every precious stone was your covering, the sardis, topaz, and the diamond, the beryl, the onyx, and the jasper, the sapphire, the emerald, and the carbuncle, and the gold." Ez. 28:13, first part. He had musical instruments incorporated in his anatomy: "The workmanship of your timbrels and your pipes was prepared in you in the day that you were created." Ez. 28:13, last part. God had given him authority, and freedom: "You were the anointed cherub that covers; and I have set you so; you were upon the holy mountain of God; you have walked up and down in the midst of the stones of fire." Ez. 28:14.

You would expect a being so favored to be forever content, adoring the Creator who had lavished such amazing attributes upon him; but in Lucifer, God's favor became seed for the first germination of sin in the universe.

"You were perfect in your ways from the day that you were created, till iniquity was found in you." Ez. 28:15. What was the nature of this iniquity that God discerned in Lucifer? Let the Bible describe the thought process that led one of heaven's most glorious creatures, an angel of great authority and beauty, to forsake heaven and opt for, of all destinies, eternal doom.

> How are you fallen from heaven,
> O Lucifer, son of the morning!
> How are you cut down to the ground,
> Who weakened the nations!
> For you have said in your heart:
> 'I will ascend into heaven,
> I will exalt my throne above the stars of God;
> I will sit also upon the mount of the congregation,
> In the farthest sides of the north:
> I will ascend above the heights of the clouds;
> I will be like the most high'. Is. 14:12-14.

Lucifer resolved to elevate himself above God. His beauty, intelligence, and authority, went to his head, and he felt himself better able to run the affairs of the universe than the Creator of all. Can you detect the terrible egoism from the number of sentences starting "I", in the foregoing verses? Lucifer knew what the result of rebellion would be. So strong, however, was the craving to satisfy the ego that he plunged on in open warfare, in his attempt to "be like the most High."

Nature of the cosmic battle

The book of Revelation summarizes what happened in heaven. "And war broke out in heaven: Michael and his angels fought with the dragon;

and the dragon and his angels fought." Rev. 12:7. There were no swords in that war; neither cannons nor missiles. It was a war of wits and words; a war between good and bad; between give and get; evil countered by love. Lucifer accused God of employing bribery to win the affection of created beings. The book of Job reveals this aspect of the controversy. When God points out His righteous servant Job to Satan, the devil accuses:

> "Does Job fear God for nothing?" Satan replied. "Have you not put a hedge around him and his household and everything he has? You have blessed the work of his hands, so that his flocks and herds are spread throughout the land. But stretch out your hand and strike everything he has, and he will surely curse you to your face." Job 1:9-11, NIV.

By reading between the lines, we can come up with the following accusations that Satan leveled against God:

- You are naturallyt an unloving and unlovable god.
- You bribe your creatures with physical comforts and material possessions in order to win their love; indeed, you created them with the sole hope of selfishly reposing in purchased adoration.
- In *My* case, you expected loyalty in return for creating *Me* more handsome than any other creature, and more powerful than all angels. *I*, Lucifer, The Giver of Light, the Morning Star, saw through your scheme and, rebelling together with other enlightened angels, we broke the prison chains and freed ourselves.

We get a glimpse of another dimension of the cosmic battle during the temptation of Jesus by Satan at the launch of the Lord's ministry. "Then the devil, taking Him up on a high mountain, showed Him all the kingdoms of the world in a moment of time. And the devil said to Him, "All this authority I will give You, and their glory; for this has been delivered to me, and I give it to whomever I wish.'" Luke 4:5-6. Note carefully that the devil, who, by virtue of his former position in heaven, would know the identity of Jesus better than most created beings, claims to His face that he, Satan, had taken delivery of the kingdoms, authority, and splendor of the earth, and that he now controlled them. Note furthermore that Christ's defense does not challenge the truthfulness of Satan's claims to earth's throne. God has indeed permitted Satan dominion over the planet earth, and all that is in it, to prove his claims that he was a better leader.

God has allowed the devil a set period in which to demonstrate to the entire universe his brands of government, socio-economy, education, philosophy, and religion. This suggests that in the battle, Lucifer had challenged his creator's style of leadership, form of government and religion. So convincing was the brilliant Sun of the Morning that he won the allegiance of some of God's angels, and left a cloud of doubt hanging over the entire universe. It was therefore necessary for God to permit Satan a platform to demonstrate his claims to a watching universe. The once glorious angel of God was for this reason confined to the planet earth.

Having led a partially successful revolt of angels in heaven, Satan proceeded to recruit adherents among earthlings, as we shall see in chapter 3. The devil has, through the agency of men and women of this world, set up the systems that are supposed to be better than God's. In the final execution of the satanic master plan, the world is to plunge into the greatest strife ever. Only the coming of the Lord Jesus will save the planet from annihilation. These things are soon to fall upon a largely unsuspecting world.

Lucifer was not alone

By the time God banished Lucifer from heaven, the wily one had managed to sway some of Heaven's angels to his corrupt way of thinking. Revelation 12 describes what happened.

> And war broke out in heaven: Michael and his angels fought with the dragon; and the dragon and his angels fought but they did not prevail, nor was a place found for them in heaven any longer. Rev. 12:7, 8.

The revelator does not leave us to speculate who the dragon was.

> So the great dragon was cast out, that serpent of old, called the devil and Satan, who deceives the whole world; he was cast to the earth, and his angels with him. Rev. 12:9.

Earlier on, in verses 3 and 4, we are told that Lucifer had corrupted one third of God's 'stars', the angels, and brought them down with him. Throughout this book, we will expose the many antics of these miscreant spirits, called demons, as they work tirelessly to install their master "upon the mount of the congregation."

Worshippers targeted—How safe are you?

Two lines in Lucifer's ego-feeding diatribe of Isaiah 14 stand out most starkly in aid of our effort to unearth the strategy of the devil. We must reveal the full implication of these two lines:

I will be like the most high. (v. 14 last part).

I will sit also upon the mount of the congregation. (v. 13 last part).

Satan cherishes the most prominent position in the hierarchy of the universe; the very position that only God, by virtue of His Creatorship, can fill. In heaven, un-fallen angels still worship and adore God: "You are worthy, O Lord, to receive glory and honor and power; for You created all things, and by Your will they exist and were created." Rev. 4:11. We see that God deserves—and receives—worship because He created the universe, and sustains it.

Glory is due to Jesus Christ for proving the wretchedness of sin and Satan to the watching un-fallen universe by His death on the cross, while conquering death and sin in the process. "Worthy is the Lamb who was slain to receive power and riches and wisdom, and strength and honor and glory and blessing!" Rev. 5:12.

God, the Creator, and Jesus the slain Lamb earned worship. They deserve worship. On the other hand, Lucifer, a created being, never qualified to receive worship. Only his pride persuaded him of his fitness for adulation. He, therefore, set out to be *like the most High.* The question we must ask now is: What strategy would he use to realize his ambition?

The answer lies in the following powerful statement of intent, loaded with meaning: "I will sit also *upon the mount of the congregation,* on the farthest *sides of the north*" Is. 14:13,last part, emphasis supplied. What is this mountain on the sides of the north? The psalmist identifies it in clear terms:

> Great is the LORD, and greatly to be praised in the city of our
> God, in His holy mountain. Beautiful in elevation, the joy of the
> whole earth, is *Mount* Zion on *the sides of the north.* Ps. 48:1, 2.

Lucifer's use of the word *congregation* should send a shiver down the spine of Christendom. A congregation can only be found within a place or community of worship! The most obvious implication of this observation is that, in general, whenever people gather to worship—be they Christian, Moslem, Hindu, Buddhist, heathen or any other religious grouping, church or family—the devil is in their midst, to establish himself as the focus of worship. More specifically, Lucifer has his eyes focused on Mount Zion, the eternal city of God and the venue of gathering for His congregation. This was clearly the target of Lucifer's ambition.

The psalmist equates those who seek the Lord and trust in Him, with Mount Zion: "Those who trust in the LORD are like Mount Zion, which cannot be moved, but abides forever." Ps. 125:1. It is plain that when banished to planet earth, Satan set out to usurp God's authority over those who sought to live under God's protection. Satan's first targets were, therefore, the families of the sons of God both before and after the flood. Next, he went after the congregation Israel, the race. Today, spiritual Israel, the Christian Church, is his target. He has succeeded almost completely in each phase, by employing various strategies that suited the times.

In ancient history, the devil presided over congregations that made many gods of idols, and sacrificed their sons at the fiery altar. Israel, the chosen of God, did not escape the lure of idolatry.

> And (Israel) left all the commandments of the LORD their God, and made them molten images, even two calves, and made a grove, and worshipped all the host of heaven, and served Baal. And they caused their sons and their daughters to pass through the fire, and used divination and enchantments, and sold themselves to do evil in the sight of the LORD, to provoke him to anger. 2 Kings 17:16, 17.

However, in keeping with 'civilization', the cunning enemy of souls has had to refine the methods used to either create or infiltrate congregations, and hence position himself as the focus of worship. Satan has had to acknowledge that the majority in the modern world have adopted Christianity, whether nominally or by true conversion, as their religion. Today's civilized society would frown at human sacrifice. The crafty old serpent has mellowed his methods to suit the times. He now employs subtle deception to keep 'Christian' congregations intact in the belief that they are worshipping God through Jesus Christ, when in fact he has firmly established himself *"upon the mount of the congregation."*

Many misled

Consider the texts below, which are the words of our Lord Jesus. The central theme in these texts is that although many people believe that they are 'saved', and are Christians, not all of them will see eternal life. This is in spite of the Lord's stated and demonstrated desire to see all humanity saved. You have probably read these verses, and heard them preached upon many times before. However, dear friend, probably for the first time ever, read these warnings again with full awareness of Satan's ambition to sit *"upon the mount of the congregation"*. Personalize these texts and consider the possibility that they may be directed at you alone.

In Luke 13:23, a worried disciple of Jesus poses the question to the Master, "Lord, are there few who are saved?" Jesus answered: "Strive to enter through the narrow gate, for many, I say to you, will seek to enter and will not be able." Luke 13:24-27. The *many* facing disqualified include self-professing Christians who have diligently carried their Bibles to church every week, returned faithful tithe and made generous offerings. Some who have participated zealously in all church programmes will be among them. You are not safe just because you have a pious and gifted pastor, priest, or prophet who preaches moving sermons and performs miracles; healing the sick and restoring the lame. You are unsafe because your spiritual leader may himself be doomed for destruction! Regarding this aspect of the matter, listen to the words of the Lord Jesus himself—He who occupies the final judgment seat: "Many will say to me in that day, 'Lord, have we not prophesied in Your name, cast out demons in Your name, and done many wonders in Your name?'" Matt. 7:22. To these men and women who have led large and vibrant 'Christian' congregations as prophets, pastors, priests, bishops and popes, Jesus will answer, "I never knew you; depart from Me, you who practice lawlessness". Matt. 7:23.

You may be the victim of a con

As you read on, divorce yourself for a moment, from the feeling of allegiance to the institution that is your church. View these lines in a very individual light, remembering always that far from being a collective matter, salvation is determined at the individual level. There is a very real possibility that you *could* be a member of a congregation which is the victim of a con. This is what the Lord suggests by the statement "Not everyone who says to Me, 'Lord, Lord,' shall enter the kingdom of heaven, but he who does the will of My Father in heaven." Matt. 7:21. How safe are we in the institutions that each one of us so dearly cherishes as '*my church*'?

If the idea of having been spiritually conned is repugnant, remembering that the conman is the most intelligent fallen angel, not some dumb half-wit spirit, may make it more palatable. It is not easy for an intelligent, educated adult, to admit that he or she has been led astray for so long. The victim of a con who has handed money eagerly to a trickster is reluctant to report the matter to the police, and is unlikely to divulge the incident to his spouse.

You and I, through studying the smoker's way of thinking—or maybe, the lack of it—in chapter 1, have revealed how wretchedly deceptive our own human hearts can be. The matters we are about to discuss are not just about lung cancer and heart disease. We are about to tackle issues of eternal life or the loss of it. The stakes are infinitely high.

Satan's doom inevitable and justified

The cross of Calvary has since conquered Satan. You may ask why God has not since destroyed the devil. The answer lies in the character of God and the need to prepare the universe for the new heaven and the new earth, which the saints will inhabit to eternity, with sin never occurring again. We will look at this in more detail in chapter 16. God's unfathomable justice and wisdom demand that He justifies the destruction of even His self-appointed arch-enemy to the entire intelligent universe, and to the devil himself! When the final sentence is passed on Satan, his angels and human sinners, every knee, including the devil's own, shall bow in acknowledgement of God's justice on the one hand, and acknowledgement of personal guilt on the other.

Through events unfolding on planet earth from Eden to the pending destruction of sin, God must give a chance for all possible scenarios which attempt to create a better world and God-like man, while sparing Satan, his angels, and human sinners, to be played out and proved impossible. God will not achieve the destruction of sin in the universe supernaturally, in an instant. A situation must evolve where all remaining created beings will make a conscious decision never again to sin. God will not turn his creatures into loving robots; they will have to abhor sin by deliberate choice. This, God will facilitate partly by addressing all the possible questions that may arise regarding His justice in destroying Satan, demons and human sinners. If He does not do this, one can imagine some man or angel in the new dispensation asking questions in sympathy with men and angels whom they deem unjustly executed by God, leading to a second round of rebellion. By the time that God finally destroys sin and sinners, He will have permitted the drama of the earth's history to remove all potential doubt regarding the need for such destruction.

At last, fire will destroy Satan, his angels, and those men and women who have refused to release their clutch from the devil's alluring garment. By that time, events in the final hours of the earth will have proved beyond doubt the case for such destruction. No one in the New Heaven and New Earth can ever again question the justice and love of God. Voluntarily, all creation will choose to follow the precepts of God, out of sheer love and honor for Him. Having appreciated the full nature of sin, none will want to see its ugly head rise ever again.

No man need perish

God does not intend to destroy even one soul! "'For I have no pleasure in the death of one who dies,' says the Lord GOD. 'Therefore turn and live!'" Ez. 18:32. The only creatures God would destroy are Satan, His former trusted cherub, together with His lieutenant angels. This destruction need not come upon any human being. We must just disentangle ourselves from the invisible web spun to entrap us by the enemy of God, as he slides rapidly to destruction.

Mental, moral and spiritual emancipation are required. We need to change the way we think; the way we view religion. Realizing that Satan is even now leading some of our churches to a common fiery end, we must stop taking worship for granted. We ought now to make the right *personal* decision, based on solid biblical doctrine.

As we proceed to the next chapter, to see how Satan began his ascent *'upon the mount of the congregation'* by initiating the fall of man, we ought to keep two important points uppermost in our minds.

1. Satan's ambition is to receive worship, sitting in the position that God should occupy in churches.

2. It is possible for your mind to refuse plain truth stated in the very Bible you purport to believe in, if that truth flies against what you have been brought up to believe, or what makes you feel good, or popular, or puts bread on your table.

What would hold you back from accepting God's truth today? Whatever it is, can it ever be more precious than eternity in a sinless, painless world? Jesus Christ, your Exemplar, is asking you today, "For what profit is it to a man if he gains the whole world, and loses his own soul?" Matt.16:26.

CHAPTER 3

Sin Enters the World

The two choices of Eden

When God created Adam and Eve in His own image, he placed them in Eden, to tend and enjoy the idyllic garden. They would extend dominion over the entire earth, under God's direct mentorship. God offered them access to the Tree of Life, provided they obeyed His law. Obeying God was tantamount to accepting Him as guide and sole leader in matters ecclesiastical, social, political, and economic—all facets of human endeavor. Any righteousness in them, would stem from a character developed through the in dwelling of the Holy Spirit. He would help protect them from the influence of the devil and his army of fallen angels. They would thus conquer the devil, and justify his destruction; and God would establish His theocratic government on Earth. The Creator would put in place a truly equitable world economy with no shortages, no poverty, no pain, and no tears. In religious matters, because of the perpetual presence of the Holy Spirit within him, man would continue to have direct and unlimited communion with his Maker. He would continue to partake of the Tree of Life, and live forever.

There was another tree in the Garden—The Tree of the Knowledge of Good and Evil. By choosing to partake of its fruit, Adam and Eve would, in essence, be making the conscious decision to disobey God and henceforth assume personal responsibility for setting up their religion, social structures and norms, political government, and economy. Thereafter, they would decide for themselves what was right and what was wrong to do. They would judge for themselves what constituted sin. Men would decide how, who, what and when to worship. The Holy Spirit could no longer dwell within them, and they would be exposed to the influence of Satan and his demons, leading to a continual inclination to evil. The only righteousness man could possess after disobeying God was self-righteousness, which Isaiah equates with "filthy rags" in Isaiah 64:6. God stated the warning regarding this tree and its fruit as clearly as He did the sentence for disobedience.

> And the Lord God commanded the man, saying, "Of every tree
> of the garden you may freely eat; but of the tree of the knowledge
> of good and evil you shall not eat, for in the day that you eat of
> it you shall surely die." Gen. 2:16, 17.

Notice the use of the word *surely,* to emphasize the certainty of death. The couple received a beautiful, bountiful garden. Furthermore, the Creator endowed them with something vastly more significant—the power to choose to obey or disobey, to live, or to die!

Satan's first & greatest sermon to mankind

We have seen that there was war Heaven. In any war, there is a winner and a loser. It is inconceivable that God's side should lose, and "they (the dragon and his angels) did not prevail, nor was a place found for them in heaven any longer." Rev. 12:8. The devil immediately set out to fulfill the burning ambition we identified in chapter 2—to sit *"upon the mount of the congregation"* through deception. Employing the medium of the serpent, Satan prepared his first sermon with great cunning. He chose his target audience well. God's law had reached Eve through a third party. She would thus be the more likely of the two to fall for deception, and hence become the entry point of sin.

The devil feigned ignorance of God's laws and an eagerness to learn the truth. He artfully manipulated Eve's emotions to heat up in defense of her God. In the passion of the moment, Satan sowed seeds of doubt.

> And he said to the woman, "Has God indeed said, 'You shall not eat of every tree of the garden'?" And the woman said to the serpent, "We may eat the fruit of the trees of the garden; but of the fruit of the tree which is in the midst of the garden, God has said, 'You shall not eat it, nor shall you touch it, lest you die.'" Gen. 3:1-3.

Eve's fatal mistake was to engage the devil in conversation in the very first occult experience of humanity. How many times have you and I been exposed to Satan through consulting seers, palm-readers, star-gazers, fortune tellers, witch-doctors, and healers, whose power derives from the same demonic source as imparted speech to the serpent in Eden?

Many associate all supernatural occurrences, including miracles of healing, only with God. Could you be one of them? Be warned, "do not believe every spirit, but test the spirits, whether they are of God." 1 John 4:1. Take a lesson from Eve never to engage devils in any way.

Now, the devil tells Eve, *"You will not surely die."* Gen. 3:4, emphasis supplied. To an innocent human being who had never heard a lie before, this statement must have created considerable confusion and mental anguish. It was the very opposite of what God had preached to her husband. This verse alone may stand out in all history as the most powerful sermon that Satan ever delivered to humanity.

By simply adding the word 'not' to God's warning of Genesis 2:17, the devil brought to Eve's mind a whole new dimension to the idea of death, whatever it might have been at the time. If one is not *surely* dead, what is he? Where is he? The cunning old serpent was quick to provide an answer: "For God knows that in the day you eat of it your eyes will be opened and you will be like God, knowing good and evil." Gen. 3:5. Thus, Satan delivered his first and most enduring sermon to man.

The fall of Eve

Two opposing sermons now battled in Eve's mind. The first was from He who had created her, and given her access to everything except the one tree. The second was from a charismatic, created being, who preached not only immortality, but also a state of existence equal to God! The same egoistic ambition that had triggered the fall of Lucifer now began to form itself in the woman. The prospect of rising to a position equal to God was tantalizing. Entertained freely, it soon began to look not only attractive, but possible—literally within arm's reach!

The heart began to pound faster, with the influence of adrenalin on the body increasing in unfamiliar surges as the mental faculties gave way to physical senses. Once the crafty one had sowed the seeds of doubt, and the mind began to question God's word, the five senses stepped in to tip the balance in favor of rebellion. Eve entertained wrong feelings, and then proceeded to make a crucial decision based on the feelings thus generated. She suddenly gained a keen awareness of things she had never even noticed before. "So when the woman saw that the tree was good for food, that it was pleasant to the eyes, and a tree desirable to make one wise, she took of its fruit and ate." Gen. 3:6.

Compare this with the mental resolve of the person who has set out to acquire the habit of smoking despite the pain it will bring, and in spite of all the deadly warnings in the world!

When she did not drop dead after *touching* the delicious looking fruit, Eve proceeded to *eat* it. Thus, humanity's biological mother became also the spiritual mother of all humans who have been, are, and will be enticed to err by Satan, through men and women of charisma and sweet words. She became the progenitor of those who follow preachers, seers, and miracle workers, with the subconscious agenda to have their egos boosted, their self esteem lifted, and emotions stirred by semi-scriptural oratory.

Adam's fall by deliberate choice

When Eve did not drop dead even after *eating* the forbidden fruit, "she also gave to her husband with her, and he ate." Gen 3:6. God had blessed Adam with a partner made from his own rib. That he should adore her was understandable, for her character and form were yet unmarred by sin. She must have been quite a remarkable sight, and a pleasure to have as companion. Unfortunately, Adam succumbed to Eve's sin because he loved and venerated God's beautiful gift more than he did the Giver of it.

Two lessons emerge from this episode in the garden. Firstly, we learn how easily we can fall into the error of presuming God's approval when He spares us sudden judgment. We confuse God's grace and forbearance with weakness, or ignorance, on the part of Providence. En-route from a murderous escapade, we miraculously survive an accident and feel invincible before God. How many preachers have delivered their most moving sermons barely an hour after emerging from an adulterous assignment in a seedy motel? They consider themselves so holy that God cannot see, let alone act, to punish their transgression. Yet, we must remember that God and the angelic host are forever present, in darkness as in light, though we may feel hidden and unseen. Angels record the minutest unspoken thoughts of the mind. How much more plain therefore, are the physical manifestations of those thoughts to the holy beings?

Secondly, we learn how easily we can make gods out of God's beautiful creations and gifts, and end up worshipping *them*, rather than *Him*. Eve's error came through deception. Adam's sin was premeditated! He knew that Eve's transgression had created an eternal chasm between him and his beautiful wife. Rather than let Eve walk her chosen path alone, and trusting God to create for him another wife even more beautiful, Adam chose, with his eyes wide open, to follow Eve to death across the gulf. Eve had become his god, and nothing else in the world mattered.

Adam became the spiritual father of all humans who sin by consciously choosing to act against God's precepts. They choose to do so because they are afraid of losing the physical comforts, beauties, positions, and riches of this world. Once again, we see that it is possible for humankind—you and me included—to disobey God's express commands on the strength of our personal feelings and perceptions. In so doing, we install Satan *'upon the mount of the congregation.'*

We must remember always that the smoker we met in our opening chapter is alive in each one of us! We must study, watch, and pray, if we are to keep him suppressed at all times.

Once man had fallen to sin, his mental, physical, and spiritual decline began. It will continue until the very end, when God finally eradicates sin, and creates a new world. Till then, Satan will continue to create more and more sophisticated designs, and man, in enthusiastic response, will become more and more depraved, to the extent that if it were possible for Jesus to delay His coming beyond a certain point in time, no flesh would be saved alive.

Meanwhile, let us return to the Garden of Eden. Humanity had now received two contradicting sermons. On the one hand, God declared, "the wages of sin is death." Rom. 6:23; and on the other, Satan preached: "That is not true! Man does not *actually, really, completely* die. On the contrary, he assumes a God-like state, possessing the knowledge and attributes of God. Though unseen by the eyes of the living, the dead will hover over the living, just like God." This became the setting for a controversy, which you and I should settle from the scriptures. Do sinners die or not? We shall tackle this question in chapters 13 and 14 of this book.

The Plan of Redemption

Adam and Eve did not drop dead when they sinned, as would be expected from God's warning in Genesis 2:17. This was because the moment Eve extended her hand and touched the forbidden fruit, the Godhead swung the Plan of Redemption into action. Immediately, the status of the plan, conceived before the foundation of all creation, for Jesus to die for the sins of humanity, was elevated to implementation mode.

From that very moment, Grace would allow the sinning race days on earth, to allow them the opportunity to repent. All would fall into the sleep we call death, when the time granted them was up, each at his moment. There would be a resurrection, and a judgment of all people, at the very end. God would reward some with eternal life, while others He would allow to die a second and final death (see chapter 16). In the Plan of Redemption, a way was provided for man to return to God and escape this second, eternal death decreed for sinners. All that fallen man had to do, in order to regain the eternal life that had been his original privilege, was to repent, and believe in faith in the promised Seed, the Messiah who was to come and die for his sins.

God delivered the very first promise of the Messiah in the judgment he handed to the serpent in Eden: "And I will put enmity between you and the woman, and between your seed and her Seed; He shall bruise your head, and you shall bruise His heel." Gen. 3:15. The Messiah was to be born among men, and was to die without sin, as ransom in place of all sinners who were willing to offload their sins in faith upon Him. Adam and Eve never asked for this favor; neither did they deserve it. The Plan of Redemption was a pure act of grace extending from their day, to all humanity, until the end of time.

If God was to save mankind from the death He had decreed for sin, He had to find a way to fulfill the sentence, "The soul that sins, it shall die" Ez. 18:20. This had to be, because it is impossible to reverse God's word, for "God is not a man, that He should lie, nor a son of man, that He should repent. Has He said, and will He not do? Or has He spoken, and will He not make it good?" Num. 23:19.

Man had sinned, and had to die. If sinful man was to live, an equal substitute had to die in his place. This is why Paul says: "Without the shedding of blood there is no remission." Heb. 9:22. The sacrifice of this ransom in place of humanity had to fulfill God's sense of unfathomable justice. How did the Plan of Redemption achieve this? It provided the perfect ransom in Jesus Christ, the Messiah. In the entire universe, God the Son was the only One found suitable for the role of ransom. Let us see how He qualified.

Jesus was the original Word.

> In the beginning was the Word, and the Word was with God, and the word was God . . . . All things were made by Him; and without Him was not any thing made that was made . . . . He came unto His own, and His own received Him not . . . . And

the Word was made flesh, and dwelt among us. John 1:1, 3, 11, 14.

Jesus created the universe. His single life therefore was of infinitely greater value than all humanity—indeed all creation—put together. No pot—no matter how exquisitely molded—can possibly possess greater value than the potter who fashioned it from miry clay. Only Christ, therefore, was qualified to die in the place of all human beings at once! In His one life, all the combined lives of humanity could fit and leave room. When He died on the cross, Jesus was a man just like Adam, or you and me, having been born of a human mother, and grown up from childhood like any other person. On Calvary, a human being died for *all* the sins committed by *the entirety of humanity*, and he was more than enough substitute. The Sacrifice of the Christ was an over-compensation! The Accuser can never allege now, that humanity has not received its just rewards for sin. He can no longer justify any claim that God, in sparing repentant human sinners, exercises impartiality.

From the original fall of man, until the Pentecost of Acts 2, only those specifically called out for a purpose by God received His Holy Spirit with power, to execute specific duties. The prophets, judges, and patriarchs of the Old Testament are examples of those whom God specifically endowed with the Holy Spirit. He nevertheless remained in the world and among the people of God, to guide them and strengthen them at all times. Jesus told His disciples before His departure:

Nevertheless I tell you the truth. It is to your advantage that I go away; for if I do not go away, the Helper will not come to you; but if I depart, I will send Him to you . . . Nevertheless, when He, the Spirit of truth, has come, He will guide you into all truth. John 16:7, 13.

After Jesus' conquest of sin, and unseating of the devil from the throne of planet Earth, the Holy Spirit descended visibly in great power, on those called out to form the explosive nucleus of the current phase of His congregation, the Christian Church.

In the period from Adam to the cross of Calvary, the repentant sinner in the congregation of God, as typified by Israel in the later part of the era, would show his faith in the promised Messiah, *who was to come*, by shedding the blood of an innocent beast, offered as substitute for the remission of man's own sins.

While the Bible does not explicitly tell us God outlined the Plan of Redemption, including the need to offer animals as sacrifice for their sins, to Adam and Eve, some observations reveal He did. Firstly, God's sentence to the serpent included the promise of a Seed of Adam that would crush the serpent's head. Secondly, we conclude that when Abel offered burnt offerings of animals to God, he had received instruction from his parents. His parents in turn could only have taken lecture from God. On disembarking from the ark, the casual way in which "Noah built an altar to the Lord, and took of every clean animal and of every clean bird, and offered burnt offerings at the altar," reveals the existence of a tradition long established. Gen. 8:20. The practice was later refined at Sinai in the Sanctuary rituals, and finally abolished by the death of the true sacrifice, Jesus Christ, on the cross.

After Calvary, those who sought salvation had to repent and believe in the Messiah who *had come*. This is the case with us today. We see, therefore, that throughout the history of the earth, faith in the same Messiah, Jesus Christ, in the Plan of Redemption, would be the only means to salvation.

Rapid decline—Cain

Once Satan had caused Adam and Eve to disobey God, he set about establishing himself and his systems on earth. His strategy would be to recruit to his aid, those humans who were inordinately inclined to feed their egos, and gratify their physical senses. He targeted those who would not place their trust entirely on God, but rather relied on 'common sense' and feelings to decide issues requiring spiritual discernment. The very first human offspring was the first victim.

We have learnt that without blood, remission of sin is not possible. Adam and Eve taught their two sons this truth. Abel obeyed God's instructions without question, and the Lord accepted his offering of slain animals. Meanwhile, his elder brother Cain, who was a talented gardener, reasoned that it was well for Abel to offer animals at the altar because he was a gifted animal husbandman. However, he rationalized, as for him, it was more appropriate to offer cabbages, carrots, beetroot and other produce from his plot, since his God-given talent was tilling the soil. Talk about common sense! Cain resolved that he would worship God, but in his own special way; a way that suited his lifestyle. He took the best vegetables from his plot and burnt them for an offering. God rejected his effort.

Instead of repenting and correcting his error, Cain proceeded to commit yet another sin—the first recorded murder in human history! He killed his brother out of jealousy. Unwittingly, he became the devil's agent in the attempt to thwart the coming of the Seed that God had promised would crush Satan's head. Abel had been the likely candidate to father the lineage of the *"sons of God,"* from which would most likely emerge the Seed. Hence, the devil terminated him through his fallen brother Cain. People of all societies consider the sin of murder vile and grievous. It is, therefore, an indicator of how rapidly the nature of man had degenerated, that this terrible sin should surface within the very first generation of born humans.

Cain "went out from the presence of the Lord." Gen. 4:16. This seems to suggest defiance, rather than repentance and remorse. He settled down to start his own family, stubbornly carrying with him his self-appointed way of worshipping God. Thus, Cain became the father of what the Bible calls "the sons of men." Here, we see the devil, through Cain, laying the spiritual foundation for all congregations big and small, which would purport to love and worship God the Creator, and yet do so in ways contrary to the precepts of the very God whom they claim to worship.

This was the birth of humanism, and its ascendency over the precepts of God. Today churches that profess Christ are sprouting like mushrooms, each one built on a doctrine that flies in the face of God's precepts. In these churches, the devil easily fulfills his ambition to sit *upon the mount of the congregation.* How sure are you that what you call 'my church' is leading you along the path prescribed only by God, through His Holy Word?

The sons of men & civilization

Cain soon built a city, which he called Enoch after his first son. We see here the first evidence of human civilization. The word civilization can assume different meanings in different contexts. The following is a definitions from http://wordit.com/: "The term comes from the Latin civis, meaning 'citizen' or 'townsman'. In a technical sense, a civilization is a complex society in which many of the people live in cities and get their food from agriculture, as distinguished from band and tribal societies."

As a result of the curse of God, the earth became progressively degenerate. The land gave back less and less for more and more human input. God, ever kind, has raised up inventors in every generation since the earliest history of man. These men and women have designed new methods and implements to ease human toil, increase productivity and make life better. The talents that men and women possess are God's gift to the world. We can cite an example where the Scriptures reveal God as the source of human talents and creative genius.

> Then the LORD spoke to Moses, saying: "See, I have called by name Bezalel, . . . And I have filled him with the Spirit of God, in wisdom, in understanding, in knowledge, and in all manner of workmanship, to design artistic works, to work in gold, in silver, in bronze, in cutting jewels for setting, in carving wood, and to work in all manner of workmanship. Ex. 31:1-5.

There is, unfortunately, a sad downside to human civilization. Man has sought to use God given skills for purposes other than to create a better world. The following quotation, from Ellen G. White, summarizes the problem.

> The use which men have made of their capabilities, by misusing and abusing their God-given talents, has brought confusion into the world. They have left the guardianship of Christ for the guardianship of the great rebel, the prince of darkness. Man alone is accountable for the strange fire which has been mingled with the sacred. The accumulation of many things which minister to lust and ambition has brought upon the world the judgment of God. When in difficulty, philosophers and the great men of earth desire to satisfy their minds without appealing to God. They ventilate their philosophy in regard to the heavens and the earth, accounting for plagues, pestilences, epidemics, earthquakes, and famines, by their supposed science. Hundreds of questions relating to creation and providence, they will attempt to solve by

saying. This is a law of nature. (E. G. White, Fundamentals of Christian Education 1923, 409)

The foregoing paragraphs aptly describe the opposing forces underlying human civilization from the very beginning. On the one hand, God strives by giving light, talent, and skill, to make human life better amid the *'thorns'* and *'thistles'*. On the other, man, in the main, is either corrupting God's endowments, or creating his very own, without God's direction.

Let us return to Cain and his lineage. Within five generations, we witness the first report of polygamy in the community of men. The polygamist-cum-murderer is Lamech who brags to his wives "I have killed a man for wounding me, even a young man for hurting me." Gen. 4:23. In his proud ranting, he unilaterally claims for himself a multiplied portion of the protection that God had granted Cain after he murdered Abel. "If Cain shall be avenged sevenfold, then Lamech seventy fold." Gen. 4:24.

The depravity of man increased with each succeeding generation, as population increased, and civilization advanced. In spite of this, there was always a presence of sons of God who heeded God's precepts, and worshipped Him according to His will. Sometimes their number dwindled to just a few individuals in the entire world, but they were nevertheless present at all times. We shall study this branch of Adam's children, the remnant, in a later chapter.

The female offspring of the sons of men were beautiful; and the sons of God, against His will, began to intermarry with the daughters of men. The outcome was a spiritual adulteration of the lineage of the children of God. Soon, sin pervaded every facet of human endeavor, greatly compromising the intercessory effect of the presence of a Godly people upon the world. So repugnant was the outcome that God regretted ever creating man.

Then the Lord saw that the wickedness of man was great in the earth, and that every intent of the thought of his heart was only evil continually. And the Lord was sorry that He had made man on the earth, and He was grieved in His heart. Gen. 6:5, 6.

Imagine what kind of decadent world this had become, for God to rue the day He had created man, intended as a friend, in His own image. The Lord had to make a decision that must have caused the greatest pain. "So the Lord said, 'I will destroy man whom I have created from the face of the earth, both man and beast, creeping thing and birds of the air, for I am sorry that I have made them.'" Gen. 6:7. God would destroy the majority of humanity and start over.

Heaven found only one man in the entire world worthy of grace. God commanded Noah to build the ark that would save him and his family, and any others who may repent and join him, as well as all species of animal. Providence had proved the utter wretchedness of man's systems of government, economy, and religion—in short, civilization—under the influence of Satan. You may be familiar with the account of Noah and the flood that destroyed almost the entire population of plants and animals. Only eight human beings survived, out of an entire planet. You will find the full story in chapters 6, 7 and 8 of Genesis.

The obvious lesson from this episode is confirmation that God is not so much interested in numbers as in obedience. In things spiritual, there is no safety in numbers. Many today feel safe because they belong to churches where large numbers flock. They mingle with college professors, medical doctors and state presidents in magnificent temples and church buildings. They feel that these intelligent, successful, and important citizens could not possibly be wrong, not realizing that "God has chosen the foolish things of the world to put to shame the wise, and God has chosen the weak things of the world to put to shame the things which are mighty." 1 Cor. 1:27.

It is time, to make a decision for God alone; to disentangle ourselves from the snare that has trapped the majority of humanity. The fact that the population of smokers is vast will not blot out the reality of cancer and death. Likewise, the huge turnout in misled congregations will never dilute the sinfulness of disobedience.

CHAPTER 4

Babylon

Fresh beginnings

God had wiped the slate clean and preserved seed to start life afresh. Noah brought three sons, Shem Ham and Japheth, together with their wives into the post-Diluvian world. These eight formed the remnant of humanity, linking the pre and post-flood worlds. The devil was promptly on the lookout for a possible recruit to resume the genealogy of *'the sons of men,'* to be used to fight—if possible destroy—*'the sons of God'* in this new dispensation.

The character of one of Noah's sons impressed Satan. Ham watched and ridiculed the naked form of his inebriated father. In sharp contrast to Ham's behavior, his two brothers walked backwards, and covered their father's nakedness (see Genesis 9:22, 23). Ham became the devil's choice.

We must trace the role played by the branch of Ham in man's degeneration after the flood. This time around, the slide was much more rapid and forceful than before the flood. This was due, in part, to knowledge of evil being ready at hand through personal experience, and oral history. There was no need to 're-invent the wheel', so to speak. Satan was of course nearby to exert his insidious influence to steer men further away from God.

Nimrod

"The sons of Ham were Cush, . . . Cush begot Nimrod; he began to be a mighty one on the earth. He was a mighty hunter before the Lord." Gen. 10:6-9. After the flood, the animal population increased much more rapidly than that of mankind. Man-eating carnivors became a constant threat to people. Alexander Hyslop describes how Nimrod became mighty.

> The exploits of Nimrod, therefore, in hunting down the wild beasts of the field, and ridding the world of monsters, must have gained for him the character of a pre-eminent benefactor of his race. By this means, not less than by the bands he trained, was his power acquired, when he first began to be mighty upon the earth; and in the same way, no doubt, was that power consolidated. Then, over and above, as the first great city-builder after the flood, by gathering men together in masses, and surrounding them with walls, he did still more to enable them to pass their days in security, free from the alarms to which they had been exposed in their scattered life, when no one could tell but that at any moment he might be called to engage in deadly conflict with prowling wild beasts, in defence of his own life and of those who were dear to him. Within the battlements of a fortified city no such danger from savage animals was to be dreaded; and for the security afforded in this way, men no doubt looked upon themselves as greatly indebted to Nimrod. (Hyslop 1901, The Two Babylons, Chapter II Section II Sub-section III, The Child in Greece)

As pointed out before, Satan, the ruler of this present world has always lurked around all inventions, and God-inspired human progress. His aim is to corrupt inventions and lead men to misapply them to the detriment of fellow men. It is therefore not surprising that we should witness a downside of this era of great human civilization and urbanization. Nimrod's first and most important city was at Babel. He later built many other cities filled with evil, notable among which was Nineveh, the city that God almost annihilated in the manner of Sodom. (Read the book of Jonah). However, it was at Babel that "he began to be a mighty one before the Lord." According to Strong's Hebrew-Greek Dictionary, the Hebrew word translated 'before' is paniym, a word also translated 'against'. Put another way, Nimrod "began to be a mighty one *against* the Lord." How did he achieve this dubious distinction?

According to Hyslop, Nimrod became so powerful that almost the entire ancient world fell under his realm. He called himself many names and one of them was 'He-Roe', meaning 'The Shepherd'. The people began to look on him as their savior and literally worship him. Hyslop writes that the phrase 'hero-worship' derives from the adulation of Nimrod, *He-Roe*. The man gradually began to portray himself more and more as a god, or the representative of all that men worshipped. Nimrod began to mobilize the ancient world against God's precepts. He became much more than a hunter of animals; he became a hunter of the souls of men. He rallied people behind him in a project that was a direct affront to God.

> Come let us make bricks and bake them thoroughly . . . . Come, let us build ourselves a city, and a tower whose top is in the heavens; let us make a name for ourselves, lest we be scattered abroad over the face of the earth. Gen. 11:3, 4.

We discern here the same spirit of self-elevation that led to Lucifer's rebellion in Heaven—to rise above the stars of God! Note how each sentence contains the words 'us' and 'we'. The building of the city and the tower of Babel antagonized God in more than one way.

Firstly, the motive for its construction was in direct opposition to God's command to Noah's family upon emerging from the ark: "Be fruitful and multiply; and *fill the earth*." Gen. 9:1 (emphasis supplied). In defiance, Nimrod cautioned, "lest we be scattered."

Secondly, the building of a tower to reach up to heaven (they called the city Heaven's Gate) was a move against God in two ways. In one way, Nimrod was helping fulfill Lucifer's ambition to *"ascend into heaven"* and *"be like the Most High."* We discern the same Luciferan ambition in the phrase *"let us make a name for ourselves."* In building the tower, the people were making the statement that they would live and worship the way they would; and if God should ever attempt to destroy them with a flood again, He would have to flood His own throne before he could drown them! They demonstrated a lack of trust in the God who had made a covenant with their grandfather Noah, "Never again shall all flesh be cut off by the waters of the flood; never again shall there be a flood to destroy the earth." Gen. 9:11.

So, Nimrod, the first man to study the science of warfare and use magic and the occult in hunting and in battle, went on to dominate a large portion of the ancient world and rule over it. He did this by creating protected city-states and becoming the lawgiver and ruler of each one of them. He set up local governments in these city-states, which became the precursors of today's state and municipal governments. These states, falling under one ruler became one of the earliest attempts at creating a world empire.

Sun worship

According to Hyslop, Nimrod's wife was Semiramis, a beautiful but immoral woman. The couple promoted forms of worship with the sun as the focal point. The sun was the 'giver of light' which is the meaning of the name 'Lucifer'. They enforced this religion throughout their realm. They presented Baal as the chief sun god. Gradually, the people began to regard Nimrod as the chief priest of the sun god. Fire was the earthly representation of the sun, and it featured in all ceremonies of Babylonian worship. The sacrifice of human babies at the fiery altar during wild ceremonies where worshippers had sex orgies with male and female temple prostitutes became widespread.

The sons of men (the genealogy of Ham), namely the Cushites, the Canaanites, Jebusites, Amorites, Gurgashites and the Hivites among many others, were scattered from Babel when God confounded their languages. As they migrated to fill the earth, they carried with them forms of the Babylonian religion they had learnt from Nimrod and Semiramis. Because of the confusion of languages, numerous different names are used in referring to the same couple in different cultures today. Many families, tribes, and nations patriotically cling to their traditional forms of worship. They claim that they have inherited the ways of their fore fathers, passed on from generation to generation. Little do they realize that many of the founding fathers of tribes, races and nations worldwide carried from Babylon traditions and forms of worship that were a direct affront to God. A child growing up among smoking parents will take up the habit as naturally as drinking water. Likewise, millions around the world have known no other way but the religion passed down to them by their fathers. They patriotically cling to this way, and strenuously resist any attempts to bring change. Could this possibly be the case with you?

Death of Nimrod and the rise of secret societies

Secular history records that Nimrod was assassinated, and his body cut up into small pieces which were dispatched to all regions of the world as a warning to those who would dare to rebel against God. The execution of Nimrod paralyzed the entire world with fear and had the effect of bringing about a stop to open Baal worship. However, it had a dreadful down side! Sun worship went underground. Worshippers kept pieces of Nimrod's body and venerated them as relics after his supposed deification. Semiramis revived and refined Baal worship by creating a secret society[3] of worshippers. Those who would become members took oaths of secrecy under pain of death. They conducted ceremonies far from the eyes of the uninitiated, in the mountains and hills referred to in the Bible as the 'high places'.

Semiramis perfected Babylon mystery religion, giving birth to the Eastern Mystery Cults that have taken centre stage in the religious affairs of the world today, leading the planet to a 'One World Order' soon to be instituted just before the return of Jesus Christ and the end of the age. We will read more about this in a later chapter.

The immoral Semiramis fell pregnant and claimed to her followers that she was pregnant by the gods; and that the child she carried in her womb was the reincarnation of Nimrod. When the baby was born, believers venerated it as the god Tammuz. Both Semiramis and her baby became objects of worship and it became common for followers to worship pictures and statues of mother and baby in her arms. This heathen practice of worshipping statues of these gods has found its way into 'Christian' worship, as images of the Virgin Mary with baby Jesus in her arms. The truth is that Baal worship, complete with all its festivals, has been adopted and adapted to suit the taste of 'Christians'; and so we have Sunday (sun-day; day of the sun), Christmas, Easter and many other so-called Christian holy days. Through the tradition of turning dead heroes such as Nimrod into gods, Semiramis popularized the pagan practice of ancestral worship. This practice is rampant in the so-called Third World. Even though many people have accepted Christianity, yet deep down in their psyche, ancestral veneration is alive.

In the attempt to build the Tower of Babel, we see the first unified effort of the people of the world for a common purpose. We see a large group of men and women uniting under one government designed and run by Nimrod, and one system of religion designed and perfected by Semiramis, acting in unison against God. The Almighty thwarted their effort by confounding their languages but the spirit of unifying the world under one government and one religion did not die with the tower project. The same ambition to unify the world under one government and religion has surfaced repeatedly in history. This should not surprise us because we are now aware of the existence of a common negative influence behind all phases of human civilization, though they be separated by time. Satan will continue to rally men under his government and have them worship him in fulfillment of his ambition to sit *upon the mount of the congregation.*

Israel—called to check the fall

Through Abraham, the seed of a descendent of Shem, God isolated and called out a race called Israel. God was to work with this people to demonstrate the magnificence and equity of His systems of education, religion, government, and economy to the world. He would make them a conduit of His blessing to the entire world. The two parties made a covenant in which Israel pledged to obey God's commandments while He undertook to bless them exceedingly. The blessing would extend to all who should follow their example. God gave instructions for the construction of a sanctuary, or temple, which Moses built for God to dwell among men.

So privileged was this people! Yet theirs was not a simple invitation to a sweet life. The prophet Isaiah summarizes God's vision of Israel's role in the world thus:

> The word that Isaiah the son of Amoz saw concerning Judah and
> > Jerusalem.
> Now it shall come to pass in the latter days
> That the mountain of the LORD's house
> Shall be established on the top of the mountains,
> And shall be exalted above the hills;
> And all nations shall flow to it.
> Many people shall come and say,
> 'Come, and let us go up to the mountain of the LORD,
> To the house of the God of Jacob;
> He will teach us His ways,
> And we shall walk in His paths.'
> For out of Zion shall go forth the law,
> And the word of the LORD from Jerusalem.
> Is. 2:1-3.

God promised the nation of Israel material prosperity on condition of obedience to His law. God's plan was to settle Israel in Canaan on a mission to become a model nation for the rest of the world to emulate. The form of government He envisaged was Theocratic—where He would rule directly through a system of prophets, priests, and judges that He would appoint. God achieved this form of government through Moses and Aaron during the wilderness journey, and through Joshua during the early years in the Promised Land.

Under Joshua's leadership, Israel settled down and prospered because they followed God's precepts and He was quick to fulfill His own end of the bargain in return.

> The Lord gave them rest all around, according to all that He had sworn to their fathers. And not a man of all their enemies stood against them; the Lord delivered all their enemies into their hand, not a word failed of any good thing which the Lord had spoken to the house of Israel. All came to pass. Josh. 21:44, 45.

In spite of the visible blessings and favour of God, apostasy reared its ugly head soon after Joshua's generation had passed on. "When all that generation had been gathered to their fathers, another generation arose after them who did not know the Lord nor the work which He had done for Israel." Judg. 2:10. This new generation grew up under the influence of the surrounding heathen tribes, which their fathers had spared against God's command.

> Then the children of Israel did evil in the sight of the Lord, and served the Baals; and they forsook the Lord God of their fathers, who had brought them out of the land of Egypt; and they followed other gods from among the gods of the people who were all around them, and they bowed down to them. They forsook God and served Baal and the Ashtoreths. And the anger of the Lord was hot against Israel. So He delivered them into the hands of plunderers who despoiled them; and He sold them into the hands of their enemies all around, so they could no longer stand before their enemies. Judg. 2:11-14.

Era of kings

Failing to diagnose idolatry as the root cause of their troubles, the Israelites attributed their weakness to the absence of sound leadership, and the people demanded "a king to judge us like all other nations." 1 Sam. 8:5. The attraction of human systems proved stronger that the love for God's. As had been the case since Eden, man chose the way that looked good to his eyes and felt good to his senses. This will be the common characteristic in all the stages of the continuing deterioration of man, until the second advent of the Christ.

By demanding a king, Israel was effectively rejecting God as its ruler.

> And the Lord said unto Samuel, Hearken unto the voice of the people in all that they say unto you: for they have not rejected you, but they have rejected me, that I should not reign over them. 1 Sam. 8:7.

Behind this simple statement was veiled the deep hurt and disappointment of He who had labored so patiently to nurture a people to the pinnacle of success in all the possible senses of the word; He who, being the Creator of all, knew what was best for man. With a very heavy heart, God gave Israel up to the human kings they so strenuously demanded.

However, before the coronation of the first king, God warned Israel of the oppression and injustice that their kings would bring upon them. This was a mere prediction based on God's foreknowledge, rather than a sentence imposed for their rebellion. God was simply describing a typical human king. To confirm the truth of the warning, all Israel needed to do was look at the nations around them and observe how the people suffered under the unjust and autocratic bondage of human monarchies.

The era of kings set off to a bad start with Saul. You can follow the history of this king in the two books of Samuel. However, during the reign of the second and third kings, namely David and Solomon, it began to look as if God would realize His vision of Israel as the world's torchbearer. Indeed, so powerful, peaceful and prosperous did the nation become that "King Solomon surpassed all the kings of the earth in riches and wisdom. Now all the earth sought the presence of Solomon to hear his wisdom, which God had put in his heart." 1 Kings 10:23, 24.

His fame resonated as far afield as Ethiopia in Africa, resulting in the Queen of Sheba making pilgrimage to Jerusalem to confirm "the fame of Solomon concerning the name of the LORD." 1 Kings 10:1. God had now placed Israel in a strategic position for achieving his aim. All Solomon had to do now was point all visiting monarchs to the True God! How readily they would have embraced the God of heaven. Alas, this was not to be! Instead, the lure of idolatry proved too strong for the wise king to resist. The fallen ways of the pagan nations of the world became his own.

The downfall of Solomon originated in his insatiable appetite for silver, gold, horses, chariots, palaces, and women. He failed to control his excesses. He accumulated seven hundred wives and three hundred concubines, mostly princesses from the heathen nations of the world, the very enemies of Israel and of God. When he compromised and built an altar in honour of the foreign god of one wife, he had to build one for every one of the thousand.

The immoderation of King Solomon, added to the apostasy that he introduced from the top, created irreparable cracks in the foundation of the nation. The next generation after him witnessed the division of Israel into two separate groupings, ceasing to be one united nation of twelve tribes. (Read 2 Samuel and 1 Kings, for a full account of the exploits of David and Solomon.)

Ten tribes broke away to form the Northern grouping called Israel. Samaria later became the capital of Israel. The tribes Judah and Benjamin remained in the South, loyal to the house of David, and keeping Jerusalem as their capital. Judah was the name assumed by the two tribes. (Please read 1 Kings 12).

The formation of breakaway Israel started as a reformation movement to protest the excesses of Solomon; but in true conformity to fallen human behavior, Israel adopted the very same oppressive ways they sought to escape from Solomon's legacy. Instead of continuing in reformation, even harsher taxation, repression of prophets and true worship, combined with abuse of power, marked the reign of all the kings of Israel. Not one of the northern kings is on record as having pleased God. The worst rulers of Israel were King Ahab and his wife, Queen Jezebel. They formalized and, to all intents and purposes, enforced Baal worship, becoming to Israel almost what Nimrod and Semiramis had been to Babylon. In the history of Judah, only a handful of kings pleased God by suppressing idol worship, but most came in the same mold as their Northern counterparts. You can read the history of the kings of Judah and Israel in the first and second books of Kings, and Chronicles.

Two hundred and fifty years and twenty kings later, Israel ceased to be a nation when the Assyrians conquered and scattered them. For another one hundred and thirty-five years, Judah held on, but the same fate finally befell them when King Nebuchadnezzar's Babylonian army overran them. In all, Judah had eighteen kings and one queen.

That God permitted pagans to destroy and plunder the temple at Jerusalem, was a visible indicator of the intensity of the Lord's displeasure with His chosen people, and a sure sign of the withdrawal of His glory from them. Nevertheless, God did not give up totally on Israel at that time. He meant affliction under Babylon and Medo-Persia as a wake-up call to stir the spirit of repentance.

The fall of Israel summarized

Since the time of Nimrod and Semiramis, the world had lost knowledge of the true God. Almost the entire inhabited world worshipped idols made by man's own hands and appointed names as gods. Idolatry had become the religion of the world. In order to reveal Himself, and to check the inevitable destruction of a world spinning without a knowledge of its Creator, God had given Israel the privilege of proving to the world the spiritual and material benefits of worshipping Him in obedience to His law of love. Far from Israel becoming an example to the rest of the world, they eagerly adopted the idolatry of the rest of the world. The sophistication of pagan city dwellers dazzled these simple people as they emerged from a forty-year wilderness journey. The lure of human civilization proved too strong to resist, and the chosen nation became blind to the reality of the God who had shown them His powerful, loving presence since their deliverance from Egypt; a very present help in time of need!

We must let the Bible summarize the fall of Israel. Few modern writers could put it any better.

> And the children of Israel did secretly those things that were not right against the Lord their God, and they built them high places in all their cities, . . . And they set them up images and idol poles on every high hill, and under every green tree: and there they burnt incense in all the high places, as did the nations which the Lord carried away before them, and did wicked things to provoke the Lord to anger. 2 Kings 17:9-11.

God revealed to the prophet Ezekiel activities of a cult operating right inside His temple. He showed the prophet a secret room, filled with paintings and idols of abominable animals, with the elders of Israel burning incense to them. "Then He brought me to the gate of the Lord's house which was towards the north; and, behold, there sat women weeping for Tammuz." Ez. 8:14.

Right there, within the perimeter of God's temple some women of Israel wept for the Babylonian god Tammuz.

> Then he said to me, Have you seen this, O son of man? Turn you yet again, and you shall see greater abominations than these. And he brought me into the inner court of the Lord's house, and, behold, at the door of the temple of the Lord, between the porch and the altar, were about five and twenty men, with their backs towards the temple of the Lord, and their faces towards the east; and they worshipped the sun towards the east. (vv. 15, 16).

Upon Mount Zion, Israel would install Satan in the place of God the Creator. Nothing could have given the devil greater satisfaction than to have God's favored nation worship him right inside His temple, upon the very mount of the congregation!

Note carefully that at that time, men, quite obviously the very leaders of the congregation, were using the temple of God for false worship without the knowledge of the general laity. This is the essence of Babylon mystery religion throughout the world, in all centuries and across all nations. It never stands alone, but latches onto, and corrupts, existing systems of God's truth. It employs popular and charismatic leaders who are, to look at, pious men of God.

Many cults appear on the surface to uphold high ideals of charity and equity, cloaked in a veil of deep piety and ceremony. The congregation attends regular service in a place and system from which the glory of the Lord has either long since departed, or has never been. The ordinary members of the church are unaware that their very best efforts are in fact an abomination to the very God they seek to worship.

Please note that the devil managed to achieve his ambition to *"sit upon the mount of the congregation"* of none other than Israel, right inside the very temple where the glory of the Lord, the Shekinah used to shine as God communicated directly with mortals! It is instructive to note also that even Ezekiel, a devout prophet of God, was not aware what went on behind the scenes in the very temple where he attended on a regular basis. So secretive are the mystery religions!

Dear friend, if this could happen in the congregation Israel, with all the first-hand knowledge and experience of God they had, under the very nose of a prophet of God, what earthly reason have you and I to place complete and blind trust in what we loyally call 'our' congregations, 'our' churches, 'our' elders, deacons, pastors, conferences and popes? Is it not time now to revisit the Bible and the Bible alone with a view to establishing the true expectations of our Creator in matters of worship? Should we not now begin to measure every word preached to us, every doctrine in our catechism, and every rite we participate in, against the scriptures?

Knowing Satan's motives as we do now, should we not be wary of every word, and every doctrine, unless it should come expressly from the Bible? Should we not now summon the courage to question, even abandon doctrines, rites, teachings—yeah, even congregations—should their base prove to be the shallow mind of man, with the concealed aid of the enemy of God?

Let not ego and sense take the lead in matters spiritual. Suppress the smoker within. We must use the intelligence that God graciously gave us, to study the scriptures, discern error, and "work out (our) own salvation with fear and trembling." Philippians 2:12.

In the Promised Land, pagans from Assyria and Babylon replaced Israel, as did other idol worshipping nations. About these new occupants we learn,

> they feared the Lord, and made unto themselves of the lowest of them priests of the high places . . . So these nations feared the Lord, and served their graven images, both their children, and their children's children: as did their fathers, so do they unto this day. 2 Kings 17:32, 41.

The failure of Israel to influence the world positively, and to point it to the true God, left a planet spinning under the steam of human civilization. This was a world generally acknowledging the existence of a supreme power, God, while steadfastly refusing to worship Him according to His statutes. Its inhabitants chose instead to place tangible objects in the gulf they created between themselves and God.

Idolaters took the place of Israel in the Promised Land. Veneration of cheap hand-made objects replaced true worship. The vile and the abominable overtook that which was holy. In the following chapters, we will see the same trend repeated with spiritual Israel, the end-time church of God.

The remnant of Israel—Jerusalem rebuilt

After seventy years of Israelite exile in Babylon, God supernaturally opened the way for repentant exiles to start trickling back. Their mission was to start the work of rebuilding the ruins that had once been Jerusalem. Those who did return were a small minority. They were the remnant who still treasured their spiritual heritage ahead of the advanced civilization and sophistries of Babylon. It is around this time that we meet the first reference to Jews, rather that Israel or Judah.

The repatriated Jews were determined to worship their God in the place and manner that He had originally prescribed for their ancestors. The rebuilding of the temple and the city went on in an atmosphere of vicious antagonism. Animosity came from the neighbors, in the surrounding countryside. The books Ezra, Nehemiah, Haggai, and Zechariah, among others, cover this period of Israel's history.

For over a hundred years after the first returnees arrived in Jerusalem, only the temple remained completed. The rest of the city was semi-built, and sparsely inhabited. Most of the Jews lived in the outlying villages and faced the real danger of losing their identity once again. It was Nehemiah who came on a mission to rebuild the wall around Jerusalem and succeeded against formidable opposition from neighbors hostile to the re-establishment of a powerful Jewish nation as of old.

When the wall was finally completed, the people gathered in the city before Nehemiah the Governor and Ezra the prophet. Ezra read aloud to them from the book of the law, which God had instructed Moses to write at Sinai. There was mass repentance of those present. The remnant of original Israel had lost political power. They were now subservient to Persian dictatorship. Although they had reconstructed the temple, they never again derived power and inspiration from it, as in the former days. The reading of the law provided the Jews with a new source of inspiration and rallying point—the written word of God!

Waiting for the Messiah

A new generation of leaders emerged, composed of the readers, interpreters and teachers of the written law of God. The Priests, the Scribes, and the Pharisees gradually came to represent the ruling class among the Jews. Because God's presence was no longer visible to them as the Shekinah of old, the Jews shifted their focus to His law, and tried at all costs, to obey it. The Jews hoped to gain spiritual salvation from observing the law. Obedience to the letter of the law became more important than love, the spirit of the law.

Politically, having been let down by the human kings their fathers had demanded, their only hope now lay in the Messiah, promised to the prophets and the patriarchs since Eden. According to their understanding, it was He, who would emerge from the house of David to emancipate Israel from the cruel bondage of foreign rulers.

The Jewish leaders read the prophecies of the coming Messiah from the books of Isaiah and Daniel, and correctly pinpointed the time of His arrival. They even identified Bethlehem of Judea as His birthplace from reading the book of Micah. However, they erroneously looked for a military leader who would lead them in conquest of their oppressors, and become a king in the mold of the King David.

The people remained in the grip of national expectancy during the four hundred years from the rebuilding of the walls of Jerusalem, to the birth of Christ. A Scriptural silence marks this period. Behind the scenes, the letter of the law and a blurred image of the coming King grew in importance until the nation became completely blind to the arrival of their long awaited Messiah.

Not only did the Jews fail to recognize their Messiah, but also they antagonized Him at all points of His life and ministry until the intensity of their cries "Crucify Him! Crucify Him!" left the Roman governor with no choice but to oblige. The result was the cross of Calvary. Up to this day there are Jews still awaiting the coming of the Messiah for the first time.

At the time of the birth of Christ, Israel as a nation had failed. It was under the oppressive bondage of Rome. Politically and economically, it was indeed as if they had returned to Egypt. Spiritually, in the synagogue, the image had become more important than the object. Ritual had overtaken that which it stood for. An impenetrable cloak of self-righteousness enveloped the Jewish leaders, which even the Messiah failed to pierce. The spiritual life of the nation was dead. A sense of resigned anticipation prevailed among the majority of the Jewish population. Only a handful awaited the coming of the Messiah with any zeal.

In the rest of the world, true worship had been replaced by paganism, God overtaken by manmade idols, and truth darkened by error. The mystery religion introduced by Semiramis was now the religion of the world with variations to suit local taste. The sun remained the focus of human worship with other planets, stars, and animals having important roles as deities.

The philosophy of the immortality of the human soul, perfected and institutionalized by the Greek thinkers, was now the religion of the world. The veneration of departed ancestors and ceremonies for the dead became normal, indeed necessary, acts of worship. The many philosophies, upon which today's Mystery Cults are rooted, have their origin in those ancient, dark days.

The spiritual state of the world was no different from that pertaining in the original Babel of Nimrod and Semiramis. Just as the original population of Babylon had eagerly accepted the mixture of truth with sweet-sounding error, so the latter world embraced the philosophies and myths of men as pillars of their faith. This widespread system of manmade religion was the foundation of what the Bible refers to as *Babylon* in the present, though the ancient city is no more.

It was in that hour of universal spiritual darkness that the fullness of time arrived, and the Messiah was born. Would He succeed in stemming the fall of man? Would His advent destroy the new Babylon? Would He usher in a new congregation to take up the baton from Israel, and assume the role of model to the world?

CHAPTER 5

The Fall Continues (End-Time Babylon)

Babylon—more than just a city

In the book of Daniel, we read about Babylon, the capital city of the Chaldeans. History describes the design of the magnificent city.

> At the (northeast) corner was a vaulted building consisting of
> a series of arches, some of which were superimposed upon a
> lower tier. On this structure were the famous hanging gardens.
> Herodotus states that Babylon was a square, . . . The city was
> surrounded by a wall (Jer. 51:58) . . . . The city had 100 gates of
> bronze, 25 on each side.—(Davis 1944, 54)

Satan intended the thick high walls, gates, hanging fruit gardens, and the river Euphrates flowing through the middle, to imitate God's New Jerusalem as described in Scripture. About this heavenly city, the revelator tells us:

> Also she had a great and high wall with twelve gates . . . . On
> the east three gates; on the north three gates; on the south

three gates; and on the west three gates . . . . And the city lieth foursquare . . . The length and the breadth and the height of it are equal . . . . And he showed me a pure river of water of life, clear as crystal, proceeding from the throne of God and of the Lamb. In the middle of its street, and on either side of the river, was the tree of life, which bore twelve fruits, each tree yielding its fruit every month." Rev. 21:12, 13, 16; 22:1, 2.

The devil influenced the construction of Babylon on a pattern broadly similar to the city of God. If God would establish His everlasting capital on earth, Satan, continuing in his attempt to better God in every point, would also establish his own capital among men. The arch enemy of God intended this counterfeit of the New Jerusalem as the control centre of the his earthly empire. Filled with the satanic pride of the true architect of the city, Nebuchadnezzar the king declared, "Is not this great Babylon, that I have built for a royal dwelling by my mighty power and for the honor of my majesty?" Daniel 4:30.

In the book of Genesis, we met Babel, the origin of Babylon. Babel was a direct affront to God. The tower was more than brick and mortar; it was a direct challenge to the God of Heaven. Babel was more than just a city. It was a rebellion; an uprising against the Almighty! It was a calculated attack at the root of all that was good, and of God. Babel was the spirit of enslavement. Circumstances had forced citizens to seek protection from a mighty hunter, who was the enemy of God. Nimrod and Semiramis then mesmerized them into their projects, government, and religion.

Babel represented the desire of one man to hold sway over all other men, and control their physical and spiritual being. It was a passion to rule over souls, and control their destinies. The Bible mentions the name 'Babel' only twice, both times in Genesis, rendering it 'Babylon' in the rest of the Bible. The physical city, built as a conceptual model of the city of God, represented a spirit of competition with the Supreme. It was a declaration of independence from, and equality with God. It was a loud announcement of cessation from everything heavenly. We must never forget that the ultimate schemer behind the tower, the city, and the religion was Satan himself, in his endeavor to take the place of God on earth.

The book of Daniel reveals how Babylon represented an enslavement of the peoples' minds:

> Then the king (Nebuchadnezzar) instructed . . . the master of
> his eunuchs, to bring some of the children of Israel . . . who had
> ability to serve in the king's palace, and whom they might teach
> the language and literature of the Chaldeans. Dan. 1:3, 4.

Babylon stood for a worldwide union, formed to trample upon all that God stood for. It was a bringing together of all peoples into one false religion, under one man, who wielded both religious and political power. It represented a uniting of church and state, under one man, who was Satan's very own medium. It was an enforcement of what was abominable before the God of Heaven:

> Then a herald cried aloud: 'To you it is commanded, O peoples,
> nations, and languages, . . . you shall fall down and worship the
> gold image that King Nebuchadnezzar has set up; and whoever
> does not fall down and worship shall be cast immediately into
> the midst of a burning fiery furnace.' Dan 3:3-6.

As the world wandered after the king, and worshipped his image, so they worshipped the spirit behind the scheme—Satan.

Destruction of ancient Babylon

God is patient with sinful humanity, and allows them time to repent. God pleaded His case long with Babylon through its king Nebuchadnezzar, till at last the human monarch humbled himself before the God of heaven. Becoming co-writer of the inspired word, the king gives this testimony in Daniel 4:

> I, Nebuchadnezzar, lifted my eyes to heaven, and my understanding returned to me; and I blessed the Most High and praised and honored Him who lives forever: for His dominion is an everlasting dominion, and His kingdom is from generation to generation. All the inhabitants of the earth are reputed as nothing; He does according to His will in the army of heaven and among the inhabitants of the earth. No one can restrain His hand or say to Him, 'What have You done?' (vv. 34, 35).

Through the humbled king, the world received knowledge of the true God. Unfortunately, after just one generation, Belshazzar a grandson of Nebuchadnezzar became another proud and idolatrous king. As a king is, so are the subjects, and the old satanic order was restored once more in Babylon. Soon the patience of the longsuffering God had to end. "We would have healed Babylon, but she is not healed; . . ." Jer. 51:9 (first part).

The proverbial last straw that broke the camel's back was the desecration of the vessels that the Chaldeans had plundered from God's temple in Jerusalem. King Belshazzar of Babylon organized a feast for his lords. He ordered servants to bring the precious and holy vessels to the party,

> that the king and his lords, his wives, and his concubines might drink from them. Then they brought the gold vessels that had

been taken from the temple of the house of God which had been in Jerusalem; and the king and his lords, his wives, and his concubines drank from them. They drank wine, and praised the gods of gold and silver, bronze and iron, wood and stone. Dan. 5:2-5.

The dirtiest hands of the lowest of society fondled the vessels that only the scrubbed and consecrated hands of priests of the house of Levi should touch. The painted lips of prostitutes drank profane wine from the holy vessels. At that moment, the heavenly courts reached a final verdict. Probation had closed for Babylon. The destruction foretold by Jeremiah decades earlier was now imminent,

> for (Babylon's) judgment reaches to heaven and is lifted up to the skies. . . . I will dry up her sea and make her springs dry. Babylon shall become a heap!; a dwelling place for jackals, an astonishment and a hissing, without an inhabitant. Jer. 51:9, 36, 37.

It so happened therefore, that in the hour of celebration and wild revelry, the Babylonian empire came to an abrupt end. "That very night Belshazzar, king of the Chaldeans, was slain. And Darius the Mede received the kingdom, being about sixty-two years old." Daniel 5:30, 31.

The city held up by the Chaldeans as the impregnable and indestructible capital of the world was no more. The Medes and the Persians razed Satan's pride to the ground, as prophecy had predicted. No one would rebuild or inhabit the city, ever! "Because of the wrath of the LORD she shall not be inhabited, but she shall be wholly desolate. Everyone who goes by Babylon shall be horrified." Jer. 50:13.

End-time Babylon in Revelation

That the book of Revelation is a prophecy of the future is a point that few will refute. At its very opening, the revelator himself describes the book as

> the Revelation of Jesus Christ, which God gave Him to show His servants—*things which must shortly take place*; . . . Blessed is he who reads and those who hear the words of this *prophecy*, and keep those things which are written in it; *for the time is near.* Rev.1:1, 3 (emphasis supplied).

The Old Testament prophecy of Jeremiah 50:13, quoted above has withstood the test of time. No man has been able to rebuild the city of Babylon since its destruction, which began with the Medes in 539 B. C. The city of Babylon is no more. Today, no map bears the name 'Babylon'. God vowed through Jeremiah that the city of Babylon would never be again; yet in the book of Revelation, we meet the same God addressing an *existing* Babylon. Is this a contradiction? Did God lie? Certainly not! For God *cannot* lie! There has to be a simple explanation.

The answer lies in our earlier observation that Babylon was *more than just a city.* Babylon is a fallen spiritual condition. It is a proud unilateral declaration of human independence from God. It is idolatry. Derived from Babel, Babylon means confusion. It is an imposition of the will of a few upon the masses. It is the spirit of enticing others to the same depraved and fallen condition as oneself. It is an autocratic system of government, which also controls the religion of the people. It is a uniting of the world against the precepts of the Lord. It is the root of all apostasy; the nucleus of all wars and strife. As an invisible institution possessing all the foregoing attributes, it is Satan's instrument for accomplishing on earth, that for which he forsook heaven—to sit *upon the mount of the congregation*.

Here is a profile of present-day Babylon, as described in Revelation:

> Babylon the great is fallen, is fallen, and has become a dwelling place of demons, a prison for every foul spirit, and a cage for every unclean and hated bird! For all the nations have drunk of the wine of the wrath of her fornication, the kings of the earth have committed fornication with her, and the merchants of the earth have become rich through the abundance of her luxury . . . . that great city, because she has made all nations drink of the wine of the wrath of her fornication. Rev. 18:2, 3; 14:8.

We easily discern the following characteristics of modern Babylon:

- It is spiritually decayed.
- It is steeped in spiritualism, and therefore must be religious.
- It is international in scope and extent.
- It has a close relationship with world political leaders, and together they are unfaithful to God.
- It is extremely rich, and by this means, it controls world trade and economy.
- It has caused all nations, worldwide, to turn their backs on God and true worship.

In Revelation 17, we receive further details to help us identify Babylon. This time the revelator depicts Babylon as a prostitute who has the entire world eating out of her hand.

Come, I will show you the judgment of the great harlot who sits on many waters, with whom the kings of the earth committed fornication, and the inhabitants of the earth were made drunk with the wine of her fornication. Rev. 17:1, 2.

The many waters referred to "are peoples, multitudes, nations, and tongues." (v. 15).

In the Bible, a wicked woman represents an apostate church. The Old Testament makes this clear. Addressing Israel, which had turned to idolatry, the Lord had this to say:

"Surely, as a wife treacherously departs from her husband, so have you dealt treacherously with Me, O house of Israel," says the LORD. Jer. 3:20.

Now then, O harlot, hear the word of the LORD! Thus says the Lord GOD: "Because your filthiness was poured out and your nakedness uncovered in your harlotry with your lovers, and with all your abominable idols." Ez. 16:35, 36.

We can confidently claim, therefore, that present day Babylon is an apostate church practicing idolatry in the house of God just as Israel had done in its time, to earn the tag of 'harlot'.

Continuing with Revelation 17, we read:

So he carried me away in the Spirit into the wilderness. And I saw a woman . . . The woman was arrayed in purple and scarlet, and adorned with gold and precious stones and pearls, having in her hand a golden cup full of abominations and the filthiness of her fornication. (vv. 3, 4).

The woman is dressed in the colors of earthly royalty. We must therefore identify a church whose leaders dress in expensive apparel, fit for kings. The reference to gold and jewelry is a pointer to the immense wealth of the fallen church.

The next text leaves no doubt that this apostate church is indeed modern day Babylon: "And on her forehead a name was written: Mystery, Babylon the great, the mother of harlots and of the abominations of the earth" (v.5).

The Inspired Word credits this church with the current idolatrous state of the world. We also learn here that the church has offspring daughters who are also harlots. In other words, there are churches worldwide that emerged from this rich church, that inherited and adopted some of the apostasy of the parent. "I saw the woman, drunk with the blood of the saints and with the blood of the martyrs of Jesus." (v. 6). We are looking for a church that was responsible for a great persecution and massacre of true Christians. Just as a man needs to imbibe much wine to become drunk, so the massacre had to be excessive to make the church 'drunk'.

There is only one church in history, which fits this profile in all points—the Roman Catholic Church, under the papacy! It is evidently one of the richest institutions in the entire world, running, charities, schools, colleges, universities, and cathedrals in almost every corner of the world. It fits the description of a mother harlot in that during the Reformation, many Christians who stood for truth left the Catholic Church, to follow leaders such as John Calvin and Martin Luther in forming the Protestant churches. These churches earned the label "protestant" because they were a result of protest against the substitution of the laws of God with traditions of men, in the Roman church. Many Protestant denominations were formed—Anglican, Baptist, Dutch Reformed, Lutheran, Methodist and others. This was the beginning of modern denominationalism. Each denomination was a grouping of those who were protesting against some particular error of the Catholic Church, while adopting and incorporating some other of its traditions. By clinging onto some of the human traditions introduced by Babylon, most protestant churches thus became the harlot daughters of Babylon.

It is important to distinguish between the papacy as a corporate institution, and individual members of the Roman Catholic Church. Many members are unaware of the true history of their church. As a result, they have earnestly embraced the errors taught, as truth.

How do the 'scarlet and purple' apparel relate to this church? You and I have seen popes, bishops, and cardinals dressed in flowing, royal regalia of these colors. The robes are of the finest material, and exquisitely cut. Although the wearing of expensive robes originated in the Catholic Church in A.D.500, many protestant priests and ministers have since adopted it.

As for being "drunk with the blood of the saints and with the blood of the martyrs of Jesus," we only need to visit history textbooks to confirm the cruel extermination of Christians who refused to bow to the god of the fallen church. Historians refer to this era of massacre as The Dark Ages. It spanned 1,260 years from A.D. 538 to A.D. 1798. The Dark Ages were a parallel of the persecution of those who refused to bow down to the king's image in Nebuchadnezzar's original Babylon.

Prophecy reveals the geographical co-ordinates of the throne of the present day Babylon as it shifts the meaning of 'Babylon' to a physical location. John sees the harlot sitting astride a beast with seven heads about which by the angel explains:

The seven heads are seven mountains on which the woman sits. (v 9).

Rome is popularly known as *the city of seven hills* because that is a geographical fact.

> No other city in the world has ever been celebrated, as the city of Rome has, for its situation on seven hills. Pagan poets and orators, who had not thought of elucidating prophecy, have alike characterized it as 'the seven hilled city' . . . To call Rome the city 'of the seven hills' was by its citizens held to be as descriptive as to call it by its own proper name. (Hyslop 1901, Introduction)

Rome is the home to the Vatican City, a kingdom whose monarch is the Pope, who heads both a state, as well as a worldwide church. We see here the recurrence of a characteristic of ancient Babylon—combining state and church leadership under one man.

Finally, the revelator shows that Rome controls world governments.

> And the woman whom you saw is that great city which reigns over the kings of the earth (v. 18.)

One historian concurs.

> Propertius, in the same strain, speaks of it (only adding another trait, which completes the Apocalyptic picture) as 'The lofty city on seven hills, which governs the whole world.' (Hyslop 1901, Introduction)

If you doubt the influence of the papacy over world leaders, then think back to the death and funeral of Pope John Paul II in 2001. Few events have attracted as much media attention as the dying hours of this man. No single event in modern history has attracted, at once, so many diverse leaders from politics, commerce, entertainment, and religion as the funeral of John Paul II. No wonder the unerring scriptures describe the papacy as reigning over the kings of the earth.

Revelation 17:2 tells us "the inhabitants of the earth were made drunk with the wine of her fornication." What does this mean? The cup that the harlot holds out to the world represents false teachings and doctrines. It was by this means that the world was 'made drunk'. Just as an inebriated man fails to present or understand simple logic, so the masses have been mentally and spiritually poisoned, to the point where they are incapable of appreciating simple biblical truth. Instead, just as one who is drunk craves for more wine, so the ears of Christendom itch for more fables and traditions of men.

We must now look back and see how the papacy gained the dubious distinction of 'the enemy of God' and how the world wandered after her.

The advent of Christ—hostile reception

The last paragraph of chapter 4 left off where the Messiah was coming into the world. We have seen that the Jews were in the privileged position to know exactly when and where the Saviour would be born. They had all the prophecies at their disposal, to use in identifying Him when He should arrive. Unfortunately, they locked their expectation onto an earthly king, the mark of whose identity would be the successful mobilization of the Jews in battle to conquer Rome. He would then rule the entire world from Jerusalem.

Because of this flawed expectation, the Jews failed to recognize the Messiah when He came. His lifestyle and ministries of healing, preaching, and teaching fulfilled the prophecies, but they saw it not. Instead, they became jealous, and sought to antagonize their Savior throughout His working life.

Through nurturing a spirit of legalistic self-righteousness in the Jewish leadership, Satan had recruited a willing ally in his war to derail the Plan of Redemption. The Pharisees accused and disparaged Jesus at every turn, on behalf of the unseen archenemy of God. Three and half years into His ministry, they crucified the innocent Son of Man on trumped up charges, after a make-believe trial.

Again, Israel had let God down. It had been the original plan of Jesus to preach the gospel to a receptive Jewish nation: "I was not sent except to the lost sheep of the house of Israel." Matt. 15:24. This chosen race was to be, in turn, the means for spreading the good news of the Kingdom to the rest of the world. However, when He came, the Son of Man met only apathy and hostility among the Jews.

> O Jerusalem, Jerusalem, the one who kills the prophets and stones those who are sent to her! How often I wanted to gather your children together, as a hen gathers her chicks under her wings, but you were not willing! Matt. 23:37.

Jesus picked only twelve men to form the nucleus for the great work of evangelizing the world. Not one of the dozen was from the Jewish ruling class. They were all common men, most of them engaging in menial work to earn a living.

When the Roman soldiers nailed the Lord to the cross, at the insistence of the Jewish leaders, Jesus' disciples, scattered into hiding. They emerged dejected, only to resume their former trades. They too, had failed to discern the true nature of Jesus' Messiah-ship, despite the time they had spent with Him. It was the resurrection of the Lord that transformed these frail beings into the most influential team of men, apart from Jesus Christ, this world has ever witnessed. The death, resurrection, and ascension of Jesus Christ ended another scenario; the one where God Himself dwells among humanity as example. That phase of the earth's history, proved beyond doubt that for as long as Satan was also in the world, even the physical presence of God Himself could not reverse the fall of man. The creation of a sinless utopia is not possible under such conditions. It was now time for the next scenario in the Plan of Redemption.

The Christian church era begins

Just before His ascension, the Lord spoke to the disciples and said,

> But you shall receive power when the Holy Spirit has come upon you; and you shall be witnesses to Me in Jerusalem, and in all Judea and Samaria, and to the end of the earth. Acts 1:8.

Two points are worth noting here. Firstly, this was a promise to release the Holy Spirit, in power, to the generality of men. Hitherto, the Holy Spirit had only manifested in the prophets and those specifically called out by God, for a special duty or purpose. Secondly, the disciples were to preach the gospel first to the Jewish people in Jerusalem, before spreading out progressively to cover the entire globe. This was because the period of probation given to the Jews as a corporate entity by the grace of God was still in force. The Book of Daniel reveals this.

> Seventy weeks are determined for your people (Jews) and for your holy city (Jerusalem), to finish the transgression, to make an end of sins, to make reconciliation for iniquity, to bring in everlasting righteousness . . . Dan. 8:24.

The counting of the weeks is "from the going forth of the command to restore and build Jerusalem . . ." (v.25). The command was given by king Artaxerxes in 457 B. C. Seventy weeks is 70 x 7 = 490 days. A day in prophecy is reckoned a year in fulfillment[4]. Bible scholars have tested the day-year principle and proved it when events predicted in prophecy have come to fulfillment at the exact times predicted[5]. Applying this principle, we find that Jewish corporate probation was set to end in A. D. 34.

The visible down pouring of the Holy Spirit upon the gathered disciples marked beginning of the Christian church era. Under the influence of the Spirit, these men were able to preach in diverse languages and with extraordinary power. As a result, there was a massive conversion to the new faith. From then on, the apostles of Jesus, under direction of the Holy Spirit, preached the good news of the resurrected Christ and the coming Kingdom of God. Many were converted and baptized into the Christian faith, "and the Lord added to the church daily those who were being saved." Acts 2:47 (last part).

The Sadducees were the first to act against the new faith, which preached resurrection. The Jewish leaders imprisoned the Apostles on different occasions as the spirit of intolerance to the Christian faith gained momentum. Three and a half years after the cross of Calvary, the first Christian martyr perished under a hail of stones, thrown by the Jews.

At that moment, the period of probation granted by the grace of God for Israel's repentance ended. Their sin? Stephen summarizes it, just before they stoned him:

> You stiff-necked and uncircumcised in heart and ears! You always
> resist the Holy Spirit; as your fathers did, so do you. Which of
> the prophets did your fathers not persecute? Acts 7:51, 52.

The baton of God's model and messenger to the world changed hands from Israel, the race, to spiritual Israel, the Christian church; a universal gathering of all who believe in Jesus Christ as the Messiah. The new congregation comprised all tongues, races, tribes, and nations. Many people repented. On baptism, they received the Holy Spirit, and went out to preach the good news with extraordinary power.

When did they stone Stephen? A. D. 34! This event marked the end of the seventy-week probation period for the Jews, prophesied by Daniel. It also marked the beginning of a period of persecution of the Church of God, which caused the new recruits to flee to "all Judea and Samaria, and to the end of the earth." As they went, they spread the gospel and soon, knowledge of Jesus Christ and the kingdom of God had filled the earth.

Love and unity, transcending border, race, and gender, characterized the early apostolic church. Though squabbles did arise here and there, the presence of the Holy Spirit was conspicuous in all the activities of the early church. Many sold their worldly possessions to share with the poor. The apostles and other leaders dressed and lived after the simplicity of the Man Jesus. They made no demands on the members, and were to them more like servants than masters. The book of Acts gives an exciting historical insight into the formative years of the church. You may want to read it for yourself.

Progressive fall of the early church

As in the days of King Solomon, it looked as if the new Christian era would usher in the utopia of a sinless world, united under God's law. Again, as in the former days, the continued presence of Satan among men brought the promising time to an early end. The decay that was to result in today's church wearing the tag of 'Babylon' had already started even in the formative days of the church. Revelation 2 says of this early church,

> I know your works, your labor, your patience, and that you cannot
> bear those who are evil. And *you have tested those who say they*
> *are apostles and are not, and have found them liars;* and you have

persevered and have patience, and have labored for My name's
sake and have not become weary. (vv. 2, 3.) (Emphasis supplied.)

Evil men were masquerading as Christ's apostles and leading people
astray. One example of such men was Simon Margus, whom we meet in
the Bible in Acts chapter 8. History records that he was "the founder of
Gnosticism . . . believed to have gone to Rome, and there actively opposed
the teaching of S. Peter, by his heretical doctrine and magical acts."
(Whitham, *A History of the Christian Church*, 104.) Gnosticism is a belief
that flesh is evil and spirit pure. It therefore rejects the claim that Jesus
Christ came in the flesh.

The Lord praises the early church for its vigilance in weeding out such
evil men, as well as for giving untiring service to the Christian cause. He
nevertheless also reprimands the church: "Nevertheless I have this against
you, that you have left your first love" (v. 4). The love for Christ as the
author and finisher of the faith was slowly fading. Dependence on human
power and intellect was gaining ground.

The Lord had this to say regarding the next phase of church history:

I know your works, tribulation, and poverty (but you are rich);
and I know the blasphemy of those who say they are Jews and
are not, but are a synagogue of Satan. Do not fear any of those
things which you are about to suffer. Indeed, the devil is about
to throw some of you into prison, that you may be tested, and
you will have tribulation ten days. Be faithful until death, and I
will give you the crown of life. (vv. 9, 10)

By the turn of the first century, impostors, taking advantage of the need
for administrative structures in the expanding church, were entrenched
within the ranks of church leadership. Some were even establishing

churches, ostensibly in the name of Jesus, which were in reality Satan's congregations. In this era, about A. D. 100 to A. D. 538, the church faced persecution from successive the pagan Roman emperors.

Persecution had begun in the days of Emperor Nero in A. D. 64 or 65. It was to continue intermittently until A. D. 538. During this period

> a large number were seized and put to horrible deaths, dressed
> in skins and worried by wild beasts, crucified or burnt to death
> in the Vatican gardens—to serve as torches while the Emperor,
> dressed as a charioteer, took part in circus performances for the
> admiration of the mob. (Whitham 1957, 21)

The "ten days" specifically highlighted by this prophecy are the ten years of intense persecution under Emperor Diocletian. This was the "longest and most severe attempt of paganism to stamp out the Church." It lasted from February 23, 303 and ended in 313 when Emperors Lucinius and Constantine jointly issued the edict of Milan, proclaiming liberty for all people to worship according to their own choice. (Ibid, 165-169.)

The Lord has this to say of the next phase of the church: "I know your works, and where you dwell, where Satan's throne is." We have already identified Satan's seat in the end times as Rome. As we shall see shortly, the church at Rome had gained prominence as the headquarters of the Christian churches worldwide.

> And you hold fast to My name, and did not deny My faith even
> in the days in which Antipas was My faithful martyr, who was
> killed among you, where Satan dwells.

The Lord targeted this praise at the remnant that remained faithful to God, even standing up against the papacy in the face of persecution and death in Rome (Antipas, anti-pope). He reprimanded the wolves that had entered the church wearing sheepskins, only to entice the congregation away from God's precepts:

> But I have a few things against you, because you have there those who hold the doctrine of Balaam, who taught Balak to put a stumbling block before the children of Israel, to eat things sacrificed to idols, and to commit sexual immorality. (vv. 13, 14, 15.)

By A. D. 538, the church was poised for the accelerated fall that would transform the once pure apostolic church into a caricature of Babylon. As you read on, bear in mind that the true church of God, pure, and with no visible bounds, never fell, nor can it ever! What we are studying here is the history of the visible institutions we call the 'Christian' churches today. Let us trace the steps of the fall of the church, and the rise of a counterfeit in its place.

The rise of end-time Babylon

In A. D. 284, Diocletian became the Roman Emperor. "He forsook the old capital with its traditions of freedom, and made Nicomedia the new imperial residence." This move marked the beginning of the disintegration of the pagan empire, which had spanned almost the entire inhabited world since 168 B. C. This eastward shift of the seat of government left a power vacuum in the former capital, Rome. (Whitham 1957, 162)

Meanwhile, the Christian church had been growing rapidly. There were churches in many of the world's cities such as Jerusalem, Rome, Corinth, Alexandria, Athens and many more. By virtue of its location in the capital city of the world, the Christian Church of Rome began to gain prominence over all others, and became more important than even the church of Jerusalem.

As the church in Rome gained prominence, so the bishop of Rome increased his influence over churches in other locations. He grew increasingly powerful in debates and councils, regarding church administration and interpretation of doctrine. Here is how a historian explains the rise of papal Rome.

> No other city in history, not even Athens, exercised such a fascination over the thoughts of men. It was the centre of an organised rule such as the world had never known before; . . . And the glamour of the eternal city naturally invested also the church of Rome in the eyes of Christians. It was an easy transition for the Bishop of Rome in later days to assume the place and style of the Emperor, and for the Roman Church to exert, even without any set purpose of state-craft, the old influence and prestige of the Empire. (Ibid. 144.)

A timely twist of fate accelerated the rise of the Bishop of Rome to worldwide supremacy. This came in the person of Emperor Constantine.

Constantine

Emperor Constantine claimed he saw a mysterious vision in 312. It was a cross of light accompanied by the words "In this conquer!" Constantine became a Christian whose "attitude towards the faith and the Christian Church is that of a convicted if not always consistent believer." He was only baptized in A. D. 337, at the approach of his death, but his positive and tolerant attitude towards the church had calamitous consequences for that institution. Political gamblers and social hangers-on followed the Emperor and flocked to church, as

insincerity and worldliness became now the foes of the Church.
It paid to be a Christian, and converts, uninstructed and desiring
chiefly to be in fashion, poured into the Church. Consequently,
it became much more difficult to exert discipline and maintain
a high Christian standard. Bishops and clergy, dazzled by their
unaccustomed honours, grew often worldly, avaricious, and
timeserving. Moreover, the spiritual character of the Church and
of her authority was imperiled as never before. (Ibid. 178)

The arrival of Constantine on the scene gave the Bishop of Rome a
golden chance to manipulate him into a coalition of the church and the
state. In return for declaring the Bishop of Rome supreme ecclesiastical
leader over all Christian churches worldwide, the Bishop would declare
the Emperor political head over all Christians worldwide. The state would
harness its military machinery to reign in those nations and tribes who
would not freely convert to the new Christian faith. An individual or
nation, by rejecting Christianity was effectively rebelling against the state.
The empire would use its military machinery against such heretics[6].

We have seen that droves of political and social speculators joined
the leader's example and walked into the church, raw and unconverted.
Because the new members were seasoned pagan idolaters, problems arose
which required either compromise of the Christian doctrine, or divorce
with this new politically influential constituency. There were two courses
open for the church to follow in the face of this pagan influx. It could
either welcome them into its fold, or refuse them membership until they
could prove themselves willing to be converted.

The church chose the second option; it welcomed the unconverted pagans
warmly into its fold. The bishop of Rome opted to save the accursed marriage,
and to alter the doctrine where it inconvenienced the heathens in the church.
In return, the clergy gained access to the military might of the empire.

Birth of papal Rome

'Christianity' became the official religion of the Empire under the Bishop of Rome. This was the birth of the institution of the papacy, though the title *pope* would only come to official use in A. D. 607. Thus began the fulfillment of the prophecy of Daniel 7, regarding this power, which would emerge out of Rome's disintegration:

> The fourth beast shall be a fourth kingdom on earth, which shall be different from all other kingdoms, and shall devour the whole earth, trample it and break it in pieces. (v. 23).

The fourth world kingdom was the Roman Empire after Babylon (605 B. C.-539 B. C.), Medo-Persia (539 B. C.-331 B. C.) and the Greece of Alexander the Great (331 B. C.-168 B. C.)

> The ten horns are ten kings who shall arise from this kingdom. (v. 24 first part).

History confirms that the Roman Empire broke up into ten almost independent states.

> And another shall rise after them; He shall be different from the first ones, and shall subdue three kings. (v. 24 last part).

A "king" would arise out of the ashes of the Roman Empire, or at the time of Rome's disintegration, whose kingship would be different from the other monarchies of the world. The only power to emerge under these circumstances was the papacy, which fully established itself in A. D. 538 following the military conquest and annihilation of three of the ten states, namely the Ostrogoths, the Vandals, and the Heruli. Starting that year, almost the entire world fell under the realm of the pope of Rome. The Pope indeed became a ruler different from the conventional kings.

> He shall speak pompous words against the Most High, . . . (v. 25, first part).

The Pope claims to be 'God on Earth,' and to be the 'Vicar of the son of God'. He claims to possess the divine power to forgive sins and to create physically, the flesh of Jesus, during the mass. He claims to have dominion over Heaven, Earth, and Hades.[7]

This same "king", "shall persecute the saints of the Most High." (v. 25, middle part). This happened in the 1260-year period starting A. D 538. Historians call this sad phase of human history the Dark Ages. These years of papal supremacy were the most painful for the saints of God. This was an era when men of the collar hunted down and persecuted those who refused to accept the apostasy introduced by the Church of Rome. Clergymen competed in the race to create higher forms of torture, in the name of God. Historians estimate that over 50 million saints died from various forms of cruel torture for being heretics. Possessing or reading a Bible was an act of heresy. Revelation 12 had predicted this sad 1260-year era of the church:

> And she *(the virtuous woman/the church)* brought forth a man child *(Jesus)*, who was to rule all nations with a rod of iron: and her child was caught up unto God, and to his throne. And the woman *(church)* fled into the wilderness, where she hath a place prepared of God, that they should feed her there a thousand two hundred and threescore days. (vv. 5, 6, brackets added).

Those who insisted on clinging to biblical truth had to flee into the mountains and valleys of Europe, Russia and other isolated and rugged enclaves. The Waldenses, scattered in the Alpine valleys and mountain of Italy were the best known such group. We see here that *'going into the wilderness',* means entering a period of hiding. It means that the visible church[8] had to disappear from the normal society of men.

You may find it hard to believe that church authorities could inflict such pain and suffering on fellow humans, in the name of God. This, nevertheless, is what happened. In fact, some of the apologies offered publicly to the world by Pope John Paul II in 2001[9] were acknowledgements of the atrocities perpetrated by the church on humanity in that dark period.

We read further, that this pompous "king", "shall intend to change times and law." (v. 25 last part). We have already seen that when faced with the option to either compromise original apostolic church doctrine, or lose the support of pagan membership, the Church of Rome chose to alter doctrine. The major attempted change in "times" was the shift of the Sabbath from the seventh, to the first day of the week, which they effected through Constantine's imperial decree, as we shall see in chapter 12. The major change in the law of God was the removal of the second commandment, which forbade idol making and worshipping. This latter act paved the way for the introduction of images of Mary, Jesus and the cross in churches and homes, and their acceptance as objects of worship. In 1215, Pope Innocent II made auricular confession to a priest, rather than to God a requirement. Councils of the church introduced hundreds of changes, to accommodate the heathen membership

There were voices of dissent, questioning these strange doctrines. The Church sought to stem protest by a resolution of the Council of Trent of 1546. This effectively declared that the Tradition of the Fathers was equal to the Bible. 'Tradition' meant the sayings and rulings of popes and councils of the Catholic Church. This resolution conferred upon popes and councils the 'divine' right to change the scriptures.

Later on, in 1870, the church proclaimed "absolute infallibility of the pope!" The proclamation sought to confer the purity and holiness of God on mere, frail humanity. Henceforth, whatever any pope said or did, could not conceivably be wrong. It was not open to criticism, as it was impossible for popes to err!

The question posed at the end of chapter 4, 'would the first advent of the Messiah, and of the Christian church create the means for mobilizing the entire world back to God?' we must from observing history, unfortunately answer in the negative. It looked, for a century or so after the Ascension, as if every soul on earth would be Christianized and the planet restored to God's law, but soon, the apostasy cited in preceding paragraphs began to eat its way to the very core of the congregation.

The papacy receives mortal wound

So evil and corrupt did the church become; so heavily did some its bishops, cardinals, and popes tax the people that they gained a reputation as cruel property owners. Through the system of indulgences, the laity paid huge sums to buy their freedom from pending hell. The yoke of the papal system on the populations of Europe grew so heavy that the people had to do something drastic to stop it.

This 'something' came about in 1798, in the form of military invasion. In France, Napoleon Bonaparte rose to power. His General Louis Alexandre Berthier overran the Vatican and captured Pius VI, the pope in office at the time. (Wikipedia 2011) This was a fatal blow to the institution of the papacy. The true church of God could now emerge from its hiding in the "wilderness." Meanwhile, it was the turn of the papacy to enter its own "wilderness." To John on Patmos, Christ had revealed this near fatal wounding of the papacy, "and I saw one of his heads as it were wounded to death." Rev. 13:3.

The subduing of the pope, this wounding of the papal institution brought immense relief to the world. It liberated true Christians to preach and practice the truth they had secretly kept alive in the caves of the wilderness. However, just as the killing of Nimrod had produced a sinister downside many centuries before, so the conquest of the pope gave impetus to the growth of the religious secret societies that have swept over the majority of Christendom today. The Jesuit Order and other brotherhoods and societies originally formed to fight the pope's wars in the crusades, went underground, taking on a more sinister, deadlier form, with the aim of re-establishing papal supremacy.

> But men in the West had never ceased to believe in the imperishableness of the rule of Rome. The tradition of the "Eternal city," the mistress of the world, and the guarantee of settled and unified government, had survived all the changes of the last three centuries. (Whitham 1957, 341)

Whitham wrote this about 'European' mindset towards the end of the sixth century, to explain the formation of the Holy Roman Empire. He may well have written the same words at the close of the sixteenth century. Indeed, his words would still be true for our present age.

The wheels that would bring about the present "Babylon" condition of the world had already started turning in 1774, with the formation of a secret club, which drew up a long range master plan spanning centuries. This would be the blueprint for, first, destroying democracy and the separation of church and state in America; and next, bringing the rest of the world under one government, with one religion. The sum-total of the religious and political ambitions of humanity, at the instigation of Satan, would at last find expression in the most advanced ungodly human union ever forged since creation—the New World Order.

CHAPTER 6

The New World Order

Hatching a long-range plan

The history of mankind is filled with men who have aspired to rule the whole world. Modern generations have witnessed strongmen who harbored this same ambition. Since the time of Napoleon, secret societies have been influencing the politicians and aristocracy of the world to bring about a centralization of power in the hands of a few men, deemed superior to the rest of humanity, in their own estimation.

The One World Order idea began with the formation of a group of eminent persons calling themselves the *Order of the Illuminati*, the 'illuminated ones'.

> The Bavarian Illuminati, which was involved in many of the 'people's' revolutions in Europe, including the French, was founded in Germany on May 1st 1776 by the occultist, Adam Weishaupt. (Icke 1999, The Greatest Secret, 238)

This is a secret organization, an occult Brotherhood, which now virtually controls indirectly the economic, political, educational, and religious direction of nearly the entire world. As of today, it may be very close to the truth to state that no government, politician, leader of commerce or religion in any country, is entirely free from the influence of this group of extremely powerful men. Many people labeled as conspiracy theorists believe that through its many front organizations, the Illuminati has roped in national presidents, international banking families, industrialists, and military men. Their avowed ambition is to create a 'New World Order', another way of saying a 'One World Order'![10]

Countdown to the One World Order

You may do well to turn to Appendix I at this stage. After following the timeline of the one world order, you may agree there is little to add to it, to expose the objectives that drive the agenda. The chief strategy used to bring the world closer to a ready acceptance of this new order is the deliberate creation, or magnification of crises, followed by claims that only a new order of governance can solve such crises permanently. By this means, the New World Order is justified to the world. To the average person, the New World Order, as presented to the public by its creators, would be acceptable as the answer to all the problems besetting the planet today.

> When there is a problem in the world, we say "What are *they* going to do about it." At which point *they*, who have secretly created the problem in the first place, respond to this demand by introducing a 'solution'—more centralisation of power and erosion of freedom. If you want to give more powers to the police, security agencies and military, and you want the public to demand you do it, then ensure there is more crime, violence

and terrorism, and then it's a cinch to achieve your aims. Once the people are in fear of being burgled, mugged or bombed, they will demand that you take their freedom away to protect them from what they have been manipulated to fear . . . . I call this technique problem-reaction-solution. Create the problem, encourage the reaction "something must be done", and then offer the solution. It is summed up by the Freemason motto 'Ordo Ab Chao'—order out of chaos. Create the chaos and then offer the way to restore order. Your order. (Icke 1999, Introduction, xii)

We will now look at some such crises, exposing the true agenda hidden behind the solution. You will find that in each case, a crisis is presented, and a solution offered, which brings the world closer to meeting the objectives of the few men of ego, who have assigned to themselves the mandate to rule the world. The following are a few examples of world crises and the solutions presented for their mitigation.

To save us from nuclear war or disaster

That we must save the world from global annihilation by nuclear weapons is one of the most compelling reasons presented for the creation of the One World Order. The threat of atomic or nuclear war, or destruction, will cause many peace-loving citizens of the world to accept the imposition of any system of government that promises to guarantee world peace.

Experts present survival of the planet as priority number one, at many international fora where world leaders meet. However, it is those nations possessing and developing deadly arsenals of nuclear weapons, which are the loudest in telling the world how it is on the brink of a nuclear holocaust. They are offering to save the world from themselves. Those who are offering to protect the world are the very ones who would destroy it.

Go green—save the planet

The ecological argument is presented to the world as a crisis of deadly proportions. Again, the highly industrialized nations have inflicted the greatest damage upon the environment. Ozone depletion, air pollution, acid rain—all these are the result of irresponsible exploitation of the earth's resources by the same rich nations that are leading the world to the New World Order. Every day they bombard us with messages of the need for jointly becoming planetary stewards of the earth's ecology before we destroy ourselves.

'Global warming' is presented as the latest threat to the planet, but developments noted in points 34) and 35) in Appendix I would point to the possibility of a deliberate ploy to adversely temper with the planet's climate, in order to frighten its inhabitants into readily accepting a powerful overseer of the world—the One World Order!

> The Club of Rome, set up at the Rockefeller family's private estate at Bellagio in Italy, created the environmental movement. The Rockefellers and the Rothschilds have played the environmental movement like a violin. The Club of Rome has used the environment to centralize power and confiscate land. It claims to be campaigning to 'save the planet' when in truth it is just another front for the Agenda intent on controlling the world and, what's more, a front peopled by those who are demonstrably creating the very environmental problems they say they wish to stop. (Icke 1999, 263)

Economic crises

The world is still reeling under the effects of the banking crisis that swept the planet in 2008. The permanent solution proffered by the major names in banking, to pre-empt future crises, is the interlocking of the global economy, and unifying currencies in the global market. To make globalization of economies attractive, they promise equitable distribution of the world's wealth in the new dispensation.

A close look at world trends will reveal that economic growth of the smaller nations is stifled, despite the rich natural resource bases in most of them. In some economically promising African countries, governments adopted strange policies, which have destroyed thriving economies and infrastructures, in order to level the economic playing field, and enhance the chances of successful integration of economies with less developed neighbours. Entire populations must come to a point where they despise their national sovereignty in favour of globalization—joining up with the controllers of world economy in the One World Order!

Health crises

The AIDS pandemic continues to decimate populations in poor countries. The more recent bird flu, swine flu and other pandemics have all caused panic. This is good for the New World Order! People in a panic will accept solutions offering worldwide protection, dubious mass vaccination, and health insurance for all, all free of charge! These healthcare facilities can only be availed to the entire world if a single benevolent government can control the world. Therefore, in the event of a referendum, the world would readily vote for the New World Order, to usher in health for all.

Moral crisis

It is true that the moral standards of the world are rapidly deteriorating by all standards. The moral crisis has resulted from legalizing prostitution, bestiality, homosexuality, and same-sex marriages; encouraging excessive alcohol consumption, waging a half hearted war against drug peddling and abuse, ignoring organized crime, . . . the list is endless.

The breakdown of the family unit has given birth to a generation of men and women who do not valuelife, and hence, the level of violence of crimes committed is rising every day. The proposed answer to the moral crisis is to force every citizen of the world into some religion or other. This is the essence of the ecumenical[11] movement, largely driven by the World Council of Churches and the World-Wide Esoteric Community[12].

In points 18 and 44 of Appendix I, you will note the ultimate intention of ecumenism to unite all humans under one religious umbrella, whatever their beliefs. No religion or denomination must disparage the doctrine of another, but rather each should seek to unite with the rest, on whatsoever points they happen to remotely agree.

In this regard, you will find in Appendix I, notes 33, 36 and 47, that many await a spiritual messiah who will embrace peoples of all religions. They call him Lord Maitreya. His imminent advent will be the stimulus for the entire world's religious people to rally behind the leaders of the One World Order, as the plan enters its final implementation phase. Maitreya, considered Master of all the prophets in the history of men, including Jesus Christ of Nazareth, will be the most likely agent for providing the centralized leadership necessary to mobilize the world into the ten planned regions (see note 30, Appendix I).

The list of international crises and 'One World' solutions is endless—food crisis, water crisis, oil crisis, crime crisis . . . The list is endless. We are living in perilous times, as described by the Lord Jesus Christ in Mathew 24.

Even some non-Christians are beginning to feel that something is seriously wrong with the world, and that these may indeed be the end-times.

Natural disasters such as earthquakes, tornadoes, floods, mudslides, draughts and tsunamis, are striking more and more frequently. These catastrophes appear to be killing and displacing more and more people each time. Pestilences in the form of Aids, Tuberculosis (TB), malaria, swine flu, cholera, and ebola, are wreaking havoc in the less developed countries. Meanwhile, it would appear as if every adult human being is destined to suffer from high blood pressure, diabetes or other malady, and live on pills.

All this was predicted by the Lord Jesus in Matthew 24, as the beginning of the end. As a Christian therefore, what ought you to do? "Watch therefore, for you do not know what hour your Lord is coming." Matt. 24:42. Those driving the One World agenda are certainly aware that the end of the present order of things is imminent. Surprisingly, many who profess Christianity are not.

Mission accomplished

The men and women in control of the plan have done all that they have to do, to usher in the One World Order. According to them, 'it is finished'. They now await the right event to cause the world to rally willingly behind them. This may be the coming of their supernatural master, Maitreya, the cosmic christ, to assume leadership in the final fulfillment of Satan's ageless plan. We will look at this in more detail in Chapter 15.

How can we know that the foundation for the One World Order has been laid? The answer is that the executors of the plan have proudly announced the fact to the world. Here is how. Take a US$1 note. Look at the back of it, the side that says 'IN GOD WE TRUST'. On the left side you will see a pyramid. The top of the pyramid is detached from the body and there is a bright eye looking out of the apex of the pyramid. The small triangle with the eye in it is the symbol of the Egyptian god Horus, the newborn sun. In ancient Egypt each sun-rise represented Horus, the 'risen savior'.

Solar divinity originated in Babylon and was refined in Egypt. It spread throughout the world. Even professing Christians have adopted it in one form or another, as we have seen earlier. The shape of the pyramid reflects the idea of the masses—you and me—at the bottom, and fewer and fewer privileged ones as we get to the top, closer to the source of light and life. The break in the pyramid is symbolic of the separation between the masses and the small elite calling themselves the *Illuminati*, meaning 'the illuminated ones'. Do not forget that the name *Lucifer* means *'the giver of light'*, *'the illuminator'*!

Above the pyramid emblem are the words 'annuit coeptis'. Annuit means '(the) enterprise' while 'coeptis means 'is a success'. The full meaning is *'the enterprise is a success'*. Now, you may be wondering, What enterprise? Below the pyramid are the words *'nuvus ordo seclorum'*. Nuvus is 'new'; ordo is order; and seclorum (secular) means 'world'. In full—*'new world order'*. Now reading the full picture, we come up with—*'our enterprise, the one world order, has been a success.'* David Icke confirms this observation

The Latin words above and below the pyramid on the Great Seal/dollar bill announce the arrival of a new secular order. The New World Order is the insider name for the Brotherhood Agenda and George Bush used the term profusely when he was president. The date written in Latin on the bottom of the pyramid, 1776, is thought, understandably, to relate to the American Declaration of Independence in that year. But something else happened on May 1st (a date beloved by Satanists) in that same year of 1776. A very significant strand in the Brotherhood network was officially launched called the Bavarian Illuminati by the German professor, Adam Weishaupt (Icke 1999, 352)

Will God remain silent?

Will the One World Order fully materialize? Will it usher in a new age of peace and prosperity for mankind, as the leaders claim? Will God stand by and watch as men take up the Luciferan agenda to rule the world; to receive worship in His place? Will the blood of all the saints shed over millennia remain un-avenged?

It is inconceivable that God should remain silent. However, if He is to act, He will in justice, first let the world know, for "Surely the Lord GOD does nothing unless He reveals His secret to His servants the prophets." Amos 3:7.

CHAPTER 7

Come Out of Babylon!

A message for every age

God has always had a special message for the world in every era. In Noah's day, the message was a warning of pending judgment. Unless men should repent of their sins and turn back to God, the Lord would destroy all life. Humanity was given a 120-year period of probation, which they squandered. Only the messenger and his family were saved.

When God was about to destroy Nineveh, he sent the prophet Jonah with the message "Yet forty days, and Nineveh shall be overthrown." Jonah 3:4. In the case of Nineveh, there was a massive repentance, and the city escaped judgment. Jeremiah and other prophets announced the conquest and captivity of Israel, and of Judah, by the Assyrians and Babylonians respectively, long before their occurrence. The message "repent ye: for the kingdom of heaven is at hand . . . Prepare ye the way of the Lord, make his paths straight," preceded the earthly ministry of the Lord Jesus. Matt. 3:2, 3. The Lord left a message for believers to flee Jerusalem when armies encompassed the city. Those who heeded the warning message escaped, while those who ignored it perished at the hands of the Roman army within the walls of the city in A. D. 70. There is a message also for us, in these end times.

Other sheep I have

Jesus Christ assured mankind:

> I am the door. If anyone enters by Me, he will be saved, and will go in and out and find pasture . . . . I am the good shepherd. The good shepherd gives His life for the sheep. John 10:9, 11.

We have seen from preceding chapters that the thief and enemy is Satan, who has succeeded in duping the majority of men and women into following him. Despite the large number of unbelievers and lawbreakers present in the world at any one time, God has always had a remnant in "all whose knees have not bowed to Baal, and every mouth that has not kissed him." 1 Kings 19:18. We will trace the history of this remnant in the final chapter. For now, suffice it to say there has always been a remnant, the true congregation of God on earth in every generation since Adam.

In these last days, many well-meaning people have been misled. There are large numbers of worshippers, in all religions and denominations, who love God with all their hearts, but have been deceived into bowing to a counterfeit. The Lord Jesus assures us that He will not leave them in darkness: "I am the good shepherd, and know my sheep." He knows those who are zealous in genuine error. He is aware of many who live in error simply because they were born and bred into it. The omniscient God has a record of all the ears that have never heard the good news: "And other sheep I have, which are not of this fold: them also I must bring, and they shall hear my voice; and there shall be one fold, and one shepherd." John 10:14, 16. The Creator of all can read the heart of every man like an open book. He is able to isolate those who would spurn truth for the sake of position, wealth, and apparel. Likewise, the Lord knows which heart would gladly open up to let in the bright rays of light, which are truth eternal.

As in generations past, there is a solemn message for ours. If you should hear it, would your heart receive it gladly? Will you count yourself one of the sheep of the Good Shepherd, the true Jesus Christ, who is calling out to you through the pages of this very book? We have studied how humanity has progressively fallen from the God's favour. We have seen that our hearts are deceitful beyond understanding. It is possible to read and clearly understand a warning message, and then inexplicably decide to ignore it, even if doing so should lead to death. The example of the smoker has revealed this illogical human trait in the first chapter of this book.

The messages you are about to read are directed at you and I, as we live in these end-times. God is speaking to humanity as the end of the age approaches. These three messages are the last communication from heaven, before the close of probation, followed immediately after by the second advent of our Lord Jesus Christ. He is coming, this time around not as the humble lamb, but in glory as King of kings.

The first angel's message

> Then I saw another angel flying in the midst of heaven, having the everlasting gospel to preach to those who dwell on the earth—to every nation, tribe, tongue, and people—saying with a loud voice, "Fear God and give glory to Him, for the hour of His judgment has come; and worship Him who made heaven and earth, the sea and springs of water." Rev. 14:6, 7.

An angel is the messenger of God. In this prophecy, the angel represents the people of God, evangelists who carry this important message to every corner of the globe. Just as everyone around can hear a *'loud voice'*, so every ear shall receive the gospel. It may be through a book, a newspaper, satellite television, the internet, or a live sermon, but every ear will hear it. You should not expect to see an angel appear from heaven to deliver this message in mid-air—God uses the agency of frail, fallible man to minister to other men.

The 'everlasting' gospel refers to the good news of salvation by Christ alone. God Himself first preached this gospel to Adam, when He taught him to slaughter animals as sin offering. The good news of salvation by the grace that saved the patriarchs and apostles of old—Abraham, Isaac, Jacob, Noah, Peter, Paul and many others—is the same gospel for the world today. It is the original, unadulterated message from God to mankind—we need not perish, for Jesus died already in our stead. The Savior is even now located within the Most Holy Place of the heavenly temple, atoning for our sins before God the Father. The entire planet must hear this good news. This book forms part of that message. Will you also join in and spread it?

"The hour of His judgment is come," means just that. Judgment is not in the past or in the future; it *is* 'come'; it has arrived; it is now! In the earthly dramatization of the plan of redemption centered on the sanctuary, final judgment occurred on the Day of Atonement. Throughout the year, priests made daily sacrifices for sin, and sprinkled the blood of an animal inside the sanctuary. In this manner, the sins of the people were 'stored' in the sanctuary, awaiting God's decision whether to convict or forgive each sin. This judgment coincided with the Day of Atonement, when the High Priest would cleanse the temple of all accumulated sin. On this day, while the High Priest was busy inside the Most Holy Place, the entire congregation remained outside, each person praying and seeking the face of God in repentance. The Lord cut off from the fold of Israel, those who did not present themselves at the sanctuary in humble repentance.

As we shall see in chapter 9, the Lord Jesus is currently located in the Most Holy Place of the true Tabernacle in heaven. The heavenly Day of Atonement is in progress. Outside of the temple, we on earth should continually pray, seeking God's face in repentance of all sins committed. Just as the Jewish Day of Atonement coincided with judgment, the period we are living in, being the period of atonement, is also of judgment. It has to be because by the time Jesus comes again, every case should have been decided, and rewards apportioned, for He says, "behold, I am coming quickly, and My reward is with Me, to give to every one according to his work." Rev. 22:12. We are living in the period of probation much like the 120 years granted men in the days of Noah. It is my prayer that you and I do not squander ours as Noah's generation did theirs.

The Revelation 14 phrase "worship him that *made heaven, and earth, and the sea, and the fountains of waters*" reminds one of Exodus 20:11: "For in six days the LORD *made heaven and earth, the sea,* and all that in them is, and rested the seventh day: wherefore the LORD blessed the sabbath day, and hallowed it." The Exodus text is an extract from the Ten Commandments, in which God was directing men how they should relate to Him, as well as to other men.

The recognition of God as Creator is the solid foundation of all true religion. It is clear that in matters of worship, God is directing the attention of the present generation to the Ten Commandments in general, and to the fourth commandment in particular! We shall study the forth commandment in more detail in another part of this book. In short, the message of the first angel is alerting mankind to the judgment in progress and bidding them return to worshipping God as He originally prescribed!

The second angel's message

> And another angel followed, saying, "Babylon is fallen, is fallen, that great city, because she has made all nations drink of the wine of the wrath of her fornication." Rev. 14:8.

Revelation 18:1, 2 shows another angel repeating this message with greater urgency, and in more detail:

> I saw another angel coming down from heaven, having great authority, and the earth was illuminated with his glory. And he cried mightily with a loud voice, saying, "Babylon the great is fallen, is fallen, and has become a dwelling place of demons, a prison for every foul spirit, and a cage for every unclean and hated bird!

We have already seen that both the city and the kingdom of Babylon are extinct. We saw in chapter 5 that what the Bible terms Babylon is the modern system spiritually and morally similar, in many respects, to the original. The fall of Babylon referred to in the text is spiritually away from God, and into the devil's hands.

We have seen how idol worship and veneration of the dead have corrupted the Christian church. Worshippers bow their knees to Baal in the very churches claiming Christ as savior. Leading politicians and financiers have joined up with religious leaders to design a world with one government and one religion cemented by the cosmic christ, the so-called Lord Maitreya, whom they hail as master of all the prophets, of all the different religions of the world. We have seen that the development of the New World Order has a strong religious slant, albeit away from God.

As in the days of Nebuchadnezzar, a time is coming when the system will enforce devil worship, veiled in a modern form of spiritualism, as the religion of the world. This new world religion may be cloaked with deep piety, and accompanied by miracle working, but its author will still be Satan, in fulfilling his life-long ambition to sit *"upon the mount of the congregation."*

Come out of Babylon!

Revelation 18 goes further than simply informing the world of the fall of Babylon. An even more urgent warning is directed to the world today.

> And I heard another voice from heaven saying, "Come out of her (Babylon), my people, lest you share in her sins, and lest you receive of her plagues. For her sins have reached to heaven, and God has remembered her iniquities." Rev. 18:4, 5.

The greatest desire of God is to save all human beings unto eternal life. However, despite the great effort the Godhead has directed towards the salvation of men, they remain stuck in their evil ways. In spite of all the clear warnings and calls, such as the one in Revelation 18:4, 5, men will not repent. Like the smoker who ignores the death warning on his packet of cigarettes, human beings may ignore the clear warning messages from God, after reading and understanding them clearly.

Mental & spiritual extrication required

Christ is calling to His sheep, which are still outside, to now extricate themselves from all ungodly systems, and enter the fold of the Good Shepherd. His sheep recognize His voice and follow Him. Through sermons, books, and hymns, He is calling for us to come out of Babylon. In this sense, Babylon is not a physical location, but the mental and spiritual condition of the majority in world today, who live with confused and conflicting doctrines about God and religion. "Now the Spirit expressly says that in latter times some will depart from the faith, giving heed to deceiving spirits and doctrines of demons." 1 Tim. 4:1.

Coming out of Babylon is, foremost, a mental process. It is a deliberate and intelligent process of identifying every strand in Satan's imprisoning web, and cutting it loose before moving to the next one, and repeating the process. Each lie must be exposed and rejected; in its place, truth must blossom. I must place each doctrine of 'my church' under the spotlight of scripture, and evaluate it against *'thus saith the Lord'*. If the Lord said it not, then it is must be rejected as originating from the devil. There is no middle source of doctrine.

Spiritually, coming out of Babylon begins with forsaking everything that stands between us and God

> You shall have no other gods before Me. You shall not make for yourself a carved image—any likeness of anything that is in heaven above, or that is in the earth beneath, or that is in the water under the earth; you shall not bow down to them nor serve them. For I, the LORD your God, am a jealous God, visiting the iniquity of the fathers upon the children to the third and fourth generation of those who hate Me, but showing mercy to thousands, to those who love Me and keep My commandments. Ex. 20:3-6.

Worshipping of idols—be they of animals, Mary, Jesus or the cross—is explicitly forbidden and is an abomination to God. We must closely examine the practice of venerating and worshipping the dead from a biblical perspective, and make a decision whether or not to continue in it. In chapter 13, we shall study this question in some detail.

There are many things in life, which we hold dearer to us than we do God. Some are hobbies, while others are people and objects. The Bible calls on us to subordinate all things to God. "But seek first the kingdom of God and His righteousness, and all these things shall be added to you." Matt. 6:33. If we place greater value on any object or hobby, than we do on God, we are in effect placing a strange god before the Creator; it is as good as a carved idol, and we stand convicted by the second commandment. The very first step in coming out of Babylon is therefore a personal conviction to place God and His precepts ahead of all human feelings and inclinations. A thorough study of God's precepts is therefore the most important step to take in the flight from Babylon.

Most people belong to churches, groups, cults, and organizations with a religious or dubious quasi-religious humanitarian agenda. The message of our time is to re-examine the doctrines, aims, and objectives of our church or organization, in light of Satan's stated ambition to entice the hearts of men away from God. We must not be satisfied with what our pastors or leaders tell us. We must now personally carry out a diligent audit of our current doctrines with the Word of God as the infallible standard.

This book is part of the call to come out of Babylon. There are many today, belonging to the church identified in chapter 5 as the harlot, sitting on the beast that controls the politics, and economy of the world. Many more belong to the churches labeled harlot daughters of the harlot mother-church, in Revelation 17. These are the many protestant churches, which now form part of fallen Babylon, because their corporate leadership, far from building upon the gains of the original reformation movement has in fact taken steps to rejoin the mother church in the New World Order.

Many have innocently joined these churches genuinely seeking God's face. Far from being offended by the revelations in this book, which expose the insidious nature of the harlot church and its daughters, the true sheep of Jesus will personally revisit the scriptures and if convicted, abandon their current congregations and look elsewhere for God's true church. What will happen to those who cling to Babylon to the end?

The third angel's message

> Then a third angel followed them, saying with a loud voice, "If anyone worships the beast and his image, and receives *his* mark on his forehead or on his hand, he himself shall also drink of the wine of the wrath of God, which is poured out full strength into the cup of His indignation. He shall be tormented with fire and brimstone in the presence of the holy angels and in the presence of the Lamb. And the smoke of their torment ascends forever and ever; and they have no rest day or night, who worship the beast and his image, and whoever receives the mark of his name. Rev. 14:9-11.

In chapter 15, we will identify the mark of the beast and his image. For now, let it suffice to say those who refuse to heed the call to come out of Babylon, and choose to remain rooted in their fallen beliefs, congregations, cults, and cultures, will possess neither the knowledge, nor the moral fibre, to resist the mark of the beast. The trial that is to come upon the world is such that only those who are standing firmly on a solid foundation of truth will remain un-swayed. A great delusion will carry the majority in a tide of deception, and sweep them into eternal oblivion.

Soon, the probation granted the planet since Eden will close, and for a brief while, Satan will be permitted free reign over those who have refused the truth and ignored the call to come out of Babylon. This is "the wrath of God, which is poured out without mixture." The intervening mercy of

Christ the Mediator will no longer be available to plead in man's behalf. The text last quoted is extracted from the sternest warning that God issues in the entire Bible. Sinners will for the first time stand exposed before a Holy God; but the two cannot possibly co-exist, and Purity naturally incinerates sin. Unfortunately, those humans who have remained glued to sin will perish together with it, though this was never God's original intention.

As you read on, remember that Christ is addressing you and me. He is calling His sheep to the fold. He laments:

> My people have been lost sheep. Their shepherds have led them astray; they have turned them away *on* the mountains. They have gone from mountain to hill; they have forgotten their resting place. Jer. 50:6.

More importantly, as we review of some important biblical doctrines, the call is directed to you and me: "Today, if you will hear His voice, do not harden your hearts." Heb. 3:7.

CHAPTER 8

User's Manual

The word of God—what do you presuppose?

Before we begin the journey out of Babylon, through a study of Bible doctrines in the rest of this book, we must contrast our existing perception of Scripture, against the Bible's perception of itself. The scriptural view of the Bible is that, it is *the Word of God,* rather than *a book containing some words of God.* Put differently, all the messages, from Genesis 1:1 to Revelation 22:21 come to us directly from God. All thoughts were a direct inspiration from God, with men either quoting Him verbatim, or describing visions, dreams and instructions in their own words without altering the content and sense of His message. Let us study what some of the icons of the Christian faith have to say, regarding the source of the Scriptures.

Paul writes,

> *All scripture is given by inspiration of God,* and is profitable for doctrine, for reproof, for correction, for instruction in righteousness, that the man of God may be complete, thoroughly

equipped for every good work. 2 Tim. 3:16 (emphasis supplied).

Please note carefully the use of the word *all*. The Apostle Peter wrote the following in connection with the scriptures:

> We also have the prophetic word made more sure, which you do well to heed as a light that shines in a dark place, until the day dawns and the morning star rises in your hearts; knowing this first, that *no prophecy of Scripture is of any private interpretation, for prophecy never came by the will of man, but holy men of God spoke as they were moved but the Holy Spirit.* 2 Pet. 1:20, 21 (emphasis supplied).

These texts summarize what the Christian view of the source and purpose of the Bible is supposed to be. We must presuppose every written word as coming from the mouth of God Himself. Taking the view that the Bible is a book containing some words of God reduces the Holy Book to a novel; a book containing the words and folklore of men, with God quoted here and there. With such a presupposition built in our psyche, we would feel justified in choosing to accept that which suits our taste, while discarding all that goes against the grain of our established lifestyles and beliefs.

Is your present view of the Bible safe, considering what you now know about the devil's main mission on earth?

Inventions come with a manual

Every inventor of a gadget, instrument, or machine, in presenting it for public use, invariably attaches a User's Manual to it. We all accept that the user who wishes to derive maximum benefit from his newly acquired gadget must set it up and operate it exactly as recommended in its manual. Keep in mind the fact that even the simplest gadget made by man comes with a user's manual, written in a multiplicity of languages. Now consider God, whose intelligence is immeasurably greater than that of humans, creating life in its complexity. Imagine God making His masterpiece—man! Imagine the Creator expecting man to live life, and live it abundantly. Imagine God expecting him to be 'good' and not be 'evil'. Now place this God against the human inventor, and imagine this immeasurable Benefactor placing man on Earth, and then not providing for him a User's Manual for rightful living on the planet. Can you imagine him not providing a clear guideline on what constitutes 'good' and 'bad', 'right' and 'wrong'—a standard of measure to be used in fair judgment and reward of all mankind at the end? If you are a reasonable person, holding no prejudices against God, you will find it hard to imagine Him dumping man on Earth without providing a User's Manual. God's Manual for mankind is the Holy Bible!

This amazing book possesses answers to the innumerable questions of life. It tells us exactly how we are to relate to God as well as to one another, in order to derive maximum benefit and enjoyment from our existence. It describes how the world began, and predicts how it is to end. It gives us solid lessons on how we can overcome problems of sin, in the many examples of men and women whose mistakes and poor judgment at certain times of their lives the Word never hides from us. This very aspect of revealing the worst side of its heroes alongside the good, distinguishes the Bible from the books of men.

This Book defines sin and clearly identifies its origin. It reveals to mankind the nature of his temptation, fall into sin, and subsequent loss of the privilege to eternal life. It reveals also the amazing miracle of the Creator's plan of redemption. By this device, His son Jesus Christ took on the nature of sinful man, and died the death of a common criminal as ransom for man's sins. All who should choose to believe in him as Saviour and obey His will are reconciled to God. They regain the lost privilege to live forever, "for God so loved the world that He gave His only begotten Son, that whoever believes in Him should not perish but have everlasting life." John 3:16.

The life-changing book

Unlike any other book in print, the Bible is capable of touching the hardest and most callous heart, and transforming it into the softest, kindest, and most innocent of all. The word of God can transform a mass murderer into a prayer-warrior and preacher. A witchdoctor, discovering Christ in the pages of this amazing Book, will become a missionary, ready to lay down his life for Christ and for others. The writer of this book is living testimony of the transforming power of the word of God. Having started drinking just before university, I soon degenerated into a proper alcoholic and smoker. I indulged in all the vices associated with nightclubs. I knew, and befriended, many men and women of weak character. Selfishly, I spent money away from family and lost many wonderful opportunities in life because I had no time for anything but pleasing 'me.' By the time I accepted Christ through His word, I was feeling that I was going to have to stop drinking or die! However, I lacked the power within me to break the vicious cycle. In the morning, I would make a vow never again to touch the brown bottle; but before I knew it, I was at the bar counter once more, with the same noisy crowd; and, once more, the time was well after midnight.

I wasted a lot of time and money consulting witchdoctors and 'prophets', with a view to reversing the run of 'bad luck', and ridding myself of the evil spirits that they blamed for my excessive drinking. None of my would-be-helpers ever pointed to my self-acquired and self-destructive habits as the possible cause of my woes. They all blamed other people and spirits for me, and in fact succeeded in isolating me from the very people who loved me, and would have helped me the most at the time.

I was ready to commit suicide, when the grace of God intervened. I had bought the poison, and was ready to take it. It has been a long journey to where I am now. It would require a whole book to narrate. For now, please accept my humble submission, built on a solid personal experience, that the Bible is truly the Word of God.

Prophetic book

The Messianic prophecies in the books of Isaiah and others, came to fulfillment in the birth, suffering, death, and resurrection of Jesus Christ. Events on the ground have proved truthful the long-range prophecies of Daniel, which foretold the political history of the world to the very end of time. The prophecies in Revelation, full of promise for God's children, and chilling warnings for those who choose to be lost, are being fulfilled with amazing accuracy, as history unfolds.

Many shun the book

Some individuals and congregations shun the Bible because its pages reveal the evil schemes of the enemy of souls. Many in the world have chosen to do away with the Bible, finding it too incisive for comfort. It may surprise you to learn that through the Council of Valencia of 1229, the Roman Catholic Church placed the Bible on the 'Index of Forbidden Books' and outlawed its ownership or reading by laymen,

> for the word of God is living and powerful, and sharper than any
> two-edged sword, piercing even to the division of soul and spirit,

and of joints and marrow, and is a discerner of the thoughts and intents of the heart. Heb. 4:12.

Many, finding themselves convicted by the Word as sinners, have joined congregations that read scantily from Scripture, while dwelling almost exclusively on joyful celebration of free-for-all salvation; where believers receive the 'Holy Spirit' every Sunday, while they keep their sins.

There are others, like the white garmented African 'Apostolic' congregations that have taken Southern Africa by storm, who discard the Bible altogether, in favour of the 'holy spirit'. They claim the Spirit now speaks directly, through the many prophets and prophetesses of the sect. Surprisingly, although these men and women profess inspiration of the same 'holy spirit', each has his or her own following, and teaches a doctrine different from the rest.

Accused of duplicity

Some accuse the Bible of duplicity. They claim that it treacherously supports many opposing views on a single subject. However, this accusation arises because men have approached the Bible with pre-conceived agendas, and opened its pages only with a view to endorsing their fixed positions. Let us look at a hypothetical example.

An already married man covets a young lady and decides to marry her. However, desiring to do only what is righteous, the man must first seek the position of the Bible on the matter. He is led to the following text that describes Solomon: "And he had seven hundred wives, princesses, and three hundred concubines." 1 Kings 11:3. He extracts this part of the verse and justifies his desire: *If Solomon, a man of God in the Bible had a thousand wives, it cannot possibly be wrong to desire only a second wife.*

In seeking support from the holy pages he will ignore the last part of the verse which reads "and his wives turned away his heart" from God. Our polygamist researcher will not read further down the passage, where the Lord expresses His displeasure with Solomon's behaviour, and tells him so. In fact, so cross is God that He pronounces punishment for Solomon's sin upon succeeding generations. (Read 1 Kings 11:4-13). Our polygamist aspirant will not refer to God's warning regarding the conduct of future kings of Israel: "Neither shall he multiply wives for himself, lest his heart turn away." Deut. 17:17. He will not listen to Solomon's personal testimony of regret:

> Whatever my eyes desired I did not keep from them. I did not withhold my heart from any pleasure, for my heart rejoiced in all my labor; and this was my reward from all my labor. Then I looked on all the works that my hands had done and on the labor in which I had toiled; and indeed all was vanity and grasping for the wind. There was no profit under the sun. Eccl. 2:10, 11.

Our man will close his eyes to verses such as "Therefore a man shall leave his father and mother and be joined to his wife, and they shall become one flesh." Gen. 2:24. He will become blind to all Biblical texts clearly promoting monogamy, and be alert only to those apparently promoting polygamy, even though they should be only fractions of verses.

The Bible is the Word of God and He, being Who and What He is, cannot possibly contradict Himself. Should we meet any apparent contradictions between two texts of the Scriptures, we should search for further clarification. We either have collected insufficient information, or are making a wrong interpretation. Erroneous translations and paraphrasing, in some Bible versions, may also be a source of apparent conflict.

Precept upon precept

The polygamist's approach cited above is an example of reading a verse out of the context and spirit of the passage, as well as the rest of the Bible. No easy ride is promised the student of the Word of God. The Lord will teach knowledge to those who are of a humble demeanor; those who have accepted the leadership of the Holy Spirit in their study. God is ever ready to open the truth to those who accept each little light they have received, and are yearning for more. The Bible compares the humble learner, who is setting out on a study of the Holy Book, to a suckling baby. "Whom will he teach knowledge? And whom will he make to understand the message? Those just weaned from milk? Those just drawn from the breasts?" Is. 28:9, 10. Paul also employs this same analogy, and explains it more clearly:

> For though by this time you ought to be teachers, you need someone to teach you again the first principles of the oracles of God; and you have come to need milk and not solid food. For everyone who partakes only of milk is unskilled in the word of righteousness, for he is a babe. Heb. 5:12, 13.

Why should it be necessary to keep growing beyond breast suckling, in our quest to understand the scriptures? The answer is, "for with stammering lips and another tongue He will speak to this people." Is. 28:11.

God inspired the Scriptures. It should make sense that the wisdom and purity of mind imparted by the Holy Spirit alone should be the key to open up the mind to an understanding of what appears to the world a strange message. If this is so, how then should we study the Scriptures? Isaiah tells us, "precept must be upon precept, line upon line, line upon line, here a little, there a little." Is. 28:10. In order to extract true and unambiguous Biblical doctrine, it is necessary to bring into focus many different texts on a subject. For an example, one may only partially understand a line in the last book of Revelation when read in conjunction with a verse tucked away in the Old Testament book of Exodus. Finally, a text from Daniel, when superimposed upon the partial image, completes the picture. We shall use this principle in the chapters to come.

Prayerful, humble approach essential

Because the Lord shall speak "with another tongue", it is imperative that before embarking on any study of the Word of God, the Bible student should submit in prayer to the Holy Spirit, who inspired the writing of the Word in the first place. Whenever we open the Bible to read, there are two spirits at hand to influence the mind in interpreting the texts. Should we presumptuously embark on the study, driven by the steam of human intelligence, then the devil is ready to poison the mind with his slanted interpretation of the "tongue." On the other hand, the Holy Spirit is equally ready to assist those who prayerfully humble themselves in Him before they embark on Bible study.

The eunuch of Ethiopia in Acts 8 had the correct attitude of heart, and the Lord led Philip to him, to help him understand the scriptures he was reading. To Philip's inquiry "Do you understand what you are reading?" the humble man replied, "How can I, unless someone guide me?" Acts 8:30, 31. This broken-hearted approach to the Bible leads to enlightenment and spiritual growth. Those who philosophize upon the scriptures with an air of superiority will also find what they seek in the very same texts, but rather than lead them to eternal life, it will only entrench them deeper in error and stiff-necked self-righteousness.

All or part?

If we have accepted the position that the Bible is the true word of God, then we may ask the question: When are we to take the Bible as our guide in life? Put another way, "Are there situations arising in life where the Word of God is irrelevant, or can be superseded by the traditions of man, church, pastor, priest, bishop, 'prophet' or pope?" Please stop and consider this question seriously. Design your answer with all presence of mind. Before you arrive at a final position on the question, it may be worth your while to consider the following texts from the scriptures. "And in vain they worship Me, teaching as doctrines the commandments of men." Matt. 15:9. "Now the Spirit expressly says that in latter times some will depart from the faith, giving heed to deceiving spirits and doctrines of demons." 1 Tim. 4:1. "For the time will come when they will not endure sound doctrine, but according to their own desires, because they have itching ears, they will heap up for themselves teachers; and they will turn their ears away from the truth, and be turned aside to fables." 2 Tim. 4:3-4.

I urge you to study the above texts in a fresh light. Keep in mind the awakened knowledge that it is possible for man, as evidenced by the smoker, to stare daily at admonitions addressed specifically to him, and ignore them as if they only addressed others. It will require prayerful soul-searching and humility, to accept that one may have been wrong, and begin the process of reprogramming our presuppositions. Only then, can we change our course and begin anew.

In the next chapter of this book, we will begin to study a few of the doctrines that the devil has distorted the most in order to gain the supremacy over God's people, and the world's many congregations, including some with the best of intentions. Together we must interpret the Scriptures using the principle *"thus saith the Lord!"* as our only guide. We must allow only Scripture to interpret Scripture.

Your decision to study and accept Bible doctrine as the only guide to life will cause a glorious celebration in the heavenly realm. Lift up your head, square your shoulders, and embark on this spiritual journey, guided solely by God's Word, rather than human feelings, traditions and myths. You will bring untold joy to the Lord Jesus who so lovingly died that you could make just such a choice, and gain eternal life! Listen to the Lord's invitation, delivered in person to you and me:

> Behold, I stand at the door and knock. If anyone hears My voice and opens the door, I will come in to him and dine with him, and he with Me. To him who overcomes I will grant to sit with Me on My throne, as I also overcame and sat down with My Father on His throne. Rev. 3:20, 21.

Mental resolve required

It is imperative that *before* we meet with the simple Bible truths to follow, one leading logically to the next, we resolve in our hearts never to turn back and condemn any truth we have earlier accepted, because it has led us to a greater truth, which flies against our ego, personal taste, established culture, or routine. We learn the importance of establishing firm resolve before the trial, or temptation, in the book of Daniel. When the young Hebrew boys in Babylonian captivity were to be physically fattened and spiritually dulled on an 'unclean' Chaldean diet, verse 8 of Daniel 1 states: "But Daniel purposed in his heart that he would not defile himself with the portion of the king's delicacies, nor with the wine which he drank." The success of the quartet's three-year vegetarian campaign was rooted in such pre-trial resolution. Likewise, once we become determined to accept each new ray of light dawning upon the horizon of our minds from the scriptures, the Holy Spirit will allow greater light to illuminate our lives.

My dear friend, do not be like the smoker in chapter 1. Set aside personal tastes, feelings, and presuppositions and let us take a fresh look at some key biblical doctrines, and study how the devil has corrupted them to his advantage, and thus assumed prominence *"upon the mount of the congregation."*

Our first port of call will be the holiest place in the entire universe; the nerve centre of the Plan of Redemption. This is where all Christendom should focus its eyes in this, the Day of Atonement; but, alas, the enemy has nurtured a spirit of disinterest and ignorance about the sanctuary in heaven.

CHAPTER 9

Sanctuary in Heaven

Moses to build a type

When the children of Israel left Egypt, after 430 years of exile in that land, the Lord directed them to ask for all kinds of valuable gifts from their Egyptian neighbors. By softening the hearts of the Egyptians to give generously of their gold and silver, the Lord caused a great plunder. You can read about it in Exodus 12:35, 36. The children of Israel never knew the reason for this generous blessing, until Moses got the instruction from God, "Speak to the children of Israel, that they bring Me an offering. From everyone who gives it willingly with his heart you shall take My offering." Ex. 25:2. A long list of valuables follows in verses three through seven. What was the purpose of this request for an offering? Verse 8 has the answer: "And let them make me a sanctuary, that I may dwell among them." God intended to live among his chosen people, but not in just any location! He purposed to dwell in a structure called a *sanctuary*.

What was this sanctuary, and what would it look like? The Lord Himself provided the answer.

> According to all that I show you, that is, the pattern of the
> tabernacle and the pattern of all its furnishings, just so you shall
> make it. Ex. 25:9.

It is clear God showed Moses a tabernacle, then asked him to make a similar structure, after the "pattern" shown him in the vision.

Moses was to use only the most valuable and aesthetically appealing materials available on planet Earth in making the structure and its furnishings. From God's description, it was certain to be a structure of exquisite beauty. Exodus 25 through 27 gives exact measurements for each partition and article of furniture. God supplied specifications to the minutest detail. The sanctuary had to look exactly like the pattern shown to Moses on Mt. Sinai. Exodus 28 lists in the finest detail the nature of the garments of the Priests serving in the Sanctuary. Chapter 29 describes the process for consecrating the priests, in preparation for executing the various daily ceremonies and annual festivals, centred on the Sanctuary. Chapter 30 goes on to describe the altar of incense, the basin for washing and the recipe for preparing the anointing oil and the incense.

It is not the aim of this chapter to study in detail the earthly sanctuary built by Moses or to chronicle the many ceremonial services and annual festivals associated with it. The objective, rather, is two-fold. Firstly, it is to demonstrate from the scriptures, that the Mosaic sanctuary structure was a copy of one in heaven. Secondly, we should be able to see clearly, that Jesus is at this present moment located in that sanctuary, carrying out the final phase of work in the plan of mankind's redemption.

God's throne is in heaven

The purpose for building the sanctuary by Moses was that God intended to dwell amongst the children of Israel. The dimensions of this structure, designed for portability during the forty-year wilderness journey, were much smaller than the more permanent structure built by King Solomon in Jerusalem, years later. Nevertheless, in dedicating the gigantic temple to God in prayer, the king remarked "But will God indeed dwell on the earth? Behold, heaven and the heaven of heavens cannot contain You. How much less this temple which I have built!" 1 Kings 8:27. If the temple of Jerusalem could not be the true abode of God, how much less the portable sanctuary? The earthly sanctuary certainly served an important purpose, but we may have to admit from studying other texts in the Bible, that God's throne is located in Heaven, and not on Earth.

Psalm 2:4 says, "He who sits in the heavens shall laugh." Here, King David points to a heavenly headquarters for God. Psalm 11:4 is more emphatic. "The LORD is in His holy temple, The LORD's throne is in heaven . . ." In Acts 17:24, the apostle Paul explains, "God, who made the world and everything in it, since He is Lord of heaven and earth, does not dwell in temples made with hands." The Lord Himself declared, "Heaven is My throne, and earth is My footstool. Where is the house that you will build Me? And where is the place of My rest?" Is. 66:1. An even clearer picture of a heavenly tabernacle, Sanctuary, or temple, being the type or pattern of the earthly one built by Moses is painted in the book of Hebrews.

Earthly sanctuary a type

Hebrews 9:1-7 summarizes the earthly sanctuary structure and services superbly. Daily, the priests offered sacrifices for sin in the Holy Place on behalf of themselves and the children of Israel. Once a year, on the Day of Atonement, the High Priest would enter the Most Holy Place, first with the blood of a bullock to atone for his own sins, and then with the blood of a goat to atone for the sins of the congregation. He sprinkled the blood of the goat upon the congregation, as well as throughout the sanctuary structure and upon the horns on the altar of incense.

The High Priest cast lots to choose from between two goats, which he would slaughter. This was the 'sin offering' and was the shadow of the Messiah. The one allowed to live was the shadow of Satan, the 'scapegoat' or 'azazil'. Upon the head of the scapegoat, the High Priest confessed all the sins of Israel. By this ceremony was symbolized the cleansing of the sanctuary of all the sin that had accumulated from daily sin offerings made throughout the year. The High Priest symbolically transferred sin to its originator, Satan. The scapegoat, now bearing the sin of humans, was left in the distant and uninhabited wilderness, to die only as God knew how.

To demonstrate that the earthly sanctuary and its ceremonies were a shadow of the heavenly sanctuary and services, we begin by quoting Hebrews 8:1 thus: "Now this is the main point of the things we are saying: We have such a High Priest, who is seated at the right hand of the throne of the Majesty in the heavens". This text makes it clear that the Majestic God has His throne in a sanctuary in heaven.

But who is this priest, and what is he doing in the heavenly sanctuary? Hebrews 9:11-14 has the following answer to our question:

> But Christ came as High Priest of the good things to come, with the greater and more perfect tabernacle not made with hands, that is, not of this creation. Not with the blood of goats and calves, but with His own blood He entered the Most Holy Place once for all, having obtained eternal redemption. For if the blood of bulls and goats and the ashes of a heifer, sprinkling the unclean, sanctifies for the purifying of the flesh, how much more shall the blood of Christ, who through the eternal Spirit offered Himself without spot to God, cleanse your conscience from dead works to serve the living God?

Jesus our high priest in heaven

The above texts make it clear that the earthly sanctuary and its ceremonies were only a copy of the heavenly, and that Jesus, by qualification of His sacrificial death on the cross, and subsequent resurrection, has become High Priest in the heavenly temple. He has taken His own blood, pure and sinless, into the heavenly sanctuary as the true and everlasting sacrifice for the sins of humanity:

> For Christ has not entered the holy places made with hands, which are copies of the true, but into heaven itself, now to appear in the presence of God for us; not that He should offer Himself often, as the high priest enters the Most Holy Place every year with blood of another—He then would have had to suffer often since the foundation of the world; but now, once at the end of the ages, He has appeared to put away sin by the sacrifice of Himself. Heb. 9:24-26.

These texts demonstrate two points clearly. First, that there is a tabernacle or sanctuary in heaven, and this was the pattern for the earthly structure. Second, that Jesus Christ is now in that heavenly temple, mediating as High Priest between God and men.

John testifies to the existence of the temple, and of God's throne in heaven, as well as the presence of Jesus Christ in the Temple. The Revelator was carried away in the spirit and he "saw seven golden lampstands, and in the midst of the seven lampstands One like the Son of Man, clothed with a garment down to the feet and girded about the chest with a golden band." Rev. 1:12, 13. The seven lampstands remind us of the lampstands of the same number in the earthly sanctuary as described in Exodus 25:31-40. In fact, God directs Moses to "see that you make the lampstands after the pattern, which was shown you on the mount." Ex. 25:40.

Revelation 8:3, 4 reveals a golden altar located before the throne of God in heaven. This is the pattern of the earthly 'altar of incense', which was also made of gold, and stood before the Mercy Seat. This earthly seat—the spot over which the Shekinah Glory of the Lord hovered when God wished to show his presence to the people—was the earthly equivalent of the actual throne of God in the Most Holy Place, in the sanctuary in heaven.

Removing all doubt

Should there be any doubt still lingering as to the existence of a heavenly sanctuary or temple, then Revelation 11:19 should remove it.

> Then the temple of God was opened in heaven, and the ark of
> His covenant was seen in His temple. And there were lightnings,
> noises, thunderings, an earthquake, and great hail.

This verse, besides clearly emphasizing the existence of a temple in heaven, also holds the key to further profound truths, which if accepted as such, should shake Christendom to its very foundations by revealing the errors in many of the doctrines so routinely taught therein. Read it, and remember it. We shall re-visit this verse in chapter 10.

I hope the scriptures have made it clear that the earthly sanctuary and its ceremonies were only a shadow of the true heavenly sanctuary. Therein, Jesus Christ is now high priest, finishing off the work of atonement. He has offered his sinless blood in sacrifice, as "the Lamb of God who takes away the sin of the world." John 1:29.

Beauty and reverence point to heavenly origin

God selected only the most precious and aesthetically appealing materials for the construction of the Mosaic sanctuary, and demanded absolute cleanliness in the body and regalia of the ministering priests within. Israel was to approach the Sanctuary with absolute reverence at all times. Only those appointed by God to enter in service within the structure could do so without the danger of instant demise.

The reason for constructing a structure of such beauty, to such exact specifications, and for enforcing strict rules for cleanliness and order, was to give mankind only a glimpse of the exquisite beauty, splendor, and holiness of the original and true temple in heaven. God intended the almost unearthly beauty of the earthly sanctuary, as well as the extreme reverence, to point mankind to the existence of an original heavenly temple.

It has not been possible—neither is it possible—for any prophet who has received a visual glimpse of heaven, to describe what they saw in words other than those understood by humans. The references to gold, silver, topaz, sapphire and quartz, can only be earthly approximations of the actual materials in heaven. See, for example how John describes the New Jerusalem as being "of pure gold, like unto clear glass." Rev. 21:18. Can you imagine transparent gold? Clearly, these are the only words currently available to mankind, for describing splendor that is impossible even to imagine.

I hope that the following points are now fully established in our minds, and form part of our internal bank of truths:-

1. There is a Temple in Heaven.
2. The Mosaic sanctuary was an exact replica in miniature of the heavenly temple.

3. Jesus Christ is in the temple in Heaven as the High Priest, ministering between men and God.

Let us pray that whatever else we may learn after this, we will continue to uphold these now-established truths, and not seek to revisit and erase them under any prejudice, aroused by some further unsettling truth.

The counterfeit sanctuary

Many times, we see the devil anchoring his web of falsehood on pillars of truth. He is always imitating and corrupting the things of God. We saw how, under Satan's influence, Cain obeyed God in offering a sacrifice but substituted vegetables for the flesh and blood of an animal. We saw how Satan influenced the design of ancient city of Babylon along the pattern of the New Jerusalem of God. We saw how he created a counterfeit seed in Semiramis' 'miraculously' conceived son, presented to the pagan world as its savior, in a counterfeit plan of redemption. Briefly, we must study how the enemy of God has also created a counterfeit of the very seat of God, the Sanctuary.

Sadly, through the Roman Catholic Church the place of Jesus in the heavenly sanctuary, "the true tabernacle which the Lord erected, and not man" (Heb. 8:2), has been usurped and pulled down to earth. How has Satan managed this feat through this church? He has done so by employing at least five counterfeits.

The church has established a counterfeit Priesthood. The tearing of the veil in the Jerusalem temple at Jesus' death marked the end of human priesthood. Jesus would subsequently ascend to heaven to fulfill this role, of which the earthly had only been a shadow. Stephen was witness to Jesus' presence beside the father, moments before the Jews stoned him, "and said, 'Look! I see the heavens opened and the Son of Man standing at the right hand of God!'" Acts 8:56. We have already demonstrated, earlier in this chapter, that Jesus is now High priest in Heaven. Human priests exalted as 'gods' and 'christs' have taken the place of Christ, the Messiah. Members make verbal confession of sin to human priests who claim to forgive them in what is clear blasphemy. By this expedient, "the place of (God's) sanctuary was cast down." Dan. 8:11.

The Roman Catholic Church introduced a counterfeit Sacrifice. Christ's sacrifice on the cross was the 'once for all'. It was the ultimate sacrifice. The Catholic Church, in 1050, introduced 'the sacrifice of the Mass'. This effectively diverted attention from the true and pure sacrifice of Christ. Gabriel the angel described the papacy to Daniel: "He even exalted himself as high as the Prince of the host; and by him the daily sacrifices were taken away." Dan. 8:11.

The Catholic Church introduced a counterfeit Mediator. They introduced exaltation of Mary, 'Mother of God', by the Council of Ephesus (A. D. 431). In 1854, they proclaimed the unbiblical Immaculate Conception of the Virgin Mary. In 1950, the Assumption of Virgin Mary became doctrine. They claimed, with no scriptural basis, that the mother of Jesus ascended bodily to heaven soon after her death. The introduction of these doctrines in small progressive doses, was slowly preparing the congregation for the *grand finale*—the presentation of Mary as Mediatrix of mankind, the mediator between man and God. This means that humanity can only approach God and Jesus through Mary. This effectively shifts the attention of worshippers from the true mediatory work Jesus is doing in the heavenly sanctuary, to mere fallible humanity.

A counterfeit 'Vicar of Christ' was presented to Christendom. The pope's title is *'Vicarius Filii Dei'*, Latin for 'the Vicar of the Son of God.' This effectively usurps the role of the Holy Spirit as the Successor of Christ on earth. The Lord Himself promised and identified the Holy Spirit as His successor on Earth to continue the next phase of the plan of redemption.

> I tell you the truth. It is to your advantage that I go away; for if I do not go away, the Helper will not come to you; but if I depart, I will send Him to you. And when He has come, He will convict the world of sin, and of righteousness, and of judgment . . . When He, the Spirit of truth, has come, He will guide you into all truth; for He will not speak on His own authority, but whatever He hears He will speak; and He will tell you things to come. He will glorify Me, John 16:7, 8, 13, 14.

The antics of man have therefore replaced the true work of the Holy Spirit.

The Roman Catholic Church offers a counterfeit route to Salvation. The Scriptures clearly teach that salvation can only come through faith in Jesus Christ. The Catholic Church, as do many Protestant churches, teaches the doctrine of salvation by works, (by 'works' is meant long prayers and painful fasts), payment of indulgences, pilgrimages and penances where a believer inflicts pain on one's body. Works have therefore replaced salvation by the free grace of God. The church teaches that it is possible, by taking certain physical action, to gain salvation.

These five are some of the many ways by which the devil has managed to achieve his burning ambition to usurp all that is of God. By diverting the attention of professing Christians from the heavenly sanctuary, the enemy of God has effectively staged a *coup d'état*. Though, on the surface, it appears the work of popes, cardinals and bishops, the true power behind these accomplishments is no other than he whose avowed ambition is to divert the focus of human worship from the Creator, to himself.

God warns the proud human agent used by Satan:

> Thus says the Lord GOD: Because your heart is lifted up, and you say, 'I am a god, I sit in the seat of gods, In the midst of the

seas,' yet you are a man, and not a god, though you set your heart as the heart of a god . . . . Behold, therefore, I will bring strangers against you, the most terrible of the nations; and they shall draw their swords against the beauty of your wisdom, and defile your splendor. They shall throw you down into the Pit, and you shall die the death of the slain in the midst of the seas. Will you still say before him who slays you, 'I am a god'? But you shall be a man, and not a god, in the hand of him who slays you. You shall die the death of the uncircumcised by the hand of aliens; for I have spoken," says the Lord GOD. Ez. 28:1, 7-10.

Though the agent and medium of Satan may enjoy glory and adoration for a season, it is only a while longer before He is deposed from where he now sits, 'upon the mount of the congregation.'

CHAPTER 10

The Law of God

"Lightnings and thunderings" in Revelation

You may remember that in chapter 9 we met the text "The temple of God was opened in heaven, and there was seen in His temple the Ark of the Covenant: and there were lightnings and voices and thunderings, and an earthquake and great hail". Rev 11:19. Now, we have learnt that in studying the Bible, precept must be upon precept, "here a little and there a little". Is. 28:10. The prophet recommends this approach because God has weaved His message from one remote part of the Bible to another. Two or more scenes, incidents or texts, one in the Old Testament and another in the New, may appear unrelated to the casual eye, but jump up to link together in the mind of the more serious reader.

It happened that one day as I was reading Revelation 11 verse19. The reference to "lightnings and thunderings, and an earthquake" stirred something in my mind that I felt was important. I had met that exact phrase in the Old Testament, but could not remember exactly where. With the aid of a concordance, I soon found the phrase in two places, in the book of Exodus.

"Lightings and thunderings" in Exodus

The first time the phrase appears is in Exodus 19:16. "And it came to pass on the third day in the morning, that there were *thunderings and lightnings* . . . and the voice of the trumpet . . . ." and "the whole mountain quaked greatly." Ex. 19:18. The place was Mount Sinai, when God descended on the mountain to spell out, in His own voice, the Ten Commandments to the children of Israel. After such a spectacular prelude to God's speech, all the people listened in total attention and fear, and heard every word of the commandments that God spoke.

Soon after God announced the tenth and final commandment, again, "the people saw the *thunderings, and the lightnings*, and the noise of the trumpet . . ." Ex. 20:18. God came down personally, causing these fearsome phenomena as quotation marks to the Ten Commandments for two reasons. Firstly, He wanted to stress the paramount importance of the His pronouncement, the Ten Commandments. Secondly, he wanted the experience, and hence the commandments, to remain etched on the memories of the congregation. You may be wondering what the connection is between this incident at Sinai, back in the days of ancient Israel, and the temple in heaven sighted in Revelation.

History of the Ten Commandments

The answer lies in tracing the story of the Ten Commandments in the books of Exodus and Deuteronomy. Following the verbal declaration of the Ten Commandments or the Decalogue, God summoned Moses up the mountain, "Come up to me, into the mount, and be there: and I will give you tables of stone, and a law, and commandments which I have written, that you may teach them". Ex. 24:12. God did not use ink to write on the stones, rather, He gave Moses "two tables of testimony, tables of stone, *written with the finger of God.*" Ex. 31:18 (emphasis supplied).

We need to address two important questions here, before we can proceed. Moses was highly educated, and a proficient writer. It was he, many believe, who penned the books Genesis, Exodus, Leviticus, Numbers, Deuteronomy and Job.

The first question is: Why did God choose to write the Ten Commandments personally instead of delegating the work to his capable servant, Moses? The answer can only be the great importance that God attached to these laws, and His desire to make Israel appreciate that importance. Remember that God had also originally descended 'in person' onto Mount Sinai, to declare verbally the Law.

The second question is why God etched the Decalogue in rock, rather than write on papyrus or leather? The answer has to be the fact that rock gives an impression of permanence. It is clear that God intended to convey to us the eternal nature of the Ten Commandments.

Let us return now to tracing the history of the Tablets of the Testimony. Soon after handing the stones to Moses, God told him to go back to the camp, because apostasy had reared its ugly head among the congregation. When Moses had taken too long in the mount, the children of Israel implored Aaron, his brother, to make them a god that they could worship. Obligingly, Aaron had collected golden artifacts and jewelry from the congregation, and fashioned a calf.

When the aged leader arrived back in camp, he witnessed wild feasting, singing and dancing in worship of this golden calf god.

> And it came to pass, as soon as he came near unto the camp, that
> he saw the calf, and the dancing: and Moses' anger grew hot and
> he cast the tables out of his hands, and broke them beneath the
> mount. Ex. 32:19.

From this description, the breaking of the stones sounds like a pre-meditated act. Could this be so? Let Moses describe in his own words what happened.

> So I turned and came down from the mount, and the mount burned with fire: and the two tables of the covenant were in my two hands. And I looked, and, behold, you had sinned against the Lord your God, and had made you a golden calf: you had turned aside quickly out of the way which the Lord had commanded you. And I took the two tables, and cast them out of my two hands, and broke them before your eyes. Deut. 9:15-17.

It is clear from his own testimony that Moses broke the tablets of the commandments intentionally. A sharp feeling of despair and futility must have pierced his heart. Barely forty days after God's personal appearance amid thunder, lightning and quaking, and indeed with the fire of God still burning on the mountain, the congregation had violated the second commandment. Moses must have felt like most of us are bound to feel: It is impossible for people to keep the law of God; therefore let the law be obliterated; let it be done away with! Think about it. Moses broke the stones that God Himself had carved out and etched with His own finger! He *purposely* destroyed the *only* record we have of God writing anything *personally* for humanity!

Let us divert briefly, and visit another wilderness incident, much later on. In the desert of Zin, where Moses' sister Miriam died, there was no water, and the people were thirsty, "and they gathered themselves together against Moses and against Aaron." Num. 20:2. When the two leaders asked God for guidance, they received the following instruction, "Take the rod, and gather you the assembly together . . . and speak unto the rock before their eyes; and it shall bring forth its water." Num. 20:8.

The leader, strained under the immense pressure of Israel's open rebellion, instead of speaking to the rock, struck it. God was so angry with Moses that He sentenced the old leader to die on the wrong side of the River Jordan. Moses would not set foot in the Promised Land. It was a painful sentence, after all that he had done at the helm of his stiff-necked and ungrateful brethren. If you and I were to judge, we would provide some mitigation in defense of Moses.

Firstly, there had been a precedent at Horeb, where God had asked Moses to take the rod and *strike* a rock to bring forth water (see Exodus 17). Secondly, in the incident at Zin, God specifically opened his instruction with the words *"Take the rod . . .",* and this could have justifiably confused Moses. After all, almost all the miracles God had led the ancient leader to perform, had actively involved the rod. Thirdly, the unceasing murmuring of the children of Israel had exasperated him to the limit of his patience.

Second set of stones made

If you and I were to judge which of the two incidents, the breaking of God's handiwork, or the striking of the rock, warranted severe punishment, our answer would likely be the breaking of the stones. We would acquit Moses completely, on the second count. God did just the opposite. He did not display any anger against Moses for breaking the stones. In fact He never even raised the issue except in passing.

> Hew yourself two tables of stone like unto the first, and come up to me into the mount, and make an ark of wood. And I will write on the tables the words that were in the first tables which you broke. Num. 10:1, 2.

The man did as God commanded, and went up the mountain once more, and "was there with the Lord . . . and He wrote on the tables the words of the covenant, the Ten Commandments." Ex. 34:28. Comparing God's reaction in these two incidents, we may conclude that the breaking of the stones was within God's plan, and that He intended to convey some significant message from the whole drama.

We extract a crucial lesson here. The breaking of the stones and their replacement was, and still is, meant to convey the clear message that no man, leader, government, church, priest, prophet, bishop or pope can set aside the Ten Commandments because the people find any part of them difficult, unpleasant or inconvenient to keep, or because they cease to be fashionable!

We can summarize the paragraphs above in three statements:

- God announced the Ten Commandments *'personally'*, amid *thunder and lightning*
- God wrote the Ten Commandments *'personally'*, not once, but *twice.*
- God cut the law *in rock* with *His own finger.*

Considered together, these statements can only point to the omnipotent and immutable nature of the Ten Commandment law of God. There is even more irrefutable evidence, however, of the permanent nature of the Ten Commandments.

Back to the tablets

Returning to the history of the tablets, let us hear from Moses what happened next.

> And I made an ark of acacia wood, and hewed two tables of stone like unto the first, and went up into the mount . . . And He wrote on the tables according to the first writing . . . And I turned myself and came down from the mount, and put the tables in the ark which I had made; and there they are, as the Lord commanded me." Deut. 10:3-5.

Therefore, we know Moses placed the tablets of the law *inside* the ark of acacia wood, the Ark of Testimony!

What was the destination of the ark itself?

> And He took and put the testimony into the ark, and set the poles on the ark, and put the mercy seat on top of the ark: and he brought the ark into the tabernacle, and set up the veil of the screen, and screened the ark of the testimony; as the Lord commanded Moses. Ex. 40:20, 21.

From this narrative, we learn that Moses placed the Ark of the Testimony bearing the Tables of the Testimony inside it, under the mercy Seat. What was the Mercy Seat? In our study of the Mosaic Sanctuary in Chapter 9, we found that the Mercy Seat was the holiest spot in the whole planet Earth at that time. This was because it was the image of God's actual seat in the true heavenly tabernacle, not made by human hands. The mercy seat was the equivalent of heaven's Judgment Seat, God's throne. In the days of Moses, the glory of God, the Shekinah, shone above the Mercy seat to indicate the presence of God. In the earthly sanctuary, the tablets of the law were located where the Lord had instructed Moses to deposit them—inside the Ark of Testimony, which formed part of God's earthly throne. The tablets of the law formed the foundation of God's earthly throne, the Mercy Seat.

Back to the sanctuary in heaven

Now, dear reader, we have already agreed that the earthly sanctuary was only a shadow of the true Temple in heaven, and that the former was a miniature replica of the latter. The significance of this truth is overwhelming. By accepting the existence of a heavenly Sanctuary, of which the earthly was a shadow, we have logically accepted the existence of God's throne in heaven. By accepting the truth of God's throne in heaven, we have accepted in turn the truth of the true Ark of Testimony under God's real throne, as mirrored in the Mosaic sanctuary by the Mercy Seat. By accepting the reality of the Ark of Testimony under the throne in Heaven, we have naturally embraced as fact, the existence of the Ten Commandments of God written in some truly eternal fashion, of which the stones were but a mere shadow. Just as the stones of the law were stored under the mercy seat, so the same law is in Heaven deposited under the very throne of God. If we believe in the Biblical heaven, we have no option therefore but to conclude that the Ten Commandments are still there in heaven and hence very much in force. They form the foundation of God's throne, His government! The Ten Commandments will transcend into eternity, as surely as God's throne will.

Linking Up The "Lightnings and Thunderings"

In case any doubt should still linger, regarding both the omnipotent and immutable nature of the Ten Commandments, God provided an important link, to convince even the most stubborn doubter. We have seen that "lightnings and thunderings" accompanied the announcement of the Ten Commandments in Exodus. In the book of Revelation, the very same phrase, "lightnings and thunderings" accompanies almost every sighting of God's throne, as well as every act of judgment prophesied. Read the following verses.

- And out of the throne proceeded lightnings and thunderings . . . Rev. 4:5.
- And the temple of God was opened in heaven, and there was seen in His temple the Ark of the Covenant: and there were lightnings and voices and thunderings, and an earthquake and great hail. Rev. 11:19.
- And the angel took the censer, and filled it with fire from the altar, and cast it into the earth: and there were voices, and thunderings, and lightnings, and an earthquake. Rev. 8:5.
- And there came a great voice out of the temple of heaven, from the throne, saying It is done. And there were voices, and thunderings, and lightnings, and there was a great earthquake . . . Rev. 16:18.

The reference to lightings and thunderings is meant to bring Sinai into remembrance. God wishes to call our attention to the link between judgment and the His Moral Law, announced amid these phenomena back in the days of Moses.

Before God ushers in the new heaven and the new Earth, lightnings and thunderings are to continue issuing out of God's throne. These terrifying phenomena are, without doubt associated with the Ten Commandments, which form the base of God's throne. They are a sign of God's incompatibility with a world living outside His law. Compare this with the result of getting naked high voltage electric wires in contact with water. The scriptural reports of the lightnings and the thunderings direct the attention of humanity to the Ten Commandments. The book that you are now reading forms part of the effort to lead the world back to the Law.

Pray for the strength to accept this and other truths to follow, without turning back to old presuppositions.

But the lightnings and thunderings shall cease

Despite the many references to the startling phenomena of lightning and thunder, the Bible records that they shall end. In the new creation, after God has obliterated sin, the throne of God will be at peace. Only at this time does the revelator describe the throne of God without the former scary accompaniments: "And he showed me a river of water of life, clear as crystal, proceeding out of the throne of God, and of the Lamb." Rev. 22:1.

The throne of God has the Ark of the Covenant and the Ten Commandments as its foundation, in both the physical and spiritual senses. The Ten Commandments form the foundation of the heavenly throne and government. This has been the case from the very beginning of things. Mankind, through Adam and Eve, was given a choice to accept God as His unquestioned leader; to follow Him in faith, through obedience of His law. Peace and harmony would have been the result of such a choice. The throne of God would forever have issued the sparkling, peaceful waters of the river of life that we will now only see in the New Creation. Had our first parents triumphed, even as Christ triumphed, all creation would have drunk freely of this water of life, and never thirsted again. Mankind, and the rest of creation, would have derived perfect health and eternal existence from the crystal waters, flowing out of the law of love under God's seat. We would have witnessed the true meaning and beauty of David's longest Psalm; 119.

However, our parents in Eden chose the path of human passion. Choosing to live apart from the law of God, they opted to make their own rules, divorced from the Ten Commandments. They would choose which laws felt right to obey. They would decide for themselves what was right or wrong to do. They chose to worship God in their own fashion, in their own time. The decision brought immediate discord to the source of the river of life under God's throne. From that moment, lightning, thunder, and earthquakes rendered the water of life inaccessible to mankind. Instead of being a throne of peace, God's seat became a seat of judgment and righteous indignation. In place of the water of life, which should have brought peace, abundance and eternal life, came lightnings and thunders, which brought thorns, thistles, mediocrity, meagerness and death to the world. Nevertheless, praise be to God, and to our Savior Jesus Christ, the time is soon coming when we shall have access to the river of life. This will happen when God has destroyed all sin, whose clearest definition in the Bible is "the transgression of the law." 1 John 3:4.

CHAPTER 11

The Law and the Cross

Did the cross abolish the law?

You have probably heard it preached from the pulpit, dear friend, that the death of Jesus effectively nailed the law to the cross! The preacher most likely quoted a verse from one or two of Paul's letters in the New Testament. Equally likely, you have also met people who have argued that far from annulling the law, the cross in fact reinforced it. They claim the law is as much in force today, as it was in Moses' day. This group also produced scriptural evidence to support their view.

We agreed in chapter 4 that the Bible, being God's inspiration, could not contradict itself. Which doctrine then, is correct, regarding the law? Certainly, the majority in the world today believe the law of God outdated and replaced by grace. Some Christians and non-Christians alike believe that the law resides inside one's heart, and the only guide to good and bad is in one's conscience.

You may feel persuaded that indeed God abolished His law. However, if you are honest, you will admit uncertainty. This is because you cannot imagine the painful death of Jesus on the cross setting humanity free to commit adultery, or to murder, for example. In this chapter, we attempt to use the Bible itself to clarify this matter. We will show that there is no contradiction.

If chapter 10 demonstrated that the Ten Commandments are still in force, what then was the Apostle Paul referring to when he wrote in Colossians 3:13-14,

> and you, being dead in your sins and the uncircumcision of your flesh, has he made alive together with him, having forgiven you all trespasses; blotting out the handwriting of ordinances that was against us, which was contrary to us, and took it out of the way, nailing it to the cross?

This is the text quoted the most by those who claim that the law was nailed to the cross, and the Ten Commandments are no longer in force.

While Paul here describes ordinances that are contrary, many inspired writers of the Bible, including him, praise the Ten Commandments, in the most glowing terms. The psalmist dedicates the whole of Psalm 119 to praising and elevating the law, or the commandments. He sings "Great peace have they who love your law." (v.165). Read the entire song for yourself, and gain an appreciation of the beauty of God's law. Ps. 19:7 sings, "The law is perfect . . . ." Paul himself says in Rom. 13:10, "love is the fulfillment of the law." Rom. 8:4 describes the law as "righteous." The same man also wrote, "Therefore the law is holy, and the commandment holy and just and good." Rom. 7:12.

These few descriptions of the law give the impression of something perfect and desirable. They certainly do not create, in the imagination, a picture of being 'contrary' and deserving of abolition. If the law was this good, why would the coming of Christ, the Lamb of God who takes away sin, be the occasion for removing this good thing? Furthermore, why would Paul describe the same "just and good" law in such negative light, in Colossians 3:13-14? Here is an apparent contradiction staring us in the face; and contradictions are impossible in the Word of God! There has to be a way to reconcile the two positions.

There exists overwhelming scriptural evidence to show that Paul is referring to two different laws, when he makes the apparently contradicting statements. The psalmist is referring to a different law from that which Paul describes as 'contrary', and which the cross took out of the way. There is indeed scriptural evidence to support this position. Before we delve into that study, we must clear the myth that Jesus Christ introduced a new law to replace the Ten Commandments. We must also explain the difference between the new and the old covenants.

The law of love—merely a summary

When asked what the greatest commandment was, Jesus responded, "You shall love the Lord your God with all your heart, with all your soul and with all your mind. This is the first and great commandment. . . ." It is very important to note that Jesus did not stop there, but proceeded to answer what they had not asked: "And the second is like unto it. You shall love your neighbour as yourself." He did not stop there either, but added, "*On these two* hang all the law and the prophets." Matt. 22:37-40 (emphasis supplied).

Many professing Christians today believe that the Lord introduced these two laws to replace the Decalogue. They fail to realize that these two are a brief summary of the Ten Commandments, and that they do not appear for the first time in the New Testament. In fact, the Lord Jesus was simply quoting from the Old Testament, as He was fond of doing. "And you shall love the Lord your God with all your heart, and with all your soul, and with all your might" is from Deuteronomy 6:5. "You shall love your neighbour as yourself" is a quotation from the Old Testament verse, Leviticus 19:18. Even when Jesus says in John 13:34, "A new commandment I give unto you. That you love one another . . . ," He is simply highlighting love as the underlining principle of the last six commandments.

FIGURE 1. "ON THESE TWO HANG THE LAW AND THE PROPHETS"

THE TEN COMMANDMENTS	
SUMMARY OF 1-4 (OLD TESTAMENT) "And thou shalt love the LORD thy God with all thine heart, and with all thy soul, and with all thy might." Deut. 6:5	SUMMARY OF 5-10 (OLD TESTAMENT) ". . . thou shalt love thy neighbour as thyself . . ." Lev. 19:18
SUMMARY OF 1-4 (NEW TESTAMENT) "Thou shalt love the Lord thy God with all thy heart, and with all thy soul, and with all thy mind." Matt. 22:37	SUMMARY OF 5-10 (NEW TESTAMENT) "Thou shalt love thy neighbour as thyself." Matt. 22:39

 "On these two hang all the law and the prophets."
Matt. 22:40

LAWS GOVERNING RELATIONSHIP BETWEEN MAN AND GOD	LAWS GOVERNING RELATIONSHIP BETWEEN MAN AND MAN
1. Thou shalt have no other gods before me. 2. Thou shalt not make unto thee any graven image, or any likeness of anything that is in heaven above, or that is in the water under the earth: Thour shalt now bow down thyself to them, nor serve them: for I the LORD thy God am a jealous God, visiting the iniquity of the fathers upon the children unto the third and fourth generation of them that hate me; And shewing mercy unto thousands of them that love me, and keep my commandments. 3. Thou shalt not take the name of the LORD thy God in vain; for the LORD will not hold him guiltless that taketh his name in vain. 4. Remember the sabbath day, to keep it holy. Six days shalt thou labour, and do all thywork: But the seventh day is the sabbath of the LORD thy God: in it thou shalt not do any work, thou, nor thy son, nor thy daughter, thy manservant, nor thy maidservant, nor thy cattle, nor thy stranger that is within thy gates:	For in six days the LORD made heaven and earth, the sea, and all that in them is, and rested the seventh day wherefore the LORD blessed the sabbath day, and hallowed it. 5. Honour thy father and thy mother: that thy days maybe long upon the land which the LORD thy God giveth thee. 6. Thou shalt not kill. 7. Thou shalt not commit adultery. 8. Thour shalt not steal. 9. Thou shalt not bear false witness against thy neighbour. 10. Thou shalt not covet thy neigbour's house, thou shalt not covet thy neighbour's wife, nor his manservant, nor his maidservant, nor his ox, nor his ass, nor anything that is thy neighbour's.

When a Christian asks himself, 'How am I going to love my God and my neighbor?' there is no place else to look but the Ten Commandments, to learn the things one has to *do* if he loves God and man. If you study the first four commandments, you will quickly realize that they regulate how man should relate to God. "For this is the love of God, that we keep His commandments: . . ." 1 John 5:3. Which commandments? The first four of the ten! "By this we know that we love the children of God, when we love God and keep His commandments." 1 John 5:2. How do we love the children of God? Answer: We do so by keeping the last six of the Ten Commandments.

Moses ordered to write a book of law

Having announced His law, God then set out to draft an agreement with Israel. If the children of Israel kept the Ten Commandments, God would reward them. On the other hand, if they transgressed the law, He would punish them. The Lord asked Moses to write these terms of agreement in a book. The book would include detailed civil, ceremonial, health, and criminal law for Israel. Moses documented, further, the rewards for obedience, and the penal code for transgression in this book.

What was the destiny of this book of the law written by Moses?

> And it came to pass, when Moses had finished writing the words of this law in a book, until they were finished, that Moses commanded the Levites, who bore the ark of the covenant of the Lord, saying, Take this book, and put it *by the side of the ark of the covenant* of the Lord your God, that it may be there for a *witness against you.* Deut. 31:24-26 (emphasis supplied).

Here, in a few short verses, we discover the existence of a second law, hand-written by Moses and deposited *outside* the ark—not inside—and which was *against* the children of Israel! Here is proof of the existence of a set of laws that were on a level lower than the Ten Commandments, as demonstrated by their location outside the ark of the covenant. We have also identified the law that was contrary—*against*—the children of Israel.

It is important to reveal why God had to order a record of this second set of laws. "Why then the law? *It was added because of transgression,* till the descendent should come, to whom the promise was made." Gal. 3:19 (emphasis supplied.) There are two ways to look at how this text justifies the addition of the handwritten scroll, which we shall call the Mosaic Law, though we recognize God as its true author.

How transgression necessitated Mosaic Law

God introduced the ceremonial laws as an earthly pointer to the heavenly plan of redemption in response to the original fall of man, and consequent entry of sin into the world. Most of the annual festivals and daily sacrificial ceremonies, therefore, pointed to various stages of the reality which Jesus Christ, the Lamb of God, would later come to fulfill. In this respect, the ceremonial law, being a response to sin, was necessitated by sin. Men acted out the plan of redemption, as in a drama, on a stage whose centerpiece was the earthly sanctuary. The first advent of Christ would end these ceremonial laws.

The civil and criminal sections of the Mosaic Law were meant as a supplement to the Ten Commandments. Had Israel been able to identify love as the root of God's Moral Law, there would have been no need for the long list of civil and criminal laws that God added in Moses' book, after the Ten Commandments. The fact that mankind continued in sin, with the full knowledge of the Ten Commandments, necessitated additional statutes expounding the Moral Law. It is a sad reality that God had to spell out in detail, for the stiff-necked race, exactly what constituted theft, murder, adultery and coveting.

The four-hundred-and-thirty-year sojourn among pagans in Egypt had dulled the spiritual edge of the people's hearts. They were no longer able to recognize the difference between God, their Creator, and a calf fashioned from gold; yet this was the same generation that witnessed the miracles of God in Egypt, crossed a parted Red Sea on foot, drank water gushing from a rock, and eaten manna and quail from heaven! So calloused were the people's consciences, that the only deterrent to crime that God found suitable for the time was, "Eye for eye, tooth for tooth, hand for hand, foot for foot." Ex. 21:24. If they could not obey the law out of love, it was possible they may obey it out of fear. Transgression in the face of the Ten Commandments, therefore, necessitated this detailed version, together with its penal code.

This law was certainly contrary to the children of Israel. Disobedience of any of part of it led to severe punishment, even death by stoning. As Galatians 3:19 pointed out, this law was only temporary until the coming of Jesus to demonstrate, by His unstained and selfless life, just how much love could achieve. This part of the law-book of Moses, the old penal code, was certainly nailed to the cross and replaced by turning the other cheek. (Matthew 5:39).

Health laws

A large portion of the Mosaic Law had to do with health. Over a million people were on the move in the wilderness, with no proper sanitary facilities or housing. That there were no epidemics of disease under these crowded circumstances was largely due to the enforcement of the health laws that God gave to Moses. The health laws fell into two broad sections.

One section required the priests and members of the congregation to wash thoroughly, and 'purify' themselves before a ceremony or festival. By this means, God intended to impart a sense of the holiness of the Sanctuary, or ceremony in question. After the Cross, the washing of the spirit by the blood of Jesus, and the wearing of His cloak of righteousness replaced bodily cleansing.

The second section of the health laws dealt with personal and communal hygiene. God gave Moses detailed instructions on toiletry, and on how to handle dead animals and people. He recommended the best types of food for healthful living, and pointed out those foods considered unclean.

Knowledge of germs is a modern phenomenon, only acquired after the relatively recent discovery of the microscope. Back in the days of Moses, four thousand years ago, the people would never have understood, if God had given them a detailed lecture on how amoeba, bacteria, and viruses, were the cause of disease. Therefore, God simply said Don't, and Do!

There were penalties enacted for transgressing these laws in those ancient days. It is instructive to note that doctors today practice before and after surgery, the same scrubbing ordained back then. Health experts today promote the same dietary patterns that God gave to Israel through the Mosaic Laws. Medical scientists only discovered the connection between animal blood and gout and between animal fat and heart disease four millennia after God forbade men from consuming animal blood and fat.

Many consider these health laws old fashioned, yet one can imagine what benefits they could bring to our homes today, having sustained a million nomads in perfect health for forty years in the wilderness. Only a handful of congregations and groups still keep the health code as given in the Old Testament, yet it is well worth our while to obey them today, as strictly as the Israel of old did. After all, they came from He who being our Creator, knows best what is good for us.

Ceremonial law

Ceremonial laws took up the bulk of Moses' law-book. Large sections of the books of Exodus, Leviticus, Numbers, and Deuteronomy list these laws. They give details of the daily ceremonies, annual festivals and sabbaths. These ceremonies and festivals pointed to various phases of the work of the Messiah who was to come. It is to this part of the Mosaic Law that Paul is referring when he writes, after the advent of the Messiah, "So let no one judge you in food or drink, or regarding a festival or a new moon or sabbaths, which are a shadow of things to come but the substance is Christ." Col. 2:16-17.

The book of Hebrews alludes to the same laws in similar terms as

> a figure for the time then present, in which were offered both gifts and sacrifices that could not make him that did that service perfect, as pertaining to the conscience; which stood only in foods and drinks, and various washings, and carnal ordinances, imposed until the time of reformation. Heb. 9:9-10.

The ceremonial Laws were obviously temporary. The sabbaths referred to in Colossians are not the weekly Sabbaths of the Decalogue, but the annual, and seventh-year sabbaths of the Ceremonial Law, as can clearly be discerned from the context of the text.

The cross certainly annulled this section of the Mosaic Law, and the sign given for its expiry was the tearing of the veil to the Most Holy Place in the temple of Jerusalem. This happened the same hour Jesus died, on the first day of the Passover feast, when the High Priest was killing the Passover lamb in the temple. Type had at last met antitype, and the significance of the earthly priesthood, as well as the sacrificial ceremonies and festivals it administered, came to a sudden end. The last vestige of holiness departed from the temple, and henceforth, Jesus would assume His predestined role as the heaven-based High Priest and only mediator between man and God, as we saw in chapter 9, in our study of the Sanctuary in Heaven.

Terms of the contract—the first covenant

The last section of the Mosaic Law listed the terms and conditions binding the two parties in the contract. The two contracting parties were God, the moral Governor, on the one hand and Israel, the free moral agent representing humanity, on the other. The condition was obedience to the Moral Law. God was offering His law to a nation chosen as a model to the world.

The reward for obedience was prosperity in Canaan, a land of milk and honey. The penalty for disobedience and breach of the contract was a cocktail of curses.

> But it shall come to pass, if you hearken not unto the voice of the Lord your God, to observe to do all his commandments and his statutes, which I command you this day; that all these curses shall come upon you, and overtake you: Cursed shall you be in the city and cursed shall you be in the field. Cursed shall be your basket and your kneading trough. Cursed shall be the fruit of your body, and the fruit of your land, the increase of your cattle, and the offspring of your sheep. Cursed shall you be when you come in and cursed shall you be when you go out. Deut. 28:15-19.

> And Moses wrote all the words of the Lord . . . And he took the book of the covenant, and read in the hearing of the people: and they said, all that the Lord has said we will do, and be obedient.

> And Moses took the blood and sprinkled it on the people, and
> said, Behold, the blood of the covenant, which the Lord has
> made with you concerning these words. Ex. 24:4, 7-8.

The children of Israel swore to obey God's law, and accepted the blessings, should they succeed, and the curses should they fail. The High Priest used the blood of an ox to seal the agreement!

Note that it was part of the contract that if Israel should disobey the letter of God's law, they would suffer the curses listed above. It was in this respect that the Israelites regarded the Mosaic Law as being contrary. Paul is referring to this law when he writes of the law that the coming of the Messiah would abolish, to usher in a new and perfect covenant. What was the nature of this new covenant?

Terms of contract—the second covenant

The new covenant was a new contract, with God on the one hand, and Christians, as the new free moral agents replacing Israel, on the other. The condition remained obedience to the same original Moral Law. The reward for obedience was eternal life. The penalty for disobedience became eternal death. God established new rewards and penalties over the very same object of agreement. The difference between the new and the old covenants lies, not in the laws to be kept, but in the identity of the parties involved, in the spirit in which the laws are to be kept as well as in the fruits of obedience and disobedience.

The new covenant did not involve the race Israel alone, but embraced all humanity. Israel had failed to lift the banner of God's Moral Law for the world to emulate. Instead, they had proudly kept it to themselves, even corrupting it by adding their own ultra-legalistic overtones between the lines. Instead of appearing to the world a law of love, it became a chain of bondage around the necks of those seeking to be part of the covenant.

So burdensome had the leaders made the law, that some of the strongest words Jesus had to say in the whole Bible, were the woes He pronounced on the Pharisees and the Sadducees, in Matthew 23:23-29, for making the law impossible for the people to obey. He concludes by the very harsh words: "You serpents, you generation of vipers, how can you escape the judgment of hell?" (v. 33.) Therefore, the corporate responsibility for demonstrating the equity and beauty of God's Moral Law now fell on the Christian Church.

The second party in the new covenant was Jesus, the Christ, whose blood became the seal to the agreement, replacing the blood of the ox, which sealed the old. This was another important difference between the two covenants.

While the reward for obedience in the old contract was a long and prosperous life in earthly Canaan, that of the new covenant involved eternal bliss in the New Heaven and the New Earth, which the Lord would create in the future. In place of the curses and death by stoning, decreed as penalties under the old covenant, the new promised loss of the privilege to eternal life.

In considering these differences, it is important to bear in mind always, that the object of both covenants, the thing over which God drafted the contract, remained the Moral Law. God promises, not to write a new law, but to write the same old Law, not on rock this time but on the hearts of His people.

> But this *is* the covenant that I will make with the house of Israel after those days, says the LORD: I will put My law in their minds, and write it on their hearts; and I will be their God, and they shall be My people. Jer. 31:33.

The Israel referred to here is the new Israel, the Christian Church. Executed from the hearts of men, the law will spring rightly from a well of love, rather than from fear of curses and penalties. Humanity will keep God's law because they love their Creator and their neighbor, rather than because they hope to obtain salvation through obedience, for salvation is only possible through God's grace, and faith in Jesus.

Devil ascends on the ladder of felled moral law

Many Christian congregations today accept and teach the doctrine that the Ten Commandments were the old law, intended for Israel alone, and expired on Calvary. They say the Cross ushered in a new law of love. While it is true that God announced the Ten Commandments to Moses and Israel at Sinai, there are two important points to note.

The first is that the laws had always been in existence before Sinai. God put in place the Sabbath institution right at Creation, when He hallowed the day and set the example by resting on the seventh day. Adam and Eve hid from God because they were aware of sin, the transgression of the Law. Cain tried to hide his sin of murder from God because he well knew he had sinned. The destruction of Sodom was because "they were haughty, and committed abominations before me." Ez. 16:50. Rampant homosexuality was an evident abomination in the city of Sodom. This practice fell under the commandment number seven—"you shall not commit adultery". There are numerous examples of people committing sin, long before the birth of Israel. This demonstrates that the law existed for all men, before Israel, "for where there is no law there is no transgression." Rom. 4:15.

Secondly, God never intended for Israel to confine the law to their race alone. He selected this nation only as a model to demonstrate the beauty of the Moral Law to the rest of the world. Israel failed in this noble duty through national pride and selfishness. It is now the duty of new Israel, the

Christian Church, to do what biological Israel failed to do. It is your duty and mine today, to demonstrate the beauty and equity of God's Moral Law, the Ten Commandments for the entire world to emulate.

Only one law targeted for extinction

Should you closely interrogate those who teach that the Ten Commandments are no longer in force, it will emerge that they actually believe that nine of the Ten Commandments are still in force. It is only the fourth commandment that they are not obliged to keep. So, what is the truth? We must ask whether the law stands abolished or not? We cannot continue to preach that the cross abolished the Ten Commandments, while teaching, at the same time, that the laws prohibiting adultery, murder and theft are still in place. This is an example of the confusion labeled Babylon in Scripture.

The devil is having his way because the children of God are ignoring plain truth and accepting error and confusion as doctrine, to suit their personal tastes; fitting religion into their chosen lifestyles, patterns, and timetables. Few of us realize how the institutions that are our churches mislead us into ignoring the full law of God, and in the process offending Him: "For whosoever shall keep the whole law, and yet offend in one point, he is guilty of all" James 2:10.

Jesus never abolished the law

It is crucial that Christians settle, from Scripture alone, the question whether or not the Cross abolished the law. By definition, a cross is just two pieces of dead wood joined together. However the Cross that Christians have their faith focused upon, is the one on Calvary, two thousand years ago. There were many crosses on this hill at that time. In fact, one Passover afternoon, Roman soldiers nailed three men to three crosses side by side. To the two crosses on either side, long iron nails pinned the palms and ankles of two robbers.

On the middle one, a wasted, quiet man hung by the thread of his tendons from the timber, as the cruel nails tore at his flesh under the weight of his body. On his head was a crown of sharp thorns, which sent intermittent trickles of blood down the lines that fatigue had drawn on his face, onto the parched earth. A layer of blood and sweat, mingled with the thick spittle of hate-filled men, covered his body. Above his head was a note announcing his crime to the universe: *King of the Jews.*

The man fastened to the middle cross was an ordinary man only because He had foregone His divinity. He left the splendor of Heaven and the adoration of angels, in order for just this to happen: the Cross! Jesus Christ of Nazareth was the Messiah, the one the saints had been anticipating since Adam. He was the Creator of all, who condescended to die at the hands of His own creations, that He may reconcile His creations to their God. Therein lies the significance of the middle cross of Calvary.

Now, many claim that this same cross nullified the entire law of God as given to the patriarchs of old. If we walked up to the man hanging miserably on the cross that Friday afternoon and asked Him why He let it happen this way, what would His answer be? Do you, in all honesty, believe that He would say, "I have done this to free mankind from the bondage of the Ten Commandments."? Or would He explain that mankind had sinned by transgressed the Law. From the very beginning, God had decreed death as sentence for sin. God's word cannot be retracted, therefore man had to die. There were three options open to God. The first was to abolish the Law, which would be impossible. The second option was to let man die for his sins. The love of God for humanity made this option unviable. The third option was to find a way that the sentence passed on sinful mankind could be executed without humanity perishing. That way, the Law of God remains, and mankind lives. That is why He was hanging on this cross this afternoon. It would appear that the Messiah anticipated our question many centuries ago, or else His own generation had already started debating the question. Whichever is the case, He did answer the question clearly:

> Think not that I am come to destroy the law, or the prophets: I am not come to destroy, but to fulfill. For *verily* I say unto you, till heaven and earth pass away, *one jot or one tittle* shall in no wise pass from the law, till all be fulfilled. Whosoever therefore shall break *one of these least* commandments, and teach men so, he shall be called least in the kingdom of heaven, but whosoever shall do and teach them, the same shall be called great in the kingdom of heaven. Matt. 5:17-19, emphasis supplied.

It is amazing that even though this is one of very few points upon which the Lord virtually swears, many Professing Christians today simply brush it aside without second thought. The significance of the word "*verily*," and the phrase "*one jot or one tittle,*" to stress His point is purposely ignored by many. However, there you have it, straight from the Messiah's mouth. He never came to abolish the Moral Law! He who has ears has heard. He who chooses to be like the smoker may be too proud to accept new truth. Take no comfort in numbers. Remember it is possible, indeed predicted, that the millions in the majority are wrong!

CHAPTER 12

The Desecrated Day

Would you accept?

Consider the following hypothetical incident unfolding in your church. You and your family are sitting comfortably, at the opening of the main service. One of the elders mounts the pulpit and greets the congregation. It is time for announcements.

"Please pay attention. There are three items, from the General Council of our Central Conference in America. All member churches are to implement them with immediate effect.

"Starting next week our children's Sunday school classes will be receiving special lessons in pick-pocketing, and on how to lie without being detected. Renowned practitioners, men of long experience and recently released from prison, will conduct the training. We hope that our children will benefit immensely, from these life-enhancing skills.

"Before marriage, senior youth must pair up with chosen partners of the opposite sex and live together as man and wife for a trial period, with a view to establishing whether or not they are compatible. They should change partners until they identify the most ideal. This is an important courtship step, which should see the rate of divorce decrease in our church.

"All family heads will be required to keep a small statue of Jesus or the cross. They must first bring it to church for sanctification by our pastor. Each time they pray to God, they are to place the holy statue in front of them and pour out their heart to it. The statue will in turn convey their prayers to God. It is hoped that the gap between sinful man and God will be bridged by this means.

"Thank you; and God bless you as you begin to implement these new measures."

How would you feel after these announcements? How would your spouse sitting beside you react? Imagine the reaction of the older members of the congregation. Outrage may be too light a word to describe the reaction of the congregation. I doubt the congregation would even allow the elder to finish the announcements in peace. One member may even throw a hymn book at his face. You may even join in the protest. Please continue imagining.

Why protest?

After ten minutes of loud incoherent discussion, the pastor walks in and stands beside the elder. The congregation gradually settles into a tense silence.

"I interpret the noise as protest . . ." the pastor starts. He is not allowed to go on. A fresh wave of disgruntled noises breaks out. After achieving another silence, the pastor proceeds: "What is the basis of your protest? Let us have a hand up to answer."

A hundred hands go up at once, and the one given the floor stands up and shouts, "The church should not force us to sin against God by going against His precepts!" There is loud support. The Pastor holds up his hand and proceeds: "Our church has always taught what you accepted at baptism. Doctrine number eight in our church handbook is to the effect that since the Cross, we are saved by grace, as the law was effectively rendered null and void by the Cross. Well, time has come for our members to live what we have accepted all along and not putting into practice. The law was nailed to the cross, and only the grace of Christ saves us."

With the knowledge you now posses about the Sanctuary and the two different sets of God's law, would you accept this answer? I hope not! If this were to happen in real life, your congregation would feel a sense of outrage against the church hierarchy, for attempting to enforce doctrines that are clearly against the law of God.

To back your protest from Scripture, you would possibly refer to Exodus 20, where texts are available to counter each one of the elder's three announcements. "You shall not steal" and "You shall not bear false witness against your neighbor", verses 15 and 16 respectively, would make the first of the elder's announcements an affront to God. Verse 14: "You shall not commit adultery," clearly nullifies announcement number two. The third announcement would break the second commandment:

> You shall not make for yourself a carved image—any likeness of anything that is in heaven above, or that is in the earth beneath, or that is in the water under the earth; you shall not bow down to them nor serve them. (vv. 4, 5)

Self convicting

Now, the laws you have used to resist the introduction of apostasy are part of the group of ten we studied in chapter 9. You have employed the Ten Commandments to fight off error. This process of flashing the torch of Scripture on a doctrine to establish its correctness was the very same one used by the reformers—John Huss, John Calvin, John Wesley and others.

Regarding the keeping of these laws, one apostle wrote clearly:

> If you really fulfill the royal law according to the Scripture, 'You shall love your neighbor as yourself', you do well; but if you show partiality you commit sin, and are convicted by the law as transgressors. For whoever shall keep the whole law, and yet stumble in one point, he is guilty of all. James 2:9, 10.

You may question the identity of the 'royal law' in this text. James clarifies this in the next verse. "For He who said, 'Do not commit adultery', also said 'Do not murder' . . ." (v. 11) The two are clearly part of the Ten

Commandments, and James is warning against transgressing any one of them.

There are solemn implications behind this victory against error. We have used the Decalogue to prove the sinfulness of stealing and committing adultery. James 2:9-10 creates a serious problem for us—a dilemma! Once we have affirmed the validity of "Do not commit adultery" today, we must also necessarily accept the validity of the nine remaining commandments. These nine include the forth commandment:

> Remember the Sabbath day, to keep it holy. Six days you shall labor and do all your work, but the seventh day is the Sabbath of the LORD your God. In it you shall do no work: you, nor your son, nor your daughter, nor your male servant, nor your female servant, nor your cattle, nor your stranger who is within your gates. For in six days the LORD made the heavens and the earth, the sea, and all that is in them, and rested the seventh day. Therefore the LORD blessed the Sabbath day and hallowed it. Ex. 20:8-11.

Selective amnesia

Most Christian churches the world over, disobey this fourth commandment. First, they claim that the Ten Commandments were nailed to the cross. Strangely, they then condemn stealing and adultery as sins against God. However, something is seriously wrong with this thinking, since the laws against theft and adultery appear in the same set of laws as the Sabbath commandment. First, they declare the entire law null and void; next, they quietly bring back to life nine of the Ten Commandments, and enforce them, purposely forgetting one. Only the Sabbath commandment remains nullified, in spite of James' clear warning against partial obedience of God's Law. When it comes to the fourth commandment, the whole of Christendom is collectively gripped with a serious case of selective amnesia[13]. They forget this law even as they are reading it. God's foreknowledge of this selective loss of memory led Him to begin this commandment with 'REMEMBER'! Let us visit the Word of God to establish some truths regarding the Sabbath. But, firstly, we must satisfy ourselves which day of the modern day week is the seventh.

Instituted at creation

The announcement of the Ten Commandments at Sinai opens with "Remember" because God had instituted the Sabbath, and given it to the human race at Creation. If we believe that God 'rested' on the seventh day of the creation week because He was tired, then our conception of God is highly flawed, for "have you not known? Have you not heard? The everlasting God, the LORD, the Creator of the ends of the earth, neither faints nor is weary." Is. 40:28. God "rested" as an example to the created beings. On this day, He was looking over all that He had created and acknowledging that 'it was good'. The Creator was on this day not creating things tangible, He was creating the very day itself; an institution about which we are told: "God blessed the seventh day and sanctified it," and "the LORD blessed the Sabbath day and hallowed it." Gen. 2:3; Ex. 20:11.

To sanctify is 'to make sacred or holy'; 'to consecrate'; 'to set apart as sacred'. It was not Adam, who decided to make the day a holy memorial of God's Creation. In fact, even if he had wished to, Adam could never have achieved this feat, for neither man nor angel possibly can! God alone possesses the capacity of intrinsic holiness to impart upon created objects at His discretion. To attempt to declare any day or object holy which the Lord has not Himself consecrated, is vainglorious on the part of any created being; a self righteousness which is as "filthy rags" before God! (Is. 64:6). Because the Creator gave the Sabbath to the ancestors of *all* men, it was a gift to *all* men. As surely as we accept Adam as the father of all humanity, so we must recognize the universality of the Sabbath institution.

It is instructive to note that Adam and Eve celebrated their very first Sabbath *before* they had done any work at all to tire them. The first couple was simply discovering the exquisite beauty of God's creations around them and beginning to gain an appreciation of the awesome power and infinite genius of God! They were learning for the first time to love God for whom and what He was—the loving Creator. On this day, they were closer to God than on any other, for He was physically with them as He created and sanctified this special day.

Science confirms

Many Christians declare that each person is free to choose any day of the week as the Sabbath. They claim that as long as one can count seven day cycles consistently, one is justified in declaring this chosen day his or her sabbath. They are right in calling it *their* sabbath, for Saturday is in fact the Sabbath of the Lord—The Lord's Day, and any others are appointed for men, by men!

Many more claim that the Sabbath was moved from the seventh day, to the first of the week. We shall soon review the Scriptures to establish the authority for the change; whether it was God or man, but before we visit the Bible, we must first make two revealing observations.

The first is that it would be nonsensical for a man born on 26 January, to declare that he is moving his birthday to 30 June. It is not possible, by mere pronouncement, to shift the reality of the 26 January anniversary to any other date. In fact, it is not possible by any means under the sun! The man may advertise the modification in the daily newspaper, and throw a big party on June 30, yet January 26 will forever remain his birthday! The Sabbath rests on an historical event, which is as impossible to shift as the date of Abraham Lincoln's assassination. You would no doubt view any attempt to change the date of an historical event or birthday as ludicrous, because what is attempted is simply not possible. If you accept the un-changeability of human birthdays and historical landmarks, how much more so should you the memorial of God's Creation?

We must visit the realm of human science and extract the second observation—a very interesting discovery. Astronomical science confirms the existence of a real seven day week, with the first day distinguishable from the second and the third from the fifth and so on.

> Dr. J. B. Dimbley, premier chronologist to the British Chronological and Astronomical Association, after years of careful calculations asserts: 'If men refused to observe weeks, and the line of time was forgotten, the days of the week could be recovered by observing when the transits of the planets, or eclipses of the sun and moon, occurred. These great sentinels of the sky keep seven days with scientific accuracy, thundering out the seven days inscribed on the inspired page.'—(Marcussen 2004, National Sunday Law, Appendix 12, p.93)

It is clear, from these two observations, that it was a particular day of the week that God set apart as His holy Sabbath. Besides being physically unique, this day is charged with the invisible halo of God's blessing and sanctification, which no other day possesses, and which no man could possibly transfer to any other day of the week. The blessing is accessible to all who should approach this day with the worshipful reverence deserving of all the holy things of God.

Seven-day week universal

The seven-day creation week and the seventh-day Sabbath, have to be the only reason why a seven day week has been kept by all tribes, tongues and nations to this day, though years and months have been reckoned differently in different civilizations and ages.

> We find from time immemorial the knowledge of a week of seven days among all nations—Egyptians, Arabians, Indians—in a word, all nations of the East, have in all ages made use of this week of seven days, for which it is difficult to account without admitting that this knowledge was derived from the common ancestors of the human race.—*Encyclopedia of Biblical Literature*, Vol. II, art. "Sabbath," p. 655.

Many people claim that God intended the Sabbath for Jews alone. Contrary to this view, Isaiah clearly demonstrates that the Sabbath was instituted for the entire human race.

> Also the sons of the foreigner who join themselves to the LORD, to serve Him, and to love the name of the LORD, to be His servants—*everyone who keeps from defiling the Sabbath*, and holds fast My covenant—even them I will bring to My holy mountain, and make them joyful in My house of prayer. Their burnt offerings and their sacrifices will be accepted on My altar; for My house shall be called a house of prayer for all nations. Is. 56:6-7 (emphasis supplied).

You may not be a biological Jew, but you are the foreigner or gentile invited in this text to the new congregation of Israel, the Christian Church, if you desist "from defiling the Sabbath."

There is no argument, among theologians and historians worldwide, which modern day of the week is the seventh. They accept Saturday as the biblical seventh day of the week. You, dear reader, may want to satisfy yourself that the Bible places the Sabbath on Saturday. If we are able to show that Saturday is indeed the true Sabbath, you must realize how you have been partial in refusing the institutionalization of theft and adultery into your church, while condoning the institutionalized disobedience of one of the other laws linked to them. You may then want to correct the error and live in conformity with God's precept.

Easter holiday confirms which day

If you are Christian, you probably celebrate Easter every year. Christendom accepts Easter Friday as the day when Christ died on the cross. On the day, there was a flurry to bury Him before sunset. Let us find out why this was so. "Now when the evening was come, because it was the Preparation Day, that is, the day before the Sabbath, Joseph of Arimathea . . ." Mark 15:42. You probably know the story of this man who took down the body of Jesus and buried it in his own new tomb. We find that the day celebrated by Christendom as Easter Friday was the day before the biblical Sabbath. Luke confirms this in more detail:

> The day was the Preparation, and the Sabbath drew near. And
> the women who had come with him from Galilee followed
> after, and they observed the tomb and how His body was laid.
> Then they returned and prepared spices and fragrant oils. *And*

they rested on the Sabbath according to the commandment. Luke 23:54-56 (Emphasis supplied).

Two points are worth noting from this text. (a) The Sabbath follows the day of Jesus' death and burial—the one celebrated as Easter Friday. (b) The Lord's closest relatives and friends desisted from the work of anointing His body with oils, because they were still keeping the Sabbath commandment in the New Testament, after the Cross.

You may wonder why the women did not proceed with the anointing work on the night of that Friday. The answer lies in how days are reckoned in the Bible. The day begins at dusk and ends the next dusk. This is evident in the creation story of Genesis 1, where each day is described as "there was evening, and there was morning, the . . . day." In Leviticus 23:32, God commands, "from evening to evening, you shall celebrate your sabbath." God specifically instructs observance of the Sabbath from evening (end of sixth day) to evening (end of seventh day). Preparation day therefore starts on what we call Thursday evening and ends Friday at sunset, as it gives way to the Sabbath. Friday was called Preparation day because all work such as cooking, laundry and cleaning, that would otherwise be done on the Sabbath, was done on that day in preparation for the day of rest.

To confirm further that Saturday is the seventh-day Sabbath, let us return to the bereaving women in the book of Luke.

Now on the *first day* of the week, very early in the morning, they, and certain other women with them, came to the tomb bringing the spices, which they had prepared. But they found the stone rolled away. Luke 24:1-2, emphasis supplied.

Jesus had risen that night or early morning. You celebrate Easter Sunday as the day of the resurrection, confirming that Sunday is the day called the first of the week in the text.

If we have proved that Friday is day six, and Sunday is day one, then we have demonstrated that Saturday, sandwiched between these two, is the seventh. If Saturday is the seventh day of the week, then Saturday is that great unique day, sanctified as the Sabbath of the Lord.

Jesus kept the Sabbath

Scripture records that the Lord Jesus himself attended church service on the Sabbath, not only once. It was a habit.

> So He came to Nazareth, where He had been brought up. And *as His custom was*, He went into the synagogue on the Sabbath day, and stood up to read . . . Then He went down to Capernaum, a city of Galilee, and was teaching them on the Sabbaths. Luke 4:16, 31, emphasis supplied.

Added to the physical evidence of Jesus keeping the Sabbath is His teaching. In one instance, the Lord Jesus claims, "the Son of Man is also Lord of the Sabbath." This is the reason for referring to the Sabbath as the Lord's Day. Another text supports this.

> If you turn away your foot from the Sabbath, from doing your pleasure on *My holy day*, and call the Sabbath a delight, *the holy day of the LORD* honorable, and shall honor Him, not doing your own ways, nor finding your own pleasure, nor speaking

your own words, then you shall delight yourself in the LORD;
and I will cause you to ride on the high hills of the earth . . . . Is.
58:13, 14, emphasis supplied.

Other sabbaths besides the weekly

In the following text, Paul appears to imply that it is no longer necessary
to observe the original Sabbath:

So let no one judge you in food or in drink, or regarding a
festival or a new moon or sabbaths, which are a shadow of things
to come, but the substance is of Christ. Colossians 2:16, 17.

Is this the case? It is possible to clarify the issue. The first point to
note is that Paul is writing about sabbaths in connection with ceremonies
and festivals, which pointed to the coming Messiah. The question is, Were
there such sabbaths in the Scriptures? The answer is: Yes!

Let us review what the Lord teaches Moses about the relationship
between the Lord's Day Sabbath and the festival sabbath days.

These are the feasts of the LORD which you shall proclaim to
be holy convocations, to offer an offering made by fire to the
LORD, a burnt offering and a grain offering, a sacrifice and
drink offerings, everything on its day—*besides the Sabbaths of
the LORD,* besides your gifts, besides all your vows, and besides
all your freewill offerings which you give to the LORD. Lev.
23:37-38, emphasis supplied.

This text clearly shows that there were other days declared holy days by God besides the seventh-day Sabbath. A study of Leviticus 13 reveals seven such annual sabbath days:

- The first day of the Feast of Unleavened Bread (vv. 7, 8)
- The last day of the Feast of Unleavened Bread (vv. (7, 8)
- The Day of Pentecost, Feast of Weeks. (v. 21)
- The first day of the seventh month—Feast of Trumpets (v. 24)
- The tenth day of the seventh month—Day of Atonement (v. 27)
- The first day of the Feast of Tabernacles (vv. 32-36)
- The last day of the Feast of Tabernacles (vv. 32-36)

These were annual festival days commanded by God. Because they were days of rest, they were also called *sabbaths*. Unlike the weekly Sabbath, specific sacrificial ceremonies marked these sabbaths. Now, we know that all sacrifices pointed to the ultimate one, which was Christ. Thus, these annual sabbaths were a shadow of the things to come. The advent of Christ put an end to these sabbaths, and this is the essence of Paul's statement above. However, the weekly Sabbath remains untouched by the passage of time.

The supernatural rending of the veil to the Most Holy Place, exposing this inner room, which no eyes had seen except those of the Chief Priest, dramatically marked the expiry of the ceremonial law. Any vestige of holiness remaining in the temple departed at that moment. The message from God, ending the ceremonial law and the work of earthly priests was in this manner supplied for the benefit of future generations. God did not leave it up to men to guess.

The Lord's Supper replaced the Passover feast by Christ's own demonstration to the disciples. The Lord gave a clear instruction for Christians to "do this in remembrance of" He who had finally replaced the sheep and goats. (See Luke 22:19.)

Now consider the fireworks and thunder accompanying the announcement of the Decalogue, which included the Sabbath commandment at Sinai. Consider also the strong words God had against those who trampled on His holy day, throughout the Old Testament. The word Sabbath appears about two hundred times in the Bible. How likely is it that Christ would be clandestine about the abolishment of the Sabbath, after all the noise regarding its observance? Think seriously about this!

Sabbath kept after the cross

Before we take a brief look at the origins of Sunday keeping, we must conclusively demonstrate that the Sabbath was observed by the Christian church long after Jesus' death, resurrection, and ascension.

We have already met the first evidence of continued Sabbath observance where the bereaved women desisted from doing any work after Jesus died. "Then they returned and prepared spices and fragrant oils. And they rested on the Sabbath according to the commandment." Luke 23:56 (last part). Had there been any unrecorded teaching to the effect that the Sabbath was abolished or shifted to a different day, this would have been demonstrated by Jesus' close aides on this first Sabbath after His death. Nevertheless, the women continued honouring the day as before His death.

Thirty to forty-five years after the cross, we meet Paul the apostle that the Lord appointed to minister to gentiles still keeping the Sabbath, as was the case with the entire Christian church. Referring to Paul and his party, the inspired page reveals "they departed from Perga, they came to Antioch in Pisidia, and went into the synagogue on the Sabbath day and sat down. And after the reading of the Law and the Prophets . . ." Acts 13:14, 15. In verse 27 of the same chapter Paul, speaking in the present tense says, "For those who *dwell* in Jerusalem, and their rulers, because they did not know Him, nor even the voices of the Prophets which *are read every Sabbath,* have fulfilled them in condemning Him." Acts 13:27-28, emphasis supplied.

Further down the same chapter we are told, "So when the Jews went out of the synagogue, the Gentiles begged that these words might be preached to them the next Sabbath" and then, "on the next Sabbath almost the whole city came together to hear the word of God." (vv. 42, 44)

Christian congregations met for worship on the Sabbath, whether in synagogues, homes, or open spaces. Paul's companion writes, in Acts 16:13: "And on the Sabbath day we went out of the city to the riverside, where prayer was customarily made; and we sat down and spoke to the women who met there."

There is a record of Christians meeting Paul, in Thessalonica, on more than one Sabbath for study and worship: "Then Paul, *as his custom was,* went in to them, and for three Sabbaths reasoned with them from the Scriptures . . ." Acts 17:2 (emphasis supplied). Note that Sabbath keeping after the Cross was the custom of an apostle. We have already seen that it was also Jesus' custom to keep the Sabbath. Later on, Paul continues to observe the Sabbath on his visit to Athens. "And he reasoned in the synagogue *every Sabbath,* and persuaded both Jews and Greeks . . . And he continued there a year and six months, teaching the word of God among them." Acts 18:4, 11. These texts clearly demonstrate that both Jews and non-Jews alike kept the Sabbath in the early apostolic church era.

History records that Jerusalem was destroyed in A.D. 70. Looking ahead, across the decades in foretelling this event, the Lord clearly warns those who would be alive in the city at that time, "And pray that your flight may not be in winter or on the Sabbath." Matt. 24:20. In this prophecy, the Lord reveals his expectation that the Sabbath institution would still be very much in place, decades after the cross of Calvary.

John, the beloved disciple is believed to have outlived all the disciples. He was on the island of Patmos, receiving the visions of Revelation, around

A. D. 90. It is evident that John was still observing Sabbath holiness. He records: "I was in the Spirit on the Lord's Day" Rev. 1:10. We have seen that the Lord claims the Sabbath as His day. John is therefore referring to the seventh-day Sabbath in this text. There is a popular but erroneous belief that the use of the term the 'Lord's Day' in reference to the Sunday, first day of the week is Scriptural. We shall soon show the origin of this error.

Sabbath even in eternity

Another aspect of the seventh-day Sabbath is found in Is. 66:22-23.

> "For as the new heavens and the new earth, which I will make shall remain before Me," says the LORD, "So shall your descendants and your name remain. And it shall come to pass that from one New Moon to another, and *from one Sabbath to another*, all flesh shall come to worship before Me," says the LORD. (Emphasis supplied.)

This is one of the clearest declarations of the permanence of the Sabbath institution in the Bible. All professing Christians correctly believe they will live forever in a new heaven and a new earth, if they should qualify. Well, here is news for all aspirants of heaven—the seventh-day Sabbath will continue into that endless time! God has not abolished it with a view to re-establishing it in the new creation. The Sabbath remains in place even now, sanctified, hallowed and ready to bless those willing to tuck themselves under its comforting wings.

We meet the Sabbath in the alpha and the omega. We greet it the Eden of Genesis, where human history begins, and we continue in it, in the final Eden of Isaiah 66. If you believe yourself a candidate for heaven, would it not be wise to start practicing the habits of heaven now?

No divine holiness for Sunday

We have seen that God never shifted the sanctity of the original Sabbath to another day. There is not a single record in the Word of God, placing even a whiff of holiness on the first day of the week. Not a single law is on record to enforce the keeping of this day as holy. There exist no regulations on how the first day should be observed. There is therefore no sin associated with not keeping it, "for where there is no law there is no transgression." Rom. 4:15. This is one reason for the popularity of Sunday keeping within Christendom. A professed Christian can choose to do his regular work, travel or go to a movie instead of attending church on Sunday, and feel no condemnation. No penalties were ever prescribed by God for the violation of Sunday. No promises of reward were ever given for its proper observance. Any penalties or rewards associated with Sunday have to be from men and not from God, for we have no Scriptural record whatsoever of God issuing such.

If God did not ordain Sunday keeping, why does the majority in the world regard this day as the true Sabbath?

Brief history of Sunday-keeping

One historian wrote, "The worship of the sun and the heavens and of the reproductive powers of nature are almost universal features of primitive religion." (Whitham 1957, 22). The origin of Sunday 'holiness' is easily discoverable in the very name of the day itself: *'sun-day'*, or *'day-of-the-sun'*. Egypt was the first among the ancient heathen nations to influence the world to suppress the seventh day Sabbath. This was because for them the most important day was the first of the week. Egyptians venerated the sun as the source and sustainer of all life. Since it was the beginning of all, it had to be worshipped on the first day of the week! The first day of the week, now called Sunday, was considered 'chiefest of the week'. It became a feast day and was declared a national holiday, and the Sabbath relegated to a common working day.

The Egyptian sun god was Osiris, supreme among gods. Egyptian influence spread to the rest of the world and Osiris became the Baal of Assyria and the Bel of Babylon. The abominable practice of sun worship rubbed off onto the Israelites during their four hundred-year sojourn in Egypt. The Apis bull they fashioned at Sinai was a representation of Osiris[14].

So strong was this idolatrous influence that even in the days of the prophet Ezekiel, centuries after deliverance from Egypt, God exposed acts of sun-worship right inside His temple at Jerusalem.

> Then he said to me, have you seen this, O son of man? Turn you yet again, and you shall see greater abominations than these. And he brought me into the inner court of the Lord's house, and, behold, at the door of the temple of the Lord, between the porch and the altar, were about five and twenty men, with their backs towards the temple of the Lord, and their faces towards the east; and *they worshipped the sun* towards the east. Ez. 8:15-16, emphasis supplied.

"The names of the days of the week from the Roman period have been both named after the seven planets of classical astronomy and numbered, beginning with Sunday,"[15] (sun-day), a happy day with blessing pouring down from the sun. The second day became the day of the moon, Monday. Of relevance to our study was the seventh day, which became associated with the planet Saturn, considered an evil and harsh planet. God's Sabbath was Christened Saturday and declared the most evil and unlucky of all days. No person could celebrate a feast on this evil day.

The Egyptians called the first day of the week the 'Lord's Day" since the sun was lord of lords. The Romans also adopted the name the 'Lord's Day' for the first day of the week, but the 'Lord' referred to was different. Unlike the Egyptians, the Romans venerated their Emperor as the foremost god. Because the taxes due to the Emperor were collected and presented to him on the first day of the week, the day was honoured as the 'Lord's Day'. It was this Sunday 'Lord's Day', that was carried over from pagan Rome into papal Rome by the Catholic Church, in order to accommodate the horde of pagans who had become nominal Christians. Emperor Constantine was the first to enforce Sunday reverence at the direction of the clergy. Whitham, on page 176 of his book the History of the Christian Church, records that

> the principal acts of Constantine in the interests of Christianity had been the building of churches in Rome, and several significant legal enactments. Among these were . . . in 321, the command for the general observance of Sunday as a holiday throughout his dominions.

Protestants, who inherited Sunday reverence from the Catholic Church, try to justify the practice with many arguments, two of which Whitham presents as follows:

> On the 'so called day of the Sun (so chosen because it was the first day of creation, the day of light, and because on it the Saviour rose from the dead), Christians assemble (Ibid., 81)

Nevertheless, the truth of the matter is, "The observance of Sunday by Protestants is an homage they pay, in spite of themselves, to the authority of the (Catholic) Church." (Segur n.d., 213)

We have seen that God called the seventh day 'My day', the Lord's Day. Now that you know the origin of the 'Lord's Day' tag upon Sunday, what do you reckon are the chances that the Apostle John was referring to Sunday, when he wrote: "I was in the Spirit on the Lord's Day"? Of the two Lord's days, which one would *you* choose as your own, to honour and consider holy?

CHAPTER 13

The Devil's Most Enduring Deception

Rooted in pagan philosophy

The ancient philosophy of the immortality of the human soul forms the foundation of many non-Christian religions. In essence, it claims that when a person dies, his flesh decays and returns to the earth, but his spirit lives on in a more superior state, unseen by the eyes of the living. Not a few professing Christian churches too, have their doctrine of the state of the dead rooted deeply in this same human philosophy. They teach that the dead are in a state of intelligent existence, as spirit beings. They believe it possible and desirable to communicate with the dead, and to seek their intervention in the affairs of the living. Many tribal cultures, as well as some Christian churches, teach that it is impossible to reach God in prayer, except through departed ancestors or saints. What is the teaching of the Bible on the matter?

God forbids mediums and their consultation

In spite of what any church or religion may teach, God expressly forbids any attempt to communicate with, or consult the dead. God forbids any person from becoming a spirit medium:

> There shall not be found among you anyone who . . . practices witchcraft, or a soothsayer, or one who interprets omens, or a sorcerer, or one who conjurer spells, or a medium, or a spiritist, or one who calls up the dead. Deut. 18:10, 11.

King Saul was destroyed by God for consulting the medium of En Dor. "So Soul died for his unfaithfulness which he committed against the Lord, because he did not keep the word of the Lord, and also because he consulted a medium for guidance," 1 Chr. 10:13.

Many people in Christian churches today consult mediums when they feel that their troubles have become insurmountable. Like Saul, they are convinced God has let them down, and feel justified in disobedience. The presupposition behind this attitude is: *"Our departed loved ones are alive in spirit and are reachable."* This erroneous presupposition prepares the way for more error. *"God has refused to answer our prayers for deliverance; why then should we not seek the assistance of our departed fathers and mothers, who are yearning to help?"*

From reading the scriptures quoted above it sounds as if the spirits of the dead are indeed living, though God forbids their consultation. However, a study of the Bible as a whole will reveal a different story. It would be instructive to ask ourselves the following question before we proceed: Why would a loving Creator hold back from us something beneficial, despite the promises: "No good thing will He withhold from those who walk uprightly"? "For I know the thoughts that I think toward you, says the Lord, thoughts of peace and not of evil, to give you a future and a hope."

Ps. 84:11; Jer. 29:11, among many others. God so loved us that He gave up His son to a cruel death on the cross, in our stead. Why would the same God deny us something so small as to keep in touch with our departed parents and saints, especially if it is good for us? The biblical answer is very simple—God forbids communication with the dead for the sole reason that they are truly dead!

The truth—the dead know nothing!

What is the teaching of the Bible? We shall see first what probably the wisest man that ever lived was inspired to write on the subject.

> But for him who is joined to all the living there is still hope, for a living dog is better than a dead lion. For the living know that they shall die, but the dead know nothing, and they have no more reward, for the memory of them is forgotten. Eccl. 9:4-5.

These two sentences alone should form a sufficient doctrinal foundation on the subject for one who accepts the Bible as the true Word of God. The dead are in a state of oblivion, knowing nothing!

Because he was aware of the fear that paralyses the living as they imagine the anger and retribution of those, now dead, whom they wronged while they lived, King Solomon specifically added, "also their love, their hatred, and their envy have now perished; nevermore will they have a share in anything done under the sun." Eccl. 9:6. The emotions of a living person—be they of love or hatred—perish the moment he dies. Whatever threats he has issued in life, no matter how heatedly and repeatedly, become invalid on dying. Likewise, his deepest love and hottest passions vanish forever.

The dead have literally nothing more to do "under the sun." because when they rise at the final trumpet and the coming of Christ, the heavens will be rolled away like a scroll, and there will be no more sky as we know it. (Read 2 Peter 3:10.) In truth therefore, the dead will never again see the sun. Please believe, for your sake, that nothing about, or from, a dead person can come back to harm you, frighten you, talk to you, nor help you!

The dead cannot lift even their little finger to help themselves, let alone anybody else. The wise king encourages the living thus: "Whatever your hand finds to do, do it with all your might; for there is no work, or device, or knowledge or wisdom in the grave where you are going." Eccl. 9:10. In short, according to the Creator's manual for rightful living, when a person dies, there is no conscious intelligent entity of any form living on.

I hope, dear friend, that you are beginning to grasp the idea that dead people cannot plan anything. They can do nothing at all, neither for themselves, nor for or against you. This will most likely be a difficult doctrine to accept, at first. This is especially true if, like me, you grew up taking for granted the continued existence of the dead as spirit beings. But, the ultimate truth is here for us in plain and simple language: "The dead know nothing."

We must not abandon our study of the Bible at this stage because it has begun to reveal truths that go against our established presuppositions or traditions. We must pray instead that the Lord grant us the humility, as well as the mental resolve to change our presuppositions, accept Bible truth and continue to grow in spirit. We must keep the memory of the obstinate smoker of chapter 1 always in the fore.

There are many more verses in the Bible upholding the doctrine of the dead knowing nothing. Job has this to say on the subject:

> But man dies and is laid away; indeed he breathes his last and
> where is he? As water disappears from the sea, and a river becomes
> parched and dries up, so man lies down and does not rise. Till

the heavens are no more; they will not awake nor be roused from their sleep. Job 14:10-12.

Note once more the reference to the dead not living again *till the heavens disappear*. The dead may only rise at the final trumpet when the heavens are rolled away to reveal the coming King of kings, Jesus Christ. This event is to occur soon.

Immediate ascension to heaven?

Many Christians strongly believe that on dying, the righteous ascend immediately to heaven, to live with the angels and sing praises to the Lord. Whereas this is consoling news to the bereaved, yet the truth is quite different. King Hezekiah had been sick to the point of death. In prayer, he asked for an extension of life, and God granted his request. In his expression of gratitude to the Lord, these are Hezekiah's words:

> For Sheol cannot thank You, Death cannot praise You; Those who go down into the pit cannot hope for your truth. The living man, he shall praise You. Is. 38:18, 19.

In other words, had Hezekiah died, he would not be praising God.

Another verse, short and to the point, confirms the theme that there are no spirits of men in Heaven, singing and praising God. "The dead do not praise the Lord, nor any who go down into silence." Ps. 115:17. If indeed, the dead went up to heaven upon dying, would they not burst into spontaneous praise of the Lord? What with the mansions, the streets of gold, the wiped tears, and life eternal! It is evident from the foregoing texts, that the dead are not praising God, because they are not in heaven. They cannot be—not yet, anyway!

King David still in his grave

Even during the time of the apostles the flawed doctrine of the immortality of the soul, and of saints ascending straight away to heaven, was prevalent. The apostles saw a need to teach against this error. Simon Peter preached, "Men and brethren, let me speak freely to you of the patriarch David, that he is both dead and buried, and his tomb is with us to this day." Acts 2:29. The apostle specifically adds in verse 34 of the same chapter: "For David is not ascended into the heavens . . ." So, even King David is still waiting in his grave with all the other saints for the last-day resurrection.

An obvious corollary of this truth is that the spirit of a sinner does not immediately eject from his deathbed into hell either. Both saint and wicked will continue in a state of oblivion until the time appointed for their resurrection.

Mary and the saints not exempt

We have demonstrated that the dead know nothing. If this is true for one, it must be true about all, "for there is no respect of persons with God." Rom. 2:11. This has to include all the patriarchs, prophets and the Twelve Apostles—in short, the saints.

Mary, the mother of Jesus, while virtuous in her earthly life, is no more alive and active today than Judas Iscariot, who disgracefully sold his master for a paltry thirty pieces of silver. If, therefore, Mary and all the saints are resting in silence, any communication with God attempted through them, must necessarily rebound on the impenetrable wall of the grave. All prayers offered through the dead, no matter how earnestly, are themselves dead in their tracks. In fact, any attempt to worship God through the dead constitutes an attempt to communicate with the dead and is an affront to the very God to whom the worship is directed.

There is only One, qualifying as intercessor between man and God. "For there is one God and one mediator between God and men, the man Christ Jesus." 1 Tim. 2:5. Jesus Christ is clearly the only acceptable intercessor. Having died sinless and risen from the dead "not with the blood of goats and calves, but with his own blood He entered the Most Holy Place . . . And for this reason He is the mediator of the new covenant, by means of death . . ." Heb. 9:12, 15.

The death and resurrection of Jesus alone are on record as having the power to place Him before God the Father in our behalf. No other being in the entire universe was found equal to the task. Only Jesus, through His pure blood, qualifies to intercede between men and God. To bring in any other entity, (whether 'saint' or villain, dead or alive) into the chain of intercession is to introduce gross error and sin. The prayer that attempts to pass through the medium of dead people is not acceptable before God. The authority receiving the prayer, if not God, has to be His enemy, the devil!

Basis is purely human tradition

The basis for the custom of worshipping God through the saints is the human tradition of approaching respected elders through third parties. The following questions and answers, extracted from the *Catholic Baltimore Catechism No. 3, page 270* will confirm this. (The numbers appearing before each question are the numbering for the questions as they appear in the Catechism.)

Q: 1196 Do we not slight God Himself by addressing our prayers to saints?

A: We do not slight God Himself by addressing our prayers to saints, but, on the contrary, show a greater respect for His majesty and sanctity, acknowledging, by our prayers to the saints, that we are unworthy to address Him for ourselves, and that we therefore, ask His holy friends to obtain for us what we ourselves are not worthy to ask."

Q: 1189 Does the first Commandment forbid the honouring of the saints?

A: The first Commandment does not forbid the honouring of the saints, but rather approves of it; because by honouring the saints, who are the chosen friends of God, we honour God Himself.

Q: 1190 What does 'invocation' mean?

A: Invocation means calling upon another for help or protection, particularly when we are in need or danger. It is used specially with regard to calling upon God or the saints and hence it means prayer. (*Catholic Baltimore Catechism No. 3*, page 270.)

There is neither scriptural basis nor precedent, for this practice. If there was, you can be sure verses would be quoted in support of the above answers. The reverence to God's throne, sighted as the reason for approaching Him through third parties, borders on fear. But, there is no reason to fear God in prayer. We must certainly humble ourselves in His presence, but to fear Him in time of need is sin:

> For we do not have a High Priest who cannot sympathize with
> our weaknesses, but was in all points tempted as we are, yet
> without sin. Let us therefore *come boldly* to the throne of grace,
> that we may obtain mercy and find grace to help in time of need.
> Heb. 4:15-16, emphasis supplied.

The High Priest referred to here is the resurrected Jesus Christ, as we have already demonstrated in chapter 9.

Read the following question together with its answer, and note again the complete absence of any scriptural reference.

Q: 1192 Give another reason why we honour God by honouring the saints?

A: Another reason why we honour God by honoring the Saints is this: As we honor our country by honoring its heroes, so do we honour our religion by honoring its Saints. By honoring our religion, we honour our God, who taught it. Therefore by honoring the Saints we honour God, for love of whom they became religious heroes in their faith. (Ibid, 269).

This question and its answer reveal that the basis for the practice of praying through the medium of dead people is not biblical. The answer frankly admits that the practice has its origin in the human feelings of nationalism and patriotism. While there is nothing wrong with honoring the memory of departed heroes in political and civic affairs, no man is at liberty to transfer worldly practice, no matter how noble or satisfying, into the worship of the Creator, for "there is a way that seems right to a man, but its end is the way of death." Prov. 14:12.

That was the sin of Cain. He sought to worship God in his own special way, setting aside the clearly laid down guidelines for worship. Instead of a lamb, he brought cabbages, cucumbers, and carrots to the altar. He justified himself by saying he was a man of the soil, and would thus give the best from the soil. While his logic was sound to the human mind, God still demanded obedience more than sacrifice.

Saul, the first king of Israel, lost the favour of God for this very sin. He sought to worship and honour God in opposition to His prescribed statutes; but God demands and expects obedience at all times.

> Has the Lord as great delight in burnt offerings and sacrifices,
> as in obeying the voice of the Lord? Behold, to obey is better
> than sacrifice, and to hearken than the fat of rams. For rebellion
> is as the sin of witchcraft, and stubbornness is as iniquity and
> idolatry. 1 Kings 15:22-23.

Any attempt to channel prayers through intercessors other than Christ is idolatry, a sin greatly abhorred by God.

Scriptural support?

The parable of Lazarus and the rich man, found in Luke 16:19-31, is often cited as the basis for the doctrine of the immortality of the soul and immediate ascension to heaven and descent into hell. Before you proceed, you may want to read the parable from your Bible. It certainly appears to support the Catholic view, and to contradict what we have found from the rest of the Bible so far. However, it is important to realize that the story of Lazarus and the rich man is a *parable—an earthly story with a heavenly meaning!* Jesus told this parable in order to emphasize the teaching that God will reward people according to their works. (Read Revelation 22:12). The parable also reveals that there is no grace available after death.

What would you think of the person who reads about the ten virgins of Matthew 25:1-13 and concludes that only five out of all the world's virgins since Eden will enter heaven; and that all non-virgins, and certainly all males, are destined for hell? You may think him a little worse than unreasonable. Well, it is equally unreasonable to accept the *parable* of Lazarus as a literal description of what happens to saints and sinners upon dying, against all the overwhelming biblical evidence to the contrary.

Purgatory

You may have heard or read of purgatory in relation to dead people. The Bible never mentions this word. There is no place in the scriptures fitting the description of purgatory as painted by Catholic doctrine. According to their teaching, purgatory is the place where the spirit of a deceased person goes immediately upon dying. It is like a buffer zone between heaven and hell. They claim that surviving relatives can purify the soul of a sinner held in purgatory through prayers and payment of indulgences to the church. In short, the doctrine of purgatory claims repentance and forgiveness after death.

This teaching runs contrary to the whole Bible, and shakes the very foundation of Christianity. It nullifies the whole law and encourages sin, rather than obedience in this life. Many people have chosen to live a wicked life, indulging all their vile appetites, confident that their relatives will buy them a place in heaven when they die. Purgatory is a figment of human imagination proclaimed into dogma by the Council of Florence in 1439. The introduction of purgatory has created great wealth for the church, as believers have paid for the release of deceased loved sinners from this holding place into heaven. There is no scriptural basis for this creation and we will not dwell much on it.

Good news—death is not the end

Many professing Christians have willingly embraced the doctrine of the immortality of the human soul because they have found it difficult to accept that their loved ones are *surely* dead and gone. Do not despair, for there is hope for those who mourn. The dead will live again, after resurrecting from their deep sleep. The Bible predicts two resurrections—one for the saints and another for the sinners. Let us study the scriptures.

The book of Daniel has this to say regarding the two events: "And many of those who sleep in the dust of the earth shall awake, some to everlasting life, some to shame and everlasting contempt." Dan. 12:2. There will be two groups in the resurrection—those who will receive joyful tidings, and those who will meet with a bitter reception. In verse 13 of the same chapter, the prophet is assured by the angel Gabriel in farewell, "But you go your way till the end; for you shall rest, and will arise to your inheritance at the end of the days." Therefore, there is hope; but only for some and not for others. Only those who have accepted the atoning blood of Jesus, and lived according to His will, shall enter into the joy of eternity. Profession of Christianity alone will not qualify us for heaven. Jesus promises,

> I am the resurrection and the life. He who believes in Me, though he may die, he shall live. And whoever lives and believes in Me shall never die. Do you believe this? John 11:25-26.

Many people today profess knowledge of Christ. The apostle John defines what knowledge of Christ really is:

> Now by this we know that we know Him, if we keep His commandments. He who says 'I know Him,' and does not keep His commandments, is a liar, and the truth is not in him. 1 John 2:3-4.

The promise of resurrection to eternity is real, but so is the demand for righteous living. Righteousness is a natural outcome of accepting Christ and yielding to His commands.

A more detailed study of the nature and timing of the two resurrections follows in a later chapter. For now, let us look at what form the resurrected saints will take.

Real bodies

What form will resurrected beings take? Will they be airy spirits, or will they possess recognizable bodies? The Bible presents resurrected beings as having recognizable forms. Let us study some texts. The book of Matthew confirms the visibility of the resurrected beings when Jesus died as follows:

> And the graves opened; and many bodies of the saints who had fallen asleep were raised; and coming out of the graves after His resurrection, they went into the holy city and appeared to many. Matt. 27:52-53.

This suggests that we will have a recognizable body upon resurrection. The resurrected body will be visible. Jesus knew his disciples shared with all generations past and future, misconceptions about the state of the dead, and the nature of the resurrected body. He therefore made it a point to clarify the issue before His ascension. In Luke 24 Jesus demonstrates the reality of the resurrected body thus:

> Now as they said these things, Jesus Himself stood in the midst of them, and said to them, 'Peace to you.' But they were terrified and frightened, and supposed they had seen a spirit. And he said to them, 'Why are you troubled? And why do doubts arise in your hearts? Behold my hands and feet, that it is I Myself. Luke 24:36-39.

Knowing they were still not satisfied, as surely as you and I would not be satisfied, He added, "Handle me and see, for spirit does not have flesh and bones as you see I have". (v. 39, last part). Here Jesus clarifies that the only living form of human beings after death comes after resurrection and that this form is not an airy spirit, but a true body having flesh and bones.

Wishing to drive the point home for the benefit of his disciples and for ours down the centuries, Jesus went further to demonstrate another property of the resurrected body. The resurrected body takes food! Jesus demonstrated this in Luke 24:40-43.

> He showed them His hands and feet. But while they still did not believe for joy, and marveled, He said to them, 'Have you any food here?' So they gave Him a piece of a broiled fish and some honeycomb. And He took it and ate it in their presence.

This demonstration was a very necessary part of the gospel, for those of us with a sharp palate would find nothing to look forward to in a heaven where spirits take no food. We would long for the spices and sugars of Earth, just as the children of Israel in the wilderness yearned to return to the garlic and the leaks of Egypt.

Some would argue that the example used above is the special case of Christ, not mere man! To answer this challenge, we should go to the first book of Corinthians where we see that Jesus Christ is both the means to our resurrection, as well as the typical example of resurrected man.

> For since by man came death, by Man also came the resurrection of the dead. For as in Adam all die, even so in Christ all shall be made alive. But each one in his own order. Christ the first-fruits, afterward those who are Christ's at His coming. 1 Cor. 15:21-23.

The apostle describes Christ as "first-fruits" to emphasize the similarity of His experience to that of saints to rise in the future. The first mango to ripen in a tree looks and tastes no differently by mere reason of its timing, than all others after it.

I hope dear reader, we have established the fact that after death, the only state of intelligent life is a real resurrected body and not an invisible spirit. There are only dry bones, dead flesh, and breath, divided and lifeless, in death.

What is the view of Jesus?

Before we conclude, let us visit a conversation between Jesus Christ, and one of His attendants, Martha, sister to Lazarus, Jesus' close friend who was four days dead and rotting in the grave at this stage. Martha felt that had Jesus been around when Lazarus fell ill He could have healed him. Now, she held solid but distant hope for his resurrection. In John 11:23, the Lord says, "Your brother will rise again." Now, study Martha's reply: "I know that he will rise again in the resurrection at the last day." John 11:24. Those are the words of a close associate of Jesus Christ, who would know the correct doctrines of the state of the dead, and of the resurrection. The Master did not dispute or correct her statement, because it was a universal truth. We would do well to accept her word as a statement of the correct Christian doctrine of the resurrection. The dead will only rise on the last day, when the final trumpet sounds, and Christ comes as King, which event will happen soon, as we shall see in chapter 15.

Conclusion

I hope dear friend that we have managed to establish beyond doubt the following important points so far:

- The dead know nothing, and we cannot communicate with them, neither can they with us; and there is no intelligent soul or spirit that lives on when man dies

- The dead go neither to heaven nor to hell upon dying, and are in a state of oblivion awaiting a resurrection day still in the future.

I pray that you should erase all doubts from your mind regarding the subject. You must not judge yourself too harshly, should you find yourself reverting, in little ways, to the old way of assuming the dead to be alive, especially at funerals. The desire to remain alive forever is an in-born yearning of mankind. It causes him to either reject completely, or accept grudgingly, the idea of oblivion in death. However, by continually reminding ourselves of truth in the face of the natural instinct to embrace falsehood, we will cultivate in our minds the solid presupposition that *the dead know nothing.*

CHAPTER 14

Riding High on the Dead

If the dead know nothing, who are these?

The reason why many find it difficult to believe what the Bible teaches regarding the dead is that their own experiences in life have *proved* beyond doubt the existence of spirits! There are 'ancestral' spirits, avenging spirits, healing spirits, prophesying spirits, . . . The list is endless. I will not attempt to deny the existence of these spirits. I have had personal experience with almost all types. Therefore, rather than deny their existence, I affirm the reality of spirits in the affairs of the living. Whereas it is important for all Christians to accept the reality of spirits, it is even more important to uphold always, the truth they have learnt, in spite of the reality witnessed by the senses. We must maintain that the dead know nothing!

It is not difficult to reconcile the reality of 'ancestral' spirits, and avenging spirit with the doctrine of oblivion in death. Let us do so now. We should be able to answer the questions: *'If the dead know nothing, who, or what then are these, possessing an intimate knowledge of my family history and genealogy? Who are these, telling me the things I did long ago? Who is this, claiming my great-great-grandfather murdered him, and is now demanding compensation?*

Who are these . . . ?' You may be asking yourself these questions if, like me, you have had personal experience with spirits and spirit mediums. I will soon dedicate a whole book to the study of these phenomena, based on personal experiences. For now, let us explain away these apparitions.

Roots in Eden—'you will not surely die'

In order to explain the phenomenon of so-called spirits of the dead communicating with the living, we have to revisit the place where it all began—the Garden of Eden. In verse 4 of Genesis 3 the serpent said to Eve, "You will not surely die." By implication: *"Though you may appear dead and gone, yet you are not totally dead; indeed you are alive in some other form."* What form of existence could this be? The devil supplied the answer in the form of a further lie: "For God does know that in the day you eat thereof, then your eyes will be opened and you will be as gods, knowing good and evil." Gen. 3:5. In other words: *"You will now exist in a more intelligent and superior state; as a spirit, for gods are spirits. What's more? You may, in that state, receive worship from the living, as a god."* Eve chose to believe the devil and Adam soon followed suit. After them, generations have continued believing the lie. What makes it so difficult for the world to accept the plain truth as stated by God the Creator?

Lies well supported

The devil had to make his original lies appear true. He set about it in a manner that has convinced the majority through the ages that indeed, the dead continue to exist as intelligent spirits with which the living can communicate. In chapter 2, we learnt that Satan was not alone in the rebellion that led to expulsion from heaven. He brought down a third of

God's angels with him. Satan brought this host of fallen angels into his plan. If these spirit beings could pretend to be the spirits of the dear departed relatives of the living, imagine what homage they would receive from the sons of men. The devil would by this device fulfill his original ambition to be the focus of human worship.

But how do these demons convince vast numbers of men and women to worship them? With all the many warnings in Scripture concerning the devil and demons, why are so many, even in 'Christian' churches, entangled in the spiritual death traps set by Satan and his demons? To answer this question we must first realize that though fallen, these beings are still angels. They still possess some of the attributes of the un-fallen angels that we meet in the Bible. To unravel the mystery, we must therefore study the nature of angels.

Nature of angels

In our struggle against delusion, we would do well to heed the warning of Apostle Paul.

> For we wrestle not against flesh and blood, but against principalities, against powers, against the rulers of the darkness of this world, against spiritual wickedness in heavenly places. Eph. 6:12.

While angels are spirits that are normally invisible to men, they are able to manifest in visible forms, even as humans. The two 'men' who visited Lot in the account of the destruction of Sodom and Gomorrah, were in fact angels. "Now there came two angels to Sodom at the evening." Gen. 19:1. We learn lower down that passage that the angels looked just like ordinary men to the men of Sodom: "But before they lay down, the men of the city, even the men of Sodom, surrounded the house . . . . And they called unto Lot, and said unto him, *Where are the men* who came in to you this night?" Gen. 19:4, 5, emphasis supplied.

Angels can speak through the medium of animals. We first witness this phenomenon when Satan speaks through the serpent in the Garden of Eden, in Genesis 3. We meet another angel who speaks through a donkey in the narrative of Balaam, in Numbers 22. The angel in the Balaam account chose when to become visible or invisible to the donkey and to Balaam.

Fallen angels, or demons, can take possession of a person's faculties, causing delirium or 'madness', while speaking and acting through them. Read about the demon-possessed man of the Gadarenes who answered Jesus, "my name is Legion, for we are many," in Mark 5:1-14. In this same account, we obtain further confirmation that demons can possess animals, as seen when they entered the swine. Demons can possess a person and cause convulsions and sickness. Read about it in Luke 9:39. Satan's evil angels can possess a person and cause him to be blind and dumb. Matthew 12:22 records this phenomenon. Some demons possess people and cause physical infirmities and crippling: "And, behold, there was a woman who had a spirit of infirmity eighteen years, and was bowed together and could in no way lift herself up." Luke 13:11. In this story, Jesus cast out the demon and restored the woman's normal posture.

Such are only a few attributes of angels. These beings are more intelligent than humans, "for (God) hast made (man) a little lower than the angels . . ." Ps. 8:5. They have been in existence much longer than humanity, and have the advantage of possessing knowledge of heavenly court protocol, of which they used to be a part. Most frightening is the fact that fallen angels, like the devil himself, can appear as angels of light:

And no marvel; for Satan is transformed into an angel of light. Therefore it is no great thing if his ministers also be transformed as ministers of righteousness; . . . 2 Cor. 11:14, 15.

Is it any wonder that, possessing these super-human attributes, demons can easily convince and control those among us lacking a solid foundation of truth?

Superiority of numbers

The reason the devil appears to possess the same attributes of omnipresence and omniscience as God is his use of the large number of demons under his command. He has an enormous army of fallen angels in his camp. Let us do a modest estimation of the number of demons in Satan's camp. In Revelation 5:11 John the revelator estimates the number of angels he saw around the throne of God in Heaven to be "ten thousand times ten thousand and thousands of thousands". Taking 'thousands' to mean a modest 2,000 (it could mean anything above 2,000), the least number of fallen angels available to the devil can be calculated as follows[16]:

Number of angels left in God's camp:

$$=10,000 \times 10,000 \times 2,000 \times 2,000 = 400,000,000,000,000$$

_At_ _least_ four hundred trillion angels are left in God's camp. If these represent two thirds of the original number, then the original is calculated as follows:

Original number of angels in God's camp:

$$= 400,000,000,000,000 \times 3/2 = 600,000,000,000,000$$

There must have been *at least* 600 trillion angels originally; and if one third of that number represented those angels recruited by Lucifer, then their number can be calculated thus:

Number of fallen angels = 600,000,000,000,000, x 1/3:

= 200,000,000,000,000

The devil has a staggering 200 trillion demons under his command! Now, we reckon world human population today in billions; and never at any one point in the history of the earth, has the population been any higher than it is today. This suggests that on the average, the devil has always had the *capacity* to allocate at least a thousand demons to every living human being at any one moment. With this massive number of more-than-willing agents, is it any wonder that the devil appears to possess God's attribute of omnipresence? Demons have carefully recorded the memories, names, and conversations of our departed relatives in exact tones of voice for 'replay' should we ever consult a medium about the dead. Nevertheless, we must never let this large number of demons frighten us; on God's side and ours, is twice that number of *un-fallen* angels!

'Reality' of avenging spirits

Before I can recount some of my personal experiences with spirits and spirit mediums, it is important that we are able to explain a phenomenon that has made it very difficult for people in many cultures of the world to accept the truth about the dead knowing nothing. This is the phenomenon of the 'avenging spirit' known in my own Shona language as '*ngozi*'[17].

Ngozi refers to the evil manifestations that occur in the family of a person who has committed murder. Some families hold ceremonies to raise the spirit of their murdered loved one and send it on a vengeful errand to the family of the murderer. In many societies, a man who has shed blood becomes delirious and even insane. He loses any dignity and self-respect he might have had and leaves the community of his family to live on the streets or in the forest as a vagabond.

It is possible for an offender to visit the witchdoctor to protect himself from, or rid himself of the *ngozi,* by re-directing the spirit to his own children and other family members within the vast blood-linked extended family system. The *ngozi* will then manifest in the target family members by causing madness, sickness, and general bad luck. A sustained series of coincidental disasters such as fatal accidents, job losses, and un-diagnosable illness begin to occur within the family.

A visit to the witchdoctor will reveal who the perpetrator of the murder was. They will be able to converse with the 'spirit of the victim'. Through ceremonies of cleansing involving the blood of animals, they may 'wash away' the spirit and send it along to another branch of the extended family, or back to the perpetrator. This transferring of the evil spirit back and forth may continue for generations. All the while, the families involved are held firmly in the clutches of witchdoctors, and away from Christ, the only source of true atonement. The extended family members who have suffered from the effects of the *ngozi* may decide to make peace with the marauding spirit through payment of large sums of money or cattle to the family of the deceased. In some cases, the spirit demands that the harassed family appease it by giving away a girl child as wife to a male relative of the murdered man. The witchdoctor supervises all these transactions.

These things happen so really, and so painfully, that a person who has been through a *ngozi* experience and cleansing process, may find it almost impossible to accept that "the dead know nothing." My extended family has experienced the evil torture of a *ngozi* apparently originating from our great-great-grandfather's time. I will narrate our experiences later in this chapter.

Ngozi manifests in many variations throughout the world as the devil tailors it to suit local culture and beliefs. The particular type described in this paragraph is prevalent in Zimbabwe. However, despite the 'reality' and widespread nature of the *ngozi* phenomenon, we must still revert to the Bible truth that "the dead know nothing." The logical question remains—what, or who then are these avenging spirits and what is the truth behind the whole drama of spiritual manifestation, revenge, and cleansing?

Divine protection withdrawn

Let us visit the book of Job to answer this question. Job 1 records a conversation in heaven, between God and Satan. God proudly calls the attention of Satan to His devoted servant Job. In Job 1:9-11 the devil, in responding, accuses God:

> Does Job fear God for nothing? Have You not made a hedge around him, around his household, and around all that he has on every side? You have blessed the work of his hands, and his possessions have increased in the land. But now, stretch out Your hand and touch all that he has, and he will surely curse You to Your face!

From these words, we learn that God places a hedge around people, to render them inaccessible to demonic interference. God has placed a wall around us, making it impossible for the devil and his army of demons to reach us and possess us or affect our 'luck'. This wall is in the form of an angel, as Psalm 34:7 informs us. "The angel of the LORD encamps all around those who fear Him, and delivers them." In general Satan, through his demons, tempts all humans, and tries to influence their thoughts. However, for demons to possess us and seriously affect our livelihood, the protective wall we have identified above will need to be lifted away first, and this can only be done by God.

There are at least three scenarios where God removes the wall of protection. The first example is in the same chapter of Job, in verse 12. Here, Satan has challenged God that if He would lift the wall of protection surrounding Job's property and allow the devil and his demons free access, then Job would dishonor God. Job 1:12 reads: "And the LORD said to Satan, 'Behold, all that he has is in your power; only do not lay a hand on his person.' So Satan went out from the presence of the LORD." We learn therefore that one reason God can lift the wall of protection from around us is to allow for the testing of the devil's claim that mankind cannot love God without inducement. Note from these texts that God places limits on how far the demons can go in attacking the man in question.

Do you realize dear friend, that some of the suffering you have experienced, or are going through now, could be the result of God being proud of you; so proud that he is banking on you to help disprove Satan's accusation that people love God only when they enjoy peace, comfort and good health? You could even now be the centre of a cosmic battle, which the universe is watching anxiously in the hope that you will, like Job, prove the devil a liar, and score points for your Creator. You can do this by withstanding God's enemy throughout the period set for your trial. Read the rest of the book of Job whenever you feel that life is treating you unfairly. When hard questions reel through your mind in bitterness, read the book of Job. The story of his victory and final reward may help lift your spirits up in times of trial.

There is a second scenario whereby God removes—or reduces—our protection. This is at the instigation of Satan. He asks God to lift the protective wall so he can access a person to 'sift' or test him. We find this in Luke 22:31 where the Lord Jesus tells Peter:

> Simon, Simon! Indeed, Satan has asked for you, that he may sift
> you as wheat. But I have prayed for you, that your faith should
> not utterly fail; and when you have returned to Me, strengthen
> your brethren.'

The sifting in this case resulted in Peter losing his faith in his Master. He denied any knowledge of Him, not once but three times in a short space of time. What is encouraging though is to learn that we can mitigate the results of this 'sifting' or temptation through prayer. Jesus assured Peter that He had prayed that his faith should not fail (see Luke 22:32.)

We extract here the important lesson to pray for one another. In many instances, Christians look on as a brother or sister goes through temptation or strife; and all they do is gossip about it. We should learn from Christ's example and pray for others, especially leaders who happen to be the natural focus of demonic attention. Timely intercessory prayer can play an important role in strengthening those laboring under the vicious assaults of demons. Let us pray more for others than we do for ourselves. We can rest assured that God will move some hearts to pray for our own situations in return.

The third scenario whereby God creates a breach in His protective wall is more relevant to our study of the *ngozi* phenomenon. Isaiah 59:2, 3 reads:

> Behold, the LORD's hand is not shortened, that it cannot save;
> nor His ear heavy, that it cannot hear. But your iniquities have
> separated you from your God; and your sins have hidden His
> face from you, so that He will not hear. For your hands are
> defiled with blood, and your fingers with iniquity; your lips have
> spoken lies, your tongue has muttered perversity.

Our sins can cause God to lift the veil of protection from us. Separated from God, we no longer enjoy the protection of His angel. The shedding of human blood is cited in the text as a sin for which the Lord will remove His protection.

Once God withdraws protection from around the unrepentant sinner, He becomes spiritually naked and vulnerable to the full influence and manipulation of demons. Disaster follows upon disaster. You will get a glimpse of the degree of devastation the devil and his demons are able to achieve in a short space of time by reading chapters 1 and 2 of Job.

The true nature of ngozi

There are many cases in my society where the relatives of a murder victim perform rituals to 'raise the dead' in vengeance. They pronounce a curse on the family of the perpetrator, which then materializes in the course of time. This phenomenon tends to give credence to the doctrine of the immortality of the soul. However, a study of the scriptures shows the upheavals in the life of the murderer are the result of God's withdrawal of His protection.

With the connivance of the men of Shechem, Abimelech the son of Gideon (or Jerubbaal) slaughtered seventy of his brothers in order to assume rulership over that town. (Judges 9). Only one of his siblings, Jotham survived. The surviving young man pronounced the following curse loudly from a hilltop:

> If then you have acted in truth and sincerity with Jerubbaal and
> with his house this day, then rejoice in Abimelech, and let him
> also rejoice in you. But if not, let fire come from Abimelech and
> devour the men of Shechem and Beth Millo; and let fire come

from the men of Shechem and from Beth Millo and devour Abimelech!. (vv 19, 20).

After Abimelech had reigned three years over Shechem,

> God sent a spirit of ill will between Abimelech and the men of Shechem; and the men of Shechem dealt treacherously with Abimelech, that the crime done to the seventy sons of Jerubbaal might be settled and their blood be laid on Abimelech their brother, who killed them, and on the men of Shechem, who aided him in the killing of his brothers. Judges 9:23, 24.

Note that the text does not say God raised the seventy spirits of the slain men, but that He sent an evil spirit. God does not commune with evil spirits, and *sent* means that God withdrew His protecting angel, thus paving way for an evil spirit to deal with Abimelech and the men of Shechem. As a result,

> a certain woman dropped an upper millstone on Abimelech's head and crushed his skull . . . So his young man thrust him through, and he died . . . . Thus, God repaid the wickedness of Abimelech, which he had done to his father by killing his seventy brothers. And all the evil of the men of Shechem God returned on their own heads, *and on them came the curse of Jotham the son of Jerubbaal.* (vv. 53, 54, 56, 57, emphasis supplied.)

Note further, that the demon or evil spirit will deal with the exposed man in the manner pronounced in the curse. They do this to reinforce the belief that the dead are alive as spirits, and have returned as instructed, to take vengeance.

The dead know nothing and can do nothing. The spirits that manifest as *ngozi* are, in reality, Satan's army of fallen angels, the demons. They have a field day with the man whose protection Divinity has withdrawn. They wreck havoc on his property and touch his health even to the point of death, should God so permit. However, because Satan wishes to perpetuate the lie he originally told in Eden, "You will not surely die . . . but you will be as gods," his demons masquerade as the spirits of murdered victims. The affected family wastes large sums of money and other resources, including valuable time, in efforts to appease the *ngozi*. They are at the mercy of the demons, literally worshipping them and obeying their every command. The suffering family focuses its attention on mediums, and thus misses the true atoning power of Christ's blood. In this manner, Satan fulfills his ambition to be the focus of human worship.

God lifts the wall of protection from a murderer because He declared from the beginning, "Whoever sheds man's blood, by man shall his blood be shed". Gen. 9:6. He also said elsewhere, "Vengeance is Mine, and recompense; their foot will slip in due time; for the day of their calamity is at hand, and the things to come hasten upon them." Deut. 32:35. It is God therefore, who removes his protecting angel to allow vengeance for the sin of murder.

It is possible for the *ngozi* to pass on from family to family and from generation to generation within the clan because God permits this. He says:

> I the Lord your God am a jealous God, visiting the iniquity of the
> fathers upon the children unto the third and fourth generation
> of them that hate me. Gen. 20:5.

Real life experience confirms this statement. Those particular family members within the extended family system who have chosen to follow

Christ and shun witchdoctors remain untouched by marauding spirits. However, the moment one goes against God's express command and consults a spirit medium regarding the dead, demanding to learn the cause of their misfortune, they lose God's protection and open the door to receive punishment for the iniquities of their forefathers and blood-connected relatives. This explains why *ngozi* can roam freely from family to family, among those who engage in ancestral worship, and who invite the 'spirits of departed ancestors' back into their lives, and consult spirit mediums.

Biblical evidence?

Some read Genesis 4:10, where God asks Cain,

> What have you done? The *voice of your brother's blood cries* out
> to Me from the ground. So now you are cursed from the earth,
> which has opened its mouth to receive your brother's blood from
> your hand (emphasis supplied),

and take this as scriptural evidence of the spirit of a murdered person living on, to seek and execute vengeance. We will reveal that this is not a contradiction of the rest of the scriptures, and that it is merely a figure of speech, meaning an injustice had been done that demanded judgment. We will use the following text, in which emphasis is added, to illustrate the point:

> Indeed *the wages of the laborers* who mowed your fields, which
> you kept back by fraud, *cry out;* and the cries of the reapers have
> reached the ears of the Lord. James 5:4.

You and I know money cannot talk, let alone cry out. The obvious meaning of this phrase is that the *injustice* involving non-payment of wages is standing out, demanding judgment before the Lord who sees all. A *situation* has arisen, which demands divine intervention and judgment, though the sufferer or victim may be silent and helpless.

Extending the same logic to the case of Cain, the injustice of the sin of murder stood starkly before God, who had witnessed the slaying despite Cain thinking he was alone, and could hide the crime. Abel was dead and neither his spirit nor his blood could talk, but Cain's crime was a fresh record in the judgment books of Heaven.

Personal experience with spirit mediums

Before my family knew the biblical truth, "the dead know nothing," we led a miserable life. Spirit mediums led us to believe that all the misfortune in our family originated from two sources, both of them spirits of dead people. The first was a *ngozi*, the aggrieved and vengeful spirit of a man murdered most callously by our great-great grandfather. One witchdoctor, who was also a spirit medium, whom we consulted summoned the spirit of the murdered victim to talk to us through him.

The dead man[18] described how our distant ancestor had stabbed him to death. He mentioned our ancestor by a name my father recognized from oral history. We apologized on our patriarch's behalf and pointed out that we ourselves had not been involved in the murder, and were innocent. He sympathized with us and advised that we could appease him by installing him on a male member of our family at a traditional beer ceremony or *bira*[19]. The chosen family member would then become a medium of the murdered man. Through him, the *ngozi* would marry, but any children resulting from this marriage would not bear our family name but the dead victim's. The offspring would belong to him. Bearing his surname, they would be under his control throughout their lives, his to possess and to manipulate in any way he chose.

He instructed us to slaughter a black chicken at the ceremony, and to cast a black goat in the deep forest after a procedure the spirit medium would supervise. Throughout our conversation with the spirit, we had to prayerfully clap hands with heads bowed, and generally treat the spirit with worshipful respect.

The second spirit was a potentially friendly, useful, and powerful great-grandfather who intended to possess my father and use him as his medium. He intended to carry on his former work as medicine man, and generally look after his family—us. The problems besetting our family, he added, arose from his impatience to *come out* and begin his work within the family. He was causing misery and misfortune within the family to prompt us to search out the cause, as we had now done, and do his will for our own good. Our ancestor presented a further problem before us. The *ngozi* that had spoken just before him would not allow either him, or any other family spirit, to come and bless the family before the *ngozi's* case was fully appeased. The protocol of the spirit world demanded reparation first. At the *bira*, we should invite our great-grandfather to talk through my father once we had appeased the *ngozi*.

The first *bira* was a failure despite all our best efforts and adherence to instructions. The witchdoctor told us, after two nights of singing, drum beating, drinking, and worshipping, that an unexpected problem had arisen. A deceased great grandmother, who had blessed the clan with many children, had never been married into the family as custom demanded. Her bride price remained unpaid and she was demanding her right to be married properly. To aggravate the case, her husband, one of our ancient patriarchs, had not distributed the old woman's belongings among her relatives as custom demanded. He had instead allowed his younger wife to use the utensils, in what was a cultural abomination. Her case demanded settlement before the male ancestor could settle in our family and enrich us.

To appease her, we had to buy clay and wooden kitchen utensils. We should then build a hut in the forest and deposit the utensils in it for her. We should deposit the bride price of fifty cents in a clay bowl inside the hut. She ordered us to leave a white chicken to roam freely around the hut. After thus appeasing the old woman's spirit, we were to repeat the *bira* over again; the way would now be clear for the ceremony's acceptance in the spiritual courts.

To cut a long story short, we held not two but five *biras* with our great-grandfather refusing to *come out* and talk to us through our father, citing one fault after another. The all-night ceremonies repeated over time, took their toll on my father's health, and sapped the family of energy, resources, and hope. After every *bira*, there was a dramatic misfortune in the family—a job loss, maybe a car accident. We desperately needed a way out of our predicament, and it came in the form of a 'prophet' of the white garmented African Apostolic faith that has become dominant in Africa.

Personal experience with 'prophet'

A sympathetic observer advised that we were wasting our time and resources consulting traditional healers. Men of God could solve our case at no cost. We unanimously agreed we had had enough of witchdoctors. Since we were essentially a Christian family, we reasoned, it was time we turned back to God. The prophet[20] turned out to be a short, stout man who kept a baldhead and long beard. He carried the long and hooked staff of the biblical shepherd. He kept a Friday Sabbath, ate no pork and took no wine. Three wives and many children attended him. The prophet spoke in strange tongues with a few English words thrown in, as well as many Biblical names—Michael, Gabriel, Peter, John, Isaac, Jacob! He never mentioned Jesus Christ, though *Mwari*, the name for God, was the central theme in all his strange discourse.

The man of God confirmed the presence of the *ngozi* as well as the two ancestral spirits in the family. He confirmed the disheartening news that the spirits had rejected our *biras*. He made it clear that we were now in a worse situation than at the very beginning, because the avenging spirit was now very angry with us for botching the procedures. Added to that, our two departed relations were unhappy with our continual failure to appease the ngozi.

A cold and desperate fear crept into the heart of the family. The picture of our future as painted by the prophet was bleak indeed. We were beginning to feel that maybe it was better to simply give up, and die. The prophet slowly began to brighten the picture. It may be possible to get rid of the *ngozi* permanently, and divert the ancestral spirits so that they would never bother us again. It was a dangerous procedure, and could leave the prophet maimed or even dead. He told us to go away, and bring a white chicken, six eggs, and a pint of fresh milk, to begin the treatment in three days' time. Meanwhile, the prophet would begin an extended fast.

When we returned as agreed, he declared himself ready to take on the spirits. He exchanged the white garment for a red one, fastened around the waist with a belt of woven red and white rope. We sat in a row in front of him. After mumbling and shouting "Gloria . . . . Gabriel . . . deliver power! Moses! Gloria power! . . . Michael, deliver power!" many times over, he suddenly leant over my father and appeared to kiss the top of his head. He breathed in deeply and suddenly straightened up. His facial features were strangely transformed, as was his voice and dialect. We were face to face with the *ngozi* once again. It spoke in the same tone and repeated the same story it had told us through the witchdoctor.

There was, however, one notable difference. The *ngozi* was strangely subdued. He congratulated us on our success in identifying the prophet of God. He declared himself powerless against the direct power of God's messenger. For just one twenty-cent coin bound to a red cloth and tied round the neck of a black chicken and released in the wild, he was willing to depart and never bother us again. He left after warning that if we ever relaxed and neglected to seek constant help from the prophet, he may return to cause us even more harm than before. For now, he was heading for other branches of the extended family, where he would wreak havoc.

The prophet then summoned the two family spirits, one at a time, to converse once more with us. They thanked us profusely for releasing them from the grip of the *ngozi* that, according to spirit protocol, had been cruel master to them until now. The grandmother's spirit accepted a cent coin as compensation and promised never to bother our branch of the family again. Our great-grandfather, in return for a white chicken was prepared to go and find a place to stay, and a medium to possess in another branch of the family.

The three episodes left the prophet exhausted but determined to complete the job. We hurriedly supplied a chicken, which he slaughtered. The entire family bathed in water mixed with the chicken's blood, chicken eggs, and fresh milk. He then gave each one of us a bottle of holy water. We were supposed to add a dose of this water into all our drinking, cooking, as well as bath water. We should top up the bottles continually from the tap, and never allow them to run dry. In addition, he issued each one of us with a small stone, which we should keep on our person at all times. These stones were for our protection against possible re-possession by the *ngozi*, and harassment by other evil spirits. The stones, acting also as talismans, would attract good luck to us.

The prophet promised us an immediate change of fortunes. He added though, that we were never completely safe from these and other spirits, unless we visited him, or other prophets, for regular check-up and cleansing. Our safest option would be to join his congregation and gain permanent protection from evil and ancestral spirits, as well as receive timely warning of approaching danger. The prophet invited my father to have the grandfather's spirit cleansed into a holy spirit, so he could become a healing prophet of God, like him. My father, tired and disillusioned, never took up the offer.

Fortunes did change

Our fortunes changed dramatically for the better after this, but the experience left us with many doubts and unexplained questions. My father found a job easily after a long period of unemployment. There were promotions at various work places for family members. Many strange and evil coincidences that had dogged the family vanished overnight. While we appreciated relief, we also began to feel a spiritual nakedness that neither witchdoctor nor prophet could cover. We began to feel that we were at the mercy of the prophet, and had to obey his will at all times.

I can say now, that it was at that time that we should have noticed the Lord Jesus starting to intervene and influence our thinking. We jointly decided never to consult spirit mediums and prophets again. We resolved to go back to the church we were born into—the United Methodist Church. By the time my father passed away in 1994, he was a fully restored member of the church, attending regular services with my mother. My own attendance was half hearted, and soon fizzled out. I was still drinking heavily at that time. I hope to relate the story of my life, and the process of my full conversion, in a later work. For now let us use my the experiences of my family to learn how non Christians and Christians alike are worshipping the devil, as he reaps the harvest of his original sermon in Eden: "You will not surely die . . . . but you will be as gods." Gen. 3:4, 5.

Whose agents are Witchdoctors?

The spirit medium introduced us to our dead ancestors and to the aggrieved spirit of the dead. However, you and I are now convinced *the dead know nothing*! It should be clear therefore that the whole basis of the witchdoctor's therapy was a falsehood. It is impossible for the dead to communicate any demands to the living—yet this is exactly what happened before our very eyes. The spirits even mentioned names of ancestors known from family oral history! Nevertheless, compelling as the sensory evidence may be, we must revert to the scriptural truth that the dead are in a state of oblivion. If then the practitioner contradicts the word of God, what are we to conclude but that he is not serving God? If he is not serving God, he has to be serving Satan, the enemy of God, for there is no other master to serve but the two.

It may not be too difficult to reach and accept this conclusion in the case of the witchdoctor or *sangoma*[21], when we visualize his unkempt hair, weird headdress, python-skin attire, and other morbid instruments-of-trade. It may be more difficult to accept the same verdict in the case of second of my family's spiritual consultants.

Who is the prophet's master?

The next phase of our spiritual journey led my family to a 'prophet', claiming to be a man of God. He charged no fee for his services except any thanks offering we felt like making. The prophet confirmed the diagnosis already reached by the devil's messenger! It is a 'man of God', this time who claims he can communicate with the dead. From the Written Word we *know* this to be impossible! We have no choice, therefore, but to label this practitioner Satan's tool of the same order as the *sangoma*.

No loss in the devil's camp

At this point you may well be asking the question: *"If the witchdoctor and the prophet are indeed Satan's agents, are they not fighting their master by casting out demons and relieving the negative effects of demonic influence and possession among their patients?"* The answer is a big NO! This is how it works. Patients obtain physical relief in exchange for spiritual imprisonment. The devil's camp wins souls through the mere act of temporarily transferring demons from one affected person to another, or instructing them to suspend the torment for a season. The practitioner reverses the patient's demon-inflicted physical infirmities, illness, and bad luck by the mere act of instructing the active demon to "Stop it!" This relief is offered in exchange for the soul of the one who has disobeyed God and consulted the devil's human agents to seek correction for his malady.

Look at it this way: God grants demons permission to put you on trial for reasons already discussed. Troubles of all description beset you. You visit a human commander of the occult. He commands the demons to stop tormenting you, even though it is in their power so to do. He may even command them to restore whatever it is they have taken away from you; a job, health. You receive a token to carry around at all times. This is a signal for all demons not to harm you as you walk naked, without God's protection. You now belong to their camp. For as long as you bear those tokens, God's angel can never return to his former position. Can you see how there is no loss in the devil's camp?

For many in rural areas and not a few in the metropolis, consulting witchdoctors forms the core of their religion. They claim to possess irrefutable evidence, through personal experience, of solutions to physical, spiritual, as well as emotional ills, under the care of the traditional therapist. Likewise, the majority of those belonging to the many congregations of the white garmented African Apostolic Christian faith, when asked why they so belong, reply that they are grateful for the tangible results of the prophet's prayers in lifting their mountains of troubles. They wrongly attribute this demonstrated power to God. Many are thus bound to the devil in earnest error.

Because the prophets instruct their followers never to read the Bible or entertain any teachings based on the Holy Book, it is almost impossible to witness to these souls, and introduce Jesus Christ to them. They live in a vicious trap of fear, lest evil spirits should be unleashed back upon them because of any act of disobedience or disloyalty towards the prophet. I should know. I was a member of this faith for three years.

Both witchdoctor and 'prophet' employ the ritual of 'cleansing' with the blood of animals, more than two thousand years after the atoning blood of the Messiah was shed on the cross. This amounts to spitting in the face of He who so lovingly gave away *all*, in sacrifice for erring mankind. These masters of the occult divert the attention of humanity from the cross of Jesus, and from God the Creator, to cheap animal blood, little stones, bottles of water and man-made talismans. There is no loss in the devil's camp!

Conditioning the world for a great deception

The world over, many have embraced the doctrine of the immortality of the human soul, in churches and cults alike. Through modifying this philosophy, it has been easy for the devil to introduce spiritualism in many different forms, to suit different tastes. This has given rise to numerous cults, secret societies, and congregations. From the heathen tribesman tucked away in the remotest corner of the world to the sophisticated executive in one of New York's Masonic Lodges, the devil has provided suitably packaged rituals for worshiping him. He has not spared the many professed 'Christian' churches. In these, spiritualism is now widely embraced, veiled behind works of healing miracles, tongues, and chanting trances.

Though distance, race, tribe, culture, and denomination may separate those under the spell of Satan, yet he is preparing all, mentally and spiritually, for the greatest of his feats of deception. The delusion that will trigger the end-time events leading to the second advent of Christ will ensnare all those who have harbored belief in spirits of the dead, and consulted mediums as the means to reach God, or to solve their problems.

In chapter 15, we shall see demons enter the realm of the living with devastating consequences. At that time, a great fraud will sway the majority in the world to follow the devil to destruction:

> The coming of the lawless one will be in accordance with the work of Satan displayed in all kinds of counterfeit miracles, signs and wonders, and in every sort of evil that deceives those who are perishing. They perish because they refused to love the truth and so be saved. For this reason God sends them a powerful delusion. 2 Thess. 2:9-11.

Little wonder the scriptures issue the following warning to you and me, dear reader, being sojourners on planet earth: "Woe to the inhabitants of the earth and the sea! For the devil has come down to you, having great wrath, because he knows that he has a short time." Rev. 12:12.

CHAPTER 15

Steps to the Second Advent

Waiting for the two masters

Towards the end of His earthly ministry, the Lord Jesus spoke so frequently about His death, and Second Advent, which would signal the end of this present world, that His worried disciples bade Him, "Tell us, when will these things be? And what will be the sign of Your coming, and of the end of the age?" Matt. 24:3. Should we not be asking the same question today, and yearning for an answer? The Lord's response opened with a warning against deception, "Take heed that no man deceives you." (v. 4.) Shortly, we shall see the nature of this imminent, devil-engineered deception.

The expectation of a coming saviour has held the world in its grip since Eden. Throughout the earth's history, men and women have appeared in different parts of the world and claimed to be messiahs and prophets sent from God. Their teachings have attracted followers, and many different religions and churches have resulted. Jesus Christ of Nazareth laid the foundation for Christianity. The teachings of Mohammed formed the basis for Islam. The life and teachings of Buddha gave rise to Buddhism. The

Hindi faith hinged on the teachings of their Krishna. There are many more prophets and religions besides these major ones.

While the doctrines of the different masters differ in many respects, one teaching appears common to all religions—that of a coming world saviour, who will usher in a better way of life on earth. When we reconcile texts from the Bible prophecies with notes 33, 36, and 47 of the timeline of the New World Order in Appendix I, two major groups of believers emerge, each of which is waiting for the coming of its own savior.

Waiting for the Maitreya

The first group is waiting for its master with great zeal. A heightened sense of imminence is spreading rapidly throughout the world by means of the internet and roundtable meetings. This group comprises, or will soon comprise, the majority of the world's population. From the following quotation, it is easy to see why this expected master should command such a massive following. In chapter 5 we met the "Christ Lord Maitreya" who

> has been expected for generations by all of the major religions. Christians know him as the Christ, and expect his imminent return. Jews await him as the Messiah; Hindus look for the coming of Krishna; Buddhists expect him as Maitreya Buddha; and Muslims anticipate the Imam Mahdi or Messiah. Although the names are different, many believe that they all refer to the same individual: the World Teacher, whose personal name is Maitreya (pronounced my-tray-ah). (Reninger 2006, The Return of Christ: Is Maitreya in Our World Today?)

If one could mobilize the world to focus its expectation on the same 'christ', a unified religion for the entire world would easily become a reality. This, in fact, is the aim of the ecumenical movement driven by the World Council of Churches, in conjunction with the World-Wide Esoteric Community. Another website has this to say about the awaited cosmic christ:

> In the language of the Mysteries, Christ may be likened to Dionysos, Osiris, or Krishna, who will deliver the suffering Chrest (humanity) in its trial. (Report 2001)

Maitreya is therefore the supernatural being awaited by diverse peoples of the world. He comes in the mold of the ancient Egyptian sun god Osiris[22]. Those awaiting the Maitreya represent all the world's religions united under the World-wide Esoteric Community, the Freemasons, the World Council of Churches, the United Nations and many other groupings and cults sharing the same agenda. They expect Maitreya to usher in a new era of world peace and prosperity. Note carefully that although they call their coming one 'christ', they never refer to him as *Jesus* Christ.

Few professing Christians are aware of being groomed to accept the coming of this cosmic christ. They attend church services where preachers and teachers make scant reference to the Bible. They accept the word of the pastor, priest, prophet, or pope, as gospel. The laity makes no effort to measure church doctrine against Scripture. If the preachers ever quote from the Bible, it is only to reinforce the gospel of prosperity and of complete salvation by grace, outside the works of the law.

Among those drifting towards the Maitreya are people mesmerized into churches and cults by miracles of healing and prophecy, backed by a shallow man made gospel. These include the many prophet centred, white garmented 'Apostolic' and 'Zionist' sects that have mushroomed throughout Africa. There are vast numbers from the mainstream 'Christian' churches who visit the prophets of these 'African-Christian' churches. Their faith rests in the little stones and 'holy water' they receive from them for their protection and healing. Many professing Christians go to their "normal" churches for fellowship and worship; but when faced with problems, they visit these 'prophets.'

In America, Europe and other 'advanced' countries, many are today drawn to churches were mass healing and 'blessing' is administered by preachers in the name of Jesus. They flock to church in their sins, receive blessing, physical and material relief, then return home to continue in their sins. The gospel is about prosperity; about how a born again Christian should never suffer in any way. There is no preaching against sin; no true repentance is necessary before receiving manna from heaven through the pastor. The Maitreya will easily draw such people to him at his coming because they have already allowed themselves to depend on the healing signs and wonders of thinly veiled occultism.

We summarize the expectations of the vast majority who, knowingly or un-knowingly, await the coming of the Maitreya, by quoting from the same report.

> We need to get away from the religious aspect of this Coming One. He is a spiritual Being and He will not be limited to the field of religion. He will be recognized and known by His Work and Not by the faith of those who believe in Him. Perhaps he will come forth in the field of Politics or in the field of Science. The Tibetan Master indicates that he will manifest in the field of those who are doing the most work. But, He comes for all people and He will be the Teacher of Unity, Love and Wisdom. (Report 2001)

Let us now list the characteristics of this 'christ.' We should be able to identify him and flee, when the time comes.

- He will be a spiritual entity manifesting as a human being.

- He is likely to appear in the religious field, given that this is where there is greatest anticipation, and where the greatest work is underway in preparation for his coming.

- He will claim to represent and embrace all religions and cultures of the world.

- He will call for unity of all people in love and peace.

- Speaking of love, as did Jesus, and repeating many of His words, Maitreya's movements, sermons, and teachings will capture the attention of the world. Hundreds of satellite television channels, radio stations, newspaper tabloids, and magazines will cover every move he makes, and capture each word he utters. By this means, *every eye shall see him,* and many will believe prophecy fulfilled.

The same website quoted above reveals Maitreya will not come alone.

> Comparing Him to a general is an effective analogy because He will not come alone. He will reappear with His band of workers—with many of the Teachers of Humanity. There will be ashrams outside every major planetary center. The ultimate aim of course, is to improve life on our planet, to improve the quality of our day-to-day life. (Report 2001)

'Saints', 'teachers', 'masters' and 'prophets' of all religions, who died long ago, will accompany the occult christ on his mission. These impostors will represent all nations, tribes, and races. They will claim to be residing with God in Heaven, but will deliver messages that are contrary to God's precepts as given in the Bible.

(Satan) has power to bring before men the appearance of their departed friends. The counterfeit is perfect; the familiar look, the words, the tone, are reproduced with marvelous distinctness. Many are comforted with the assurance that their loved ones are enjoying the bliss of Heaven; and without suspicion of danger, they give ear to "seducing spirits, and doctrines of devils.—(E. G. White 1911, 552)

Because they refused to accept the truth that *the dead know nothing,* many will believe in these 'resurrected' beings and follow their instruction, "for this reason God will send them strong delusion, that they should believe the lie, that they all may be condemned who did not believe the truth but had pleasure in unrighteousness." 2 Thes. 2:11, 12.

These cosmic beings will issue warnings of impending danger, which predictions will come to fulfillment. This will increase the faith of the world in these occult grand masters and spirits. Some of those appearing from the dead are remembered by the living as sinners who never worshipped God when they lived. Yet these will claim to be coming from Heaven, where they have been living very happily with God. It is because of this aspect of the deception that the majority will not repent of their sins in the time of tribulation just ahead. They will believe themselves worthy candidates of Heaven even as they plan to inflict the most gruesome punishments on the saints of God. As reliance on the spirit beings increases,

fearful sights of a supernatural character will soon be revealed in the heavens, in token of the power of miracle-working demons. The spirits of devils will go forth to the kings of the earth and to the whole world, to fasten them in deception, and urge them to unite with Satan in the last struggle against the government of Heaven.—(E. G. White 1911, 624).

When spiritualism shall hold the majority of the world's population in its grip, it will be the easiest thing to mobilize the people into the One World Order with its ten regions under one central government. (See map in Appendix II).

Waiting for the King of kings

There is a second group waiting also for its Savior. It is much smaller than the first. This group bases its expectation on the Bible alone. It is looking for the appearing of Jesus Christ of Nazareth; the same that died on the cross, rose from the dead, and ascended to heaven. Strangely, there is little zeal within this group. It appears to be viewing the imminent coming of its Christ from the wrong end of a telescope—insignificantly small and very distant! Indeed the revelator describes this group, the church of the last days, as spiritually lukewarm. "I know your works, that you are neither cold nor hot. I could wish you were cold or hot." Rev. 3:15. If cold, the church would feel the need of a warming comforter; if hot, then zeal would overflow from this group. However, they are quiet and unheard, in a world reeling drunkenly on the edge of destruction. We will identify this group in the last chapter of this book. For now, let us study the nature of the Second Coming. We will quote mostly from Matthew 24

> For then there will be great tribulation, such as has not been since the beginning of the world until this time, no, nor ever shall be. And unless those days were shortened, no flesh would be saved; but for the elect's sake those days will be shortened. Matt. 24:21, 22.

The biblical Christ will not come at a time of peace, order, and prosperity in the world. He will appear when utter chaos prevails on earth. He will come at a time of greater upheaval than any man has ever witnessed. There will certainly be no sermons on peace, unity, and prosperity at that time.

> Immediately after the tribulation of those days the sun will be darkened, and the moon will not give its light; the stars will fall from heaven, and the powers of the heavens will be shaken. Then the sign of the Son of Man will appear in heaven, and then all the tribes of the earth will mourn, and they will see the Son of Man coming on the clouds of heaven with power and great glory. (vv. 29, 30.)

Supernatural signs will appear in the heavens immediately prior to the second coming of Jesus Christ. His coming will cause the majority in the world to mourn in fear, mingled with regret. There will be no time for satellite television or newspaper printing. Satellite will not be necessary to announce the arrival of the true Christ, "for as the lightning cometh out of the east, and shineth even unto the west; so shall also the coming of the Son of man be." (v. 24:27).

The coming of Jesus Christ, unlike that of Maitreya will be one of the noisiest events in the history of the world, "for the Lord himself shall descend from heaven with a shout, with the voice of the archangel, and with the trump of God." 1 Thes. 4:16. We will look at the Second Coming in more detail towards the end of this chapter.

God will permit Satan to carry out a masterpiece of deception to dupe those on earth who forsook the truths abounding in the Scriptures. Many who have allowed themselves the luxury of reclining on the comforting doctrines of men will find the false christ irresistible.

This period of waiting will soon be over, first for the majority and then for the minority. The Maitreya is to appear soon, and his efforts will bring about the final phase of the New (One) World Order—the last ten regions of the earth! Soon afterwards, Jesus Christ will appear.

One world order—the ten regions

Over four millennia ago, a man who was king of the entire populated world was wondering what would become of his solidly built capital and empire, both named Babylon. The God of Heaven answered king Nebuchadnezzar in a dream, which Daniel the prophet interpreted. In Daniel 2, we learn that the king saw in a dream a large statue whose head was of gold, torso of silver, waist of bronze and legs of iron. (See Appendix II). The feet and toes were a mixture of iron and clay. Daniel's interpretation revealed the following:

- Head of gold—World Empire of Babylon—First world empire[23]
- Torso of silver—World Empire of Medo-Persia—Second world empire
- Waist of bronze—World Empire of Greece—Third world empire
- Legs of iron—World Empire of Rome—Fourth world empire
- Feet of iron/clay—Fifth world 'empire'—Loose confederation of world states

History confirms that world empires rose and fell as prophesied. Of the fifth 'kingdom', an extension of the fourth, Daniel had this to say:

Whereas you saw the feet and toes, partly of potter's clay and partly of iron, the kingdom shall be divided; yet the strength of the iron shall be in it, just as you saw the iron mixed with ceramic clay. And as the toes of the feet were partly of iron and partly of clay, so the kingdom shall be partly strong and partly fragile. As you saw iron mixed with ceramic clay, they will mingle with the seed of men; but they will not adhere to one another, just as iron does not mix with clay. Dan. 2:41-43.

Daniel's interpretation of the ten toes is a reference to the ten political regions that will exist at the very end of the age. (See map in Appendix II). Let us study the following text in view of the knowledge of the map, and the One World Order agenda.

And, in the days of these *(ten toe)* kings the God of heaven will set up a kingdom which shall never be destroyed; and the kingdom shall not be left to other people; it shall break in pieces and consume all these kingdoms, and it shall stand forever. Dan. 2:44.

It is clear that immediately prior to the second coming of Jesus Christ to usher in His everlasting Kingdom, there will be ten 'kingdoms' in existence; a union of weak and extremely powerful economic-political blocks, exemplified respectively by the yet unfinished African Union and the completed European Union.

It is important to note that in Nebuchadnezzar's dream, the rock that destroyed the statue struck it *in the (ten) toes*. Revelation 17 reinforces this view and leaves us with little doubt.

The ten horns which you saw are ten kings who have received no kingdom as yet, but they receive authority for one hour as kings with the beast. These are of one mind, and they will give their power and authority to the beast. Rev. 17:12, 13.

The ten 'kings' are to receive power towards the end. This is after the anticipated esoteric teacher has made his appearance, and with miracles, signs, and wonders mobilized the entire world in the final realization of the One World Order. This Maitreya, the World Spiritual Leader will be instrumental in the creation of the ten world 'kingdoms'. The leaders of the ten regions will unanimously vote this cosmic christ supreme leader above them; thus will they, "give their power and strength unto the beast."

Events on the ground so far tend to confirm the veracity of this prophecy. I present, once more, note number 30 of the history of the New World Order in Appendix I, for your study:

> 1973—The Club of Rome, a U.N. operative, issues a report entitled "Regionalized and Adaptive Model of the Global World System." This report divides the entire world into ten kingdoms.

The map of the proposed new dispensation confirms that ten political regions are on the drawing board of New World. (See map Appendix II).

The nature of prophecy is such that we should continue to review and refine our interpretations as world events daily unfold, and more information becomes available to us. What we consider correct interpretation today, we should be ready to adjust tomorrow, as history unfolds and proves us not so correct in our earlier interpretation. We must be ready to discard that which appeared true yesterday, and embrace what is obviously truer today. In this way alone can we remain as ready, as the Lord expects.

> But know this, that if the master of the house had known what hour the thief would come, he would have watched and not allowed his house to be broken into. Therefore you also be

> ready, for the Son of Man is coming at an hour you do not
> expect. Luke 12:39, 40.

It is well to be morally and spiritually ready every minute; it is, better still, to be able to interpret and announce the times to the lost sheep of the world as each piece of prophecy comes to fulfillment. Imagine what credibility and impetus this would give to the call to *'Come out of Babylon!'*

The final choice—seal or mark?

While there have been many crises in the history of humanity demanding a separation of the followers of God from those opposed to Him, they all pale in importance when compared to the standoff between truth and error that is to seize the world just before the second advent of Jesus Christ. The call to 'Come out of Babylon' will continue until every ear has heard it, then the long period of grace awarded men will end. Probation will soon close; but before it closes, every human being alive must be labeled by his master. There are only two masters: God and Satan. The people of God will receive the 'Seal of God', while Satan's followers receive the 'Mark of the Beast'. Which one will you receive?

The seal of God

God is delaying the time of trouble to allow angels to complete the work of identifying and spiritually separating His followers from the rest of the people.

> Then I saw another angel ascending from the east, having the
> seal of the living God. And he cried with a loud voice to the four
> angels to whom it was granted to harm the earth and the sea,

saying, "Do not harm the earth, the sea, or the trees till we have sealed the servants of our God on their foreheads. Rev. 7:2, 3.

The angels of God are even now engaged in the essential work of identifying the true followers of God, and placing upon them an invisible seal. Only people bearing the seal of God will stand on the last terrible Day of the Lord. They will withstand, not because they have the seal, but rather, they received the seal because they could withstand.

What are the qualities of the people receiving the seal of God? The revelator first exposes which group of people will receive the Mark of the Beast; those who will certainly not survive the Day of the Lord.

> If anyone worships the beast and his image, and receives his mark on his forehead or on his hand, he himself shall also drink of the wine of the wrath of God, which is poured out full strength into the cup of His indignation. Rev. 14:9, 10.

Clearly, the coming of the Lord will destroy this group. These have received the Mark of the Beast through obedience to the Beast. They have accepted the false religious leader and the One World Order system he brought to fulfillment. The next verse reveals the character of the opposite camp.

> Here is the patience of the saints; here *are* those who keep the commandments of God and the faith of Jesus. (v. 12).

This group has refused the Mark of the Beast. They have instead received the Seal of God. How have they qualified for the Seal of God? By having the faith *of* Jesus; not just *in* Jesus! Like Him, they *kept the commandments of God!* We have seen in an earlier chapter that no man is saved through keeping the law of God; rather, men keep the law of God because they have been saved by grace, through faith in Jesus Christ. We also saw that many self-professing Christians do not keep the entire law, but desecrate the fourth commandment. Let us see if this commandment is important for salvation.

Identifying the seal of God

The Oxford English Mini Dictionary defines the word seal as "(2) a piece of wax with a design stamped into it, attached to a document; (3) a confirmation or guarantee" and, as a verb, "to make definite." A seal is therefore a symbol of finality and un-changeability. It is a mark or sign of the authority of the owner of the seal. A king, for example, confirms a law as valid by stamping his royal seal on it. A royal seal contains three important features, namely:

1. The name of the lawgiver.
2. The title (office) of the law giver.
3. The territory (domain) of the lawgiver.

Scripture portrays God as King of the universe. He has His own royal seal. In Ezekiel 20, the Lord has this to say regarding the institution of the Sabbath,

> Moreover I also gave them My Sabbaths, to be a *sign* between them and Me, that they might know that I am the LORD who sanctifies them . . . . Hallow My Sabbaths, and they will be a *sign* between Me and you, that you may know that I am the LORD your God. (vv.12, 20, emphasis supplied.)

Keeping the Sabbath is therefore a sign of those who fully recognize God as the Creator and seek to follow His precepts above all things. Though the saints keep the entire law of God, it is the fourth commandment that bears all the features of a royal seal:

1. "The Lord thy God"—Name
2. "Maker (Creator)"—Title
3. "Heaven and Earth"—Territory (Domain).

The Sabbath commandment contains the seal of God. It provides the connection between man and his origin. The Sabbath will separate the saints from the damned in the final great conflict. The hymns sung and the Bibles read will be the same for all 'Christians', and would place all in the same camp if used as the yardstick for measurement. None would advocate murder, adultery, theft, or covetousness. Humanity will walk the same path until, on the seventh day, a small group breaks away, and takes the narrow track. The two opposite extremities of the choice to be made, with no grey area in between, are made clear, paradoxically enough, by the Catholic spokesperson, Cardinal Gibbons.

> Reason and common sense demand the acceptance of one or the other of these alternatives: either Protestantism and the keeping holy of Saturday or Catholicity and the keeping of Sunday. Compromise is impossible. (*Catholic Mirror*, December 23, 1893.)

When one has made a choice in favour of God's precepts ahead of the commands of men, he is sealed with the Holy Spirit. The following two texts show that the Holy Spirit is, in fact, the seal of God. "And do not grieve the Holy Spirit of God, by whom *you were sealed* for the day of redemption," and, "having believed, *you were sealed* with the Holy Spirit of promise." Eph. 4:30; 1:13, emphasis supplied.

The mark of the beast

The 'Beast' is the New World Government, a re-created persecuting union of religious and civic power. In chapter 5, we demonstrated how Revelation 13 and 17 reveal the Vatican as the harlot sitting on the beast and controlling it. The 'Mark of the Beast' must therefore be the most conspicuous sign of Vatican authority. To qualify as the counterfeit of God's seal, the Mark of the Beast has to be the direct opposite of the 'Seal of God', which is the seventh-day Sabbath.

We saw, in chapter 12, that Sunday is the man made institution standing in direct contrast to the Sabbath of God. An estimated fifty million saints were slaughtered in the course of enforcing this counterfeit Sabbath upon the world in the Dark Ages. The papal authorities do not deny these accusations. In fact, far from denying them, they claim success in changing the day of worship, and its acceptance by the overwhelming majority of Christendom, as proof of their divine appointment on earth.

In reply to the question "Does the Catholic Church claim the act of changing the observance of the Sabbath from the seventh to the first day of the week as a mark of her power?", Cardinal Gibbons in 1895 wrote:

> Of course the Catholic Church claims that the change was her act. It could not have been otherwise, as none in those days would have dreamed of doing anything in matters ecclesiastical and religious without her. And the act is a *mark* of her ecclesiastical power and authority in religious matters.—Signed, H. F. Thomas, Chancellor for the Cardinal. (Emphasis supplied.)

Another source supports the claim that Sunday is a special mark of the Roman church.

> Sunday is our mark of authority. The church is above the Bible, and this transference of sabbath observance is proof of that fact.[24]

The Sabbath question will gain prominence in religious circles as we move towards the end of the age. One renowned writer put it this way:

> The Sabbath will be the great test of loyalty; for it is the point of truth especially controverted. When the final test shall be brought to bear upon men, then the line of distinction will be drawn between those who serve God and those who serve Him not. While the observance of the false sabbath in compliance with the law of the State, contrary to the fourth commandment, will be an avowal of allegiance to a power that is in opposition to God, the keeping of the true Sabbath, in obedience to God's law is an evidence of loyalty to the Creator. While one class, by accepting the sign of submission to earthly powers, receive the mark of the beast, the other, choosing the token of allegiance to divine authority, receive the seal of God. (E. G. White, The Great Controversy, 1911, 605).

We shall soon show how the coming system will attempt to enforce the mark of the beast upon all citizens of the world.

As we have seen in Revelation 13:15-17, the Mark of the Beast will be received in two places. First is on the 'forehead', by deliberately deciding to dishonor God's seal, the Sabbath, despite receiving and understanding truth. The group receiving the mark on the forehead will include those

Christian leaders and activists who have loudly advocated and strenuously agitated for Sunday enforcement as the only way to solve the world's moral problems.

One may also receive the mark of the beast "on the hand," by deciding to dishonour the Sabbath, citing economic pressures, and labour laws as justification for so deciding. In this group will be many who, like Cain and King Saul, present convincing human arguments to justify their course. They have small mouths to feed at home, and tithes to return to the house of God. They therefore think to join the system in order to gain access to cash and provisions, without necessarily worshipping the Beast. Their plan is to benefit from the system of the Beast, while secretly continuing to worship the God of Heaven. To them as to Saul, the prophet has the ready reprimand, "Has the Lord as great delight in burnt offerings and sacrifices as in obeying the voice of the LORD? Behold, to obey is better than sacrifice, and to heed than the fat of rams." 1 Sam. 15:22. They will discover, when it is too late, the error of their chosen path, for "There is a way that seems right to a man, but its end is the way of death." Prov. 16:25.

Enforcing the mark—commercial segregation

Revelation 13:17 reveals that in the system to come, no man will buy or sell, unless he has the mark or name of the beast, or the number of his name. Is it feasible to put such a system in place? The simple answer is, Yes! There will be one common world economic system and currency, and only those who have pledged allegiance to the new system will receive authority to buy and sell.

A decade ago, this may have sounded a mere dream, but today the technological developments in the area of plastic money and microprocessors make this easily possible. It has become possible today to assign special identity numbers to individuals, allowing them to buy and sell using an ID-cum-bank card.

The European Union, and its currency, the Euro are the models to be applied for the coming world system. As far back as the turn of this century, Time magazine could report that Europe had a single market, a single currency, and a central bank. No member country could build an airport, decide on how much milk can be produced by national cows, or call something chocolate without consulting Brussels, or conforming to the Commission's guidelines. No important merger or acquisition could proceed unless the competition commissioner had nodded his head. Can you see that prophecy is easily within fulfillment?

A new technological development may make it possible to grant some the right to buy or sell, while denying others. Trials to place a biochip under the skin on the wrist or forehead have been successfully carried out in America. This device employs radio frequency identification, RFID[25] technology, allowing a point of sale machine to pick up details from the chip in much the same way as today's till-scanners read bar codes. If the biochip should be adopted as the new technology for carrying out transactions, one can clearly see how those privileged to have the implants may be the only ones to buy and sell. There is speculation in some quarters that the biochip is the Mark of the Beast. We must make it clear that while it may be adopted as the means for achieving discrimination in the coming system, the chip is not in itself the mark of the beast. The mark is invisible. It is mentally and morally received, through worshipping the Beast. Whatever technology will be harnessed to achieve this commercial segregation, it will not itself be the Mark of the Beast; it will only be the license awarded those who have already received the mark by accepting to join the system and, directly or indirectly, worshipping the devil in the universal religion to come.

The role of America

The USA will be in the forefront of the campaign to create the world government, and enforcing the mark of the beast. By the time of the very end, the insidious work of the agents of Satan will have completely eroded America's original values of separation of church and state. Thomas L Friedman, in an article entitled *"What the World Needs Now"* published in the Sunday New York Times, March 28, 1999 wrote that for globalism to work, America can't be afraid to act like the almighty superpower that it is. This statement represents the thinking of the people spearheading the creation of the New World Order. America has now placed itself in a position where it can fulfill the prophecies by playing a leading role in the end time events now unfolding. She will lead the campaign to enforce Sunday in place of the true Sabbath as the system forces the world to accept one global religion.

> He was granted power to give breath to the image of the beast, that the image of the beast should both speak and cause as many as would not worship the image of the beast to be killed. He causes all, both small and great, rich and poor, free and slave, to receive a mark on their right hand or on their foreheads, and that no one may buy or sell except one who has the mark or the name of the beast, or the number of his name. Rev. 13:15-17.

There will be one global religious movement tolerating all beliefs, as long as the followers have accepted the World Religious Leader as their ultimate head. The enactment of Sunday law will spread from America to the rest of the world, with the new civic and religious authorities ostracizing those not accepting it.

Probation ends

When the third angel's message, 'Come out of Babylon' has been delivered to every ear, and all persons alive have made their eternal choice, God's angels will complete the work of sealing His people. Then,

> at that time Michael shall stand up, the great prince who stands watch over the sons of your people; and there shall be a time of trouble, such as never was since there was a nation, even to that time. Dan. 12:1.

God the Son is Jesus Christ to men, and Michael the Archangel to the heavenly host of angels He leads. *Standing up* is the act of leaving the work that He has been engaged in—namely the atonement and judgment. This work has occupied Him for ages in the heavenly Sanctuary, as the High Priest; but now He stands up to assume a new role, that of a conquering monarch leading a mighty army of angels headed for the harvest of the earth.

In a loud voice that rocks the universe, Jesus Christ declares, "It is done." Rev. 16:17. Heavy smoke fills the temple to keep Him away from the mediatory work that He so cherishes. His unfathomable love for humanity would keep Him in the temple forever in His effort to save every single soul. "The temple was filled with smoke from the glory of God and from His power, and no one was able to enter the temple till the seven plagues of the seven angels were completed." Rev. 15:8.

Fire from the altar

In the Old Testament Day of Atonement, before the High Priest could enter before the presence of the Lord behind the veil, he had to perform a certain prescribed procedure for his protection.

Then he shall take a censer full of burning coals of fire from the altar before the LORD, with his hands full of sweet incense beaten fine, and bring *it* inside the veil. And he shall put the incense on the fire before the LORD, that the cloud of incense may cover the mercy seat that *is* on the Testimony, *lest he die.* Lev. 16:12, emphasis supplied.

Humans carry intrinsic sin, and could never stand exposed before the holiness of God, and live. The smoke from the altar provided a symbolic veil of protection for the High Priest. There was another place in the Old Testament where fire from the altar shielded people from an angry God. Back in the days of Moses, Aaron filled a censor with fire from the altar to tone down God's wrath when He would have consumed all Israel. In Numbers 16, we read about Korah, who incited some leaders of Israel to rebel against Moses. They challenged the role of Moses as the prophet of God, and claimed equal status before the Lord. The earth opened to swallow Korah and his group, together with their families. The congregation rose up, accusing Moses of the murder of Korah and his company. An angry God commanded Moses and Aaron: "Get away from among this congregation, that I may consume them in a moment." Num. 16:45.

When the deep love of God is rejected, and His efforts to correct are rebuffed, the wrath that replaces it is equally intense. Moses knew that God was about to wipe out the entire congregation. He also knew exactly how to appease God's wrath, and moderate the effect of the plague sent from Him.

So Moses said to Aaron, "Take a *censer and put fire in it from the altar, put incense on it,* and take it quickly to the congregation and *make atonement* for them; for wrath has gone out from the LORD. The *plague has begun.*" (v 46, emphasis supplied.)

We have seen that Jesus will soon leave His intercessory work. From that moment, humanity shall stand exposed before a Holy God, with no

they are identified through this very act, and delivered to the authorities. In the home, wife will turn upon husband, brother against sister and father against son. In the community, neighbor will sell out neighbor, while in the church, pastor will deliver deacon to the authorities. Thus, shall the prophecy be fulfilled: "And ye shall be betrayed both by parents, and brethren, and kinsfolks, and friends." Luke 21:16.

By this time, of course, many of the saints have already left the big cities and towns for rural areas, forests and mountains, after reading the signs from prophecy. Those remaining in the cities and villages are forcibly evicted from their legal homes, and their properties confiscated by mobs of frenzied protesters. Precedent predicts that criminals, taking advantage of the chaotic situation, will target any properties they covet and seize them, even though the owners have accepted the Mark of The Beast. This will further heighten the level of confusion and anarchy. As conditions of living rapidly deteriorate, the hatred targeted at the saints intensifies. Many citizens of the New World begin to take the law into their own hands, against the 'obstinate' group. Zealous 'Christian' Sunday fundamentalists arrest some of the saints, and deliver them for imprisonment and trial.

This persecution of the people of God is what the Scriptures call war against Jesus Christ. "These (ten kings) shall make war with the Lamb." Rev. 17:14, first part. They will fight the Lamb in the form of His saints who have chosen to die, rather than bow the knee to the beast. The central world government passes a universal death decree against the saints of God. The Commandment keepers are granted a short period of amnesty in which to renounce their faith before the day when it shall become a legal requirement to exterminate them. Will the incensed, demon-driven mob succeed in annihilating the children of God? The answer is No, for "the Lamb will overcome them, for He is Lord of lords and King of kings; and those who are with Him are called, chosen, and faithful. Rev. 17:14, last part. The death of the saints at this stage would neither teach anyone any lesson, nor strengthen their faith any further since, by this time, the holiness or filth of all individuals is fixed forever. How will God save His people? The same way He delivered the first Israel out of Egypt—first, by the plagues!

The seven last plagues

Just as the hate-filled majority believes it is bringing the situation under control by persecuting and imprisoning the children of God, a scene is unfolding in Heaven, which we should now visit.

> And out of the temple came the seven angels having the seven plagues, . . . then one of the four living creatures gave to the seven angels seven golden bowls full of the wrath of God who lives forever and ever. . . . Then I heard a loud voice from the temple saying to the seven angels, "Go and pour out the bowls of the wrath of God on the earth." Rev. 15:6, 7; 16:1

In Eden, humanity opted for human wisdom and civilization, led on by the enemy of the Creator. For six millennia, the Godhead has laboured through prophets, pastors, evangelists, and literature, to lead humanity back to God; but many have spurned the invitation. Now, their Creator abandons them to their choices.

The first plague are 'noisesome and grievous' sores that fall on those who have received the mark of the beast (Rev. 16:2.) The civilization of men has included the laboratory design of potent, instant cancer-causing microbes and chemicals, to be unleashed on fellow humans in biological warfare. Now, humanity receives a taste of its very own inventions. The saints remain unscathed, and this increases the ire of the afflicted, who seek to inflict even greater harm on the people of God.

The second plague turns the waters of the seas to blood—the blood of a dead man—and all sea life dies (v. 3.) The water of the rivers turns to blood in the third plague (v. 4.) In choosing Satan as its king, the earth chose pollution instead of purity, as its daily reality. The rate of pollution of the world's water bodies is accelerating so rapidly that if the planet were to continue on its present course, it would soon run out of potable water. Now, man experiences another result of the Edenic choice. While the sinner faints for want of water to drink, it is said of the saint, "His water will be sure." Is. 33:16.

There is a terrible heat wave as the sun scorches the earth in the fourth plague; worse than anything ever experienced on the planet (Rev 16:8). Since the earliest days, mankind has abandoned God the Creator, and chosen to worship the sun. God now abandons the world to its chosen god. Their god is unmerciful, and scorches men and plants alike. Hunger and thirst are the result, since water is now blood, and crops and fruits have withered and died. John saw into the future that they still "blasphemed the name of God who has power over these plagues; and they did not repent and give Him glory." Rev. 16:9, last part. Meanwhile, the hand of God will protect the saints from all the mayhem.

> They shall neither hunger nor thirst, neither heat nor sun shall strike them; for He who has mercy on them will lead them, even by the springs of water He will guide them. Is. 49:10.

In the fifth plague, "the throne of the beast, and his kingdom became full of darkness; and they gnawed their tongues because of the pain." Rev. 16:10. The abrupt and complete withdrawal of the scorching sun provides only momentary relief before the plummeting temperatures soon cause everything to freeze. The freezing cold, and pitch darkness aggravate the cancerous blisters, the thirst, and the hunger. It is plain from the description of this darkness that man-made lighting and central heating systems derived from hydro-electricity, coal and nuclear power-stations are not functional during this plague. Is it any wonder those affected should *"gnaw their tongues for pain"*?

At this stage, the lost multitudes are in a state of quandary, with men and women yearning for answers from the scriptures, but there is no evangelist to either interpret the word, or preach sermons to them.

> "Behold, the days are coming," says the Lord GOD, "that I will send a famine on the land, not a famine of bread, nor a thirst for water, but of hearing the words of the LORD. They shall wander from sea to sea, and from north to east; they shall run to and fro, seeking the word of the LORD, but shall not find it. In that day the fair virgins and strong young men shall faint from thirst." Amos 8:11-13.

By this time, it is too late to seek the face of the Lord. The very end is very near.

> And the sixth angel poured out his vial upon the great river Euphrates; and the water thereof was dried up, that the way of the kings of the east might be prepared. Rev. 16:12.

We saw in chapter 5 that the Euphrates was the river flowing through the middle of the ancient city of Babylon. The thick wall of the city extended over the surface of the water, so that no enemy could enter that way into the city. In preparing to conquer ancient Babylon, Darius the Mede and his army diverted the course of the Euphrates, so that the riverbed under the wall became exposed. The enemy was able to march into the city along the riverbed. Babylon fell that same night. In the revelation of the future, the drying up of the Euphrates refers to the opening up of the vast water body above the starry heaven. Remember, in creation "God made the firmament, and divided the waters which were under the firmament from the waters which were above the firmament; . . . and God called the firmament Heaven." Gen 1:7, 8. The phrase "kings of the east" is a reference to Michael and the vast army of angels in His company, when He comes this time around: "For as the lightning comes from the east and flashes to the west, so also will the coming of the Son of Man be." Matt. 24:27. A strange opening develops in the eastern heavens; the breach through which the heavenly host are to enter the earthly realm, just as the Medo-Persian army entered Babylon through a breach in the Euphrates.

Human astronomers will quickly detect the developments in the heavens and raise a worldwide alarm. The world has lived for a long time under the fear of an asteroid collision. Asteroids are masses of rock debris from broken up heavenly bodies that are spinning in orbit around the sun. They vary in size from a few kilograms to thousands of tons. Should they enter the earth's gravitational field, their speeds would be in the range of twenty thousand kilometres per hour. Collision with a large asteroid could cause catastrophic damage to the planet. All countries considered major powers of the earth have, over the years prepared to pre-empt any asteroid collision by firing a missile at it, and destroying it before it strikes the earth.

Now, when the heavenly passage materializes, the forces of evil and deception mobilize the entire world's firepower, and direct it at the eastern sky.

> And I saw three unclean spirits like frogs coming out of the mouth of the dragon, out of the mouth of the beast, and out of the mouth of the false prophet. For they are spirits of demons, performing signs, which go out to the kings of the earth and of the whole world, to gather them to the battle of that great day of God Almighty. Rev. 16:13, 14.

Who are the dragon, the beast, and the false prophet? The three froglike spirits are the wave of lying propaganda emanating from the three major forces influencing human opinion and action in the earth's final hours. The beast is of course the One World government system, which is a union of political and religious power, persecuting the saints once again. The papacy is an intimate component of this beast. The false prophet refers to the World Spiritual Leader, the cosmic being who has received authority to control the affairs of the One World government. Who is the dragon?

> So the great dragon was cast out, that serpent of old, called the Devil and Satan, who deceives the whole world . . . having great wrath, because he knows that he has a short time. Rev. 12:9, 12.

Realizing the shortness of his time, Satan proceeds to use his trump card. Hitherto, he has used men and demons under his command to do his work of deception, but now he must appear on the scene himself!

Satan appears in glory

The persecuted saints of God are scattered in jails and caves, as the evidence of imminent conquest by the evil forces mounts in their visual estimation. They realize that only the coming of their Savior can save them now; and they look up to the sky in mounting despair. Each begins to question his moral standing before God, and wonder if indeed he has confessed all his sins; if they have been blotted out of the heavenly records. The prophet foresees this brief period of intense anguish for the saints. "Alas! For that day *is* great, so that none *is* like it; and it *is* the time of Jacob's trouble, but he shall be saved out of it." Jer. 30:7. Just as Jacob struggled with doubts of God's forgiveness, given the facts of his deliberate sin, so the saints will agonize whether they are fit to stand the sight of the King of kings.

In their moment of greatest anguish, the enemy of souls recognizes his greatest opportunity to con the remnant, and deliver them out of God's hand. Satan summons all his brilliance in an appearance so closely approximating the scripturally described coming of Christ, that the agitated and wearied minds of the elect would almost accept it as authentic.

> For false christs and false prophets will rise and show great signs
> and wonders to deceive, if possible, even the elect . . . . And no
> wonder! For Satan himself transforms himself into an angel of
> light. Matt. 24:24; 2 Cor. 11:14.

The saints, nevertheless, remain resolute in faith as they witness 'Christ' gathering the armies of the world to prepare to destroy the asteroid from the east. While appearing as The Lamb, yet he shall speak as the dragon, for he is Satan in reality. The saints' solid knowledge of the scriptures fortifies them against the strong visual evidence of their senses.

Meanwhile, the lost multitudes leap out of their heavy cloak of despair and bewilderment. They rally behind the brilliant leader who displays great signs and wonders, summoning a fresh bout of energy for the final onslaught against the approaching King of kings, as they unite in arms behind the dragon, the beast, and the false prophet.

Armageddon: the battle for your soul

What is happening to the saints meanwhile? Having kept their faith in the face of the greatest trial and deception, God has now placed them out of harm's way. Just prior to His coming, Christ will ensure the safety of His sheep.

Behold, I come as a thief. Blessed is he that watcheth, and keepeth his garments, lest he walk naked, and they see his shame. And he gathered them together into a place called in the Hebrew tongue Armageddon. Rev. 16:15, 16.

Two questions arise here.

1. Who has been gathered?
2. Who is gathering them?

To answer these questions we need to look at the texts immediately preceding verse 16. Verse 14 talks about "the spirits of devils, working miracles, which go forth unto the kings of the earth and of the whole world, to gather them to the battle of that great day of God Almighty." Note that the gathering here is done by a plurality of entities, which can, therefore, not be the "he" of verse 16. In verse 15, the revelator introduces a second group of people, the "blessed," before the gathering of verse 16. Someone introduces himself in verse 15, coming "as a thief". In Revelation 3:3, the Lord Jesus has warned the world through John, "If therefore thou shalt not watch, I will come on thee *as a thief,* and thou shalt not know what hour I will come upon thee." (Emphasis supplied.) Many other texts use the exact same phrase "as a thief," to describe the nature of the Second Coming. (Read 1 Thessalonians 5:2; 1 Thessalonians 5:4; 1 Peter 4:15 and 2 Peter 3:10). It is therefore logical to assume that the person introducing Himself in Revelation 16:15 is Jesus Christ.

In Revelation 13:13, a beast "performs great signs, so that he even makes fire come down from heaven on the earth in the sight of men." We have seen before that the revelator uses certain phrases to connect us to Old Testament scenes. The phrase "makes fire come down from heaven" takes us back to Mount Carmel, where Elijah, the prophet of God instructs the apostate King Ahab to gather all Israel, together with Baal's prophets on Mount Carmel.

> So Ahab sent for *all the children of Israel, and gathered the prophets* together unto mount Carmel. And Elijah came to all the people, and said, "How long you falter between two opinions? If the LORD is God, follow Him: but if Baal, then follow him. And the people answered him not a word. 1 Kings 20, 21, emphasis supplied.

He challenged Baal's prophets to bring down fire from heaven. They failed the test. In one of the most spectacular scenes in the Bible, Elijah prayed to God, "then the fire of the LORD fell." (v. 38). In Revelation 13:13, the beast is counterfeiting the prophet's miracle; making out that he is either God, or of God. There is therefore a need to return to Mount Carmel once more, spiritually this time, for another showdown. It is the Lord therefore, who gathers those whom the frog-like spirits have mobilized against Him, as well as the "blessed," who have kept their clothes on, to Armageddon, to witness the final confrontation.

You may well be asking yourself what the connection is between Mount Carmel and Armageddon. In Hebrew, the word is "Harmagedôn." "Har" is Hebrew for "mountain." "Harmagedôn makes some sort of reference to a mountain. In fact, one could translate the word 'Mountain of Magedon.'" (Paulien Ph.D. 2010, 2) Here is how a visitor to Israel describes the connection:

> Mount Carmel is actually a long ridge that marks the southern edge of the Valley of Jezreel. It starts right on the coast in Haifa and runs sort of southeast for a dozen miles toward the Jordan Valley. The best way to cross it is a pass that feeds right into Megiddo at

the base of the mountain. In fact, we visited the site where they think Elijah defeated the prophets of Baal. It is the highest point on the ridge, just overlooking Megiddo. (Ibid. 2, 7)

Dr. Paulien then goes on to explain:

It was on Mount Carmel that fire was called down from heaven to prove that Yahweh was the true God. But in the case of Revelation 13, it is the land beast who calls fire down from heaven. Like the magicians of Pharaoh, the land beast seeks to prove that the counterfeit god is really the true one. And in the end-time showdown, the outcome of Mount Carmel is reversed. In Revelation, the fire falls on the wrong altar. Thus the Battle of Armageddon will include a major deceptive action on the part of Satan and his earthly supporters. (Ibid., 8)

It has been repeatedly stated throughout this book that Satan's ambition is to take the place of God and receive worship, by installing himself *upon the mount of the congregation*.

The gathering of the kings of the world by the three unclean spirits (Rev 16:13-14) is the demonic counterpart to the gathering call of the three angels of Rev 14:6-11, who represent the followers of the Lamb. Therefore, the battle of Armageddon serves as the climax of the spiritual battle over worship outlined in chapters 13 and 14 (Rev 13:4, 8, 12, 15; 14:7, 9, 11), a battle in which the whole world would be brought to a fateful decision with permanent results. The spiritual nature of Armageddon is confirmed by the spiritual challenge of verse 15, just prior to the mention of harmagedôn. As in the original instance, the issue is settled in Revelation 19:20, 21 by fire and by sword. (Ibid., 8)

Armageddon is therefore not a reference to a geographical location, but a universal confrontation, which must reveal the final victor in the controversy of ages. It is God and Satan who will fight out the battle. It is a battle for the minds, hearts, and allegiance of men. The controversy has always been between the good and evil, and the prize has always been the hearts and worship of men. No military battle is possible against the Creator. He routes those who would mobilize their military might against Him before the battle. He will destroy Satan and those who choose to remain on his side to the end.

The seventh seal: destruction!

We left off where the way was ready for the appearance of the "kings of the east." Immediately after announcing this development, the Lord reveals, "Behold, I come as a thief." Rev. 16:15. To the uninformed, the coming of Jesus Christ as King of kings will look at first like the approach of a meteorite through the breach in the heavens. There will begin to appear a small ball in the distant eastern heaven, which will grow larger and larger. The rulers will convince the majority it is a dangerous meteorite headed for earth,

In the sense that the lost will mistake the approaching King for a meteorite, and even seek to destroy Him, the Second Advent of the Lord Jesus Christ will come upon the scientists, and the military strongmen of the world, as a thief. When they expect a huge meteorr to appear in the sights of their powerful telescopes,

> then the sign of the Son of Man will appear in heaven, and then
> all the tribes of the earth will mourn, and they will see the Son

of Man coming on the clouds of heaven with power and great glory . . . . and every eye will see Him, even they who pierced Him. And all the tribes of the earth will mourn because of Him.". Matt. 24:30; Rev. 1:7.

Note, that they will fire no bullets, nor dispatch missiles. They simply mourn and wail! The general populace, having continued with its daily routine—eating and drinking, marrying and partying, will also be caught by surprise (Matthew 24:38.) Thus, everyone will mourn.

By this time, the end is very near. "Then the seventh angel poured out his bowl into the air, and a loud voice came out of the temple of heaven, from the throne, saying, 'It is done!'" Rev. 16:17. These words of finality declare the very end of the present world as we see it today. They close a six thousand year phase of the history of redemption. The destruction of a sinful world has begun; the dreadful Day of the Lord has arrived!

And there were voices, and thunders, and lightnings; and there was a great earthquake, such as was not since men were upon the earth, so mighty an earthquake, and so great. (v. 18).

In chapter 10, we saw symbolic 'lightnings and thunderings' emanating from the base of the God's throne in heaven. We learnt that they were a signal of God's incompatibility with a world that trivialized the law that constituted the foundation of the throne. Now, in the end we meet the real-life manifestation of the fearful "voices and thunders and lightnings," as the destruction of life on the planet begins.

A little foretaste of the Day of the Lord?

I have had to revisit an almost completed manuscript in order include real life events currently happening, that could be useful in painting a picture of the Day of the Lord. On March 11, 2011 a massive earthquake measuring 8.9 on the Richter scale, shook Japan. The eastern coastal city of Sendai received the greatest impact. Video clips showed perplexed people at rail stations, in shops, and in apartments who, evidently, had never witnessed a tremor of this magnitude before. Goods were tumbling off supermarket shelves, windows shattering into the streets, while pots and pans tumbled off shelves in the homes. Bridges snapped and sagged, while cracks appeared on major highways. Railway tracks buckled; factories, and other buildings burst into flames. The cooling system of one nuclear reactor packed up while scientists had to shut down five others urgently. The first shockwave lasted only five minutes, but worse was to follow.

The under-sea movement that caused the earthquake triggered a ten metre *tsunai*[26] that caused more damage than the quake. In the end, there were more than seven thousand confirmed dead. An estimated 30 thousand lives were lost. Eight million homesteads went without power. Added to all this misery, was the serious threat of a nuclear meltdown, and radiation leaks in damaged nuclear plants.

There were video clips showing only lines of foundations were hundreds of houses had stood in a suburb just hours before. One CNN clip summarized the extent of the devastation with a picture of grim irony. It showed a ship left marooned on the flat roof of the remains a two-storey building, miles inland. This level of destruction led a South African staff reporter of a *City Press* editorial of March 13, 2011, to ask in a page 5 headline, IS THIS THE APOCALYPSE? The article proceeded: "Speculation about the end of the world is rife among the many impassioned responses to events in

Japan, . . . In concert with other recent disasters across the world, . . . this earthquake is seen by some as more than a natural event."

Now dear reader, imagine the scenes described above happening at once throughout the world. Japan, with more than fifty nuclear power plants, is in third place behind the United States and China. Now, add up all the nuclear plants in other developed countries, and a picture of the Day of the Lord will begin to form. With nuclear plants destroyed in the quake of Jesus' approach, and accompanying *tsunamis*, there will be total blackouts in most parts of the world. Nuclear radiation will spread unchecked. The world's mightiest earthquake will rattle the tall buildings to the ground. Entire cities, towns, suburbs, and villages, will become rubble.

It is inconceivable that the wrath of God should by-pass Babylon in this universal destruction. In the culmination of the battle of Armageddon,

> the great city was divided into three parts, and the cities of the nations fell. And great Babylon was remembered before God, to give her the cup of the wine of the fierceness of His wrath. Rev. 16:19.

As the world quakes at the approach of the heavenly host, the multitudes who so recently were seeking to annihilate the elect of God are themselves at the receiving end of wrath.

They run back and forth in utter fear, begging the mountains and rocks, "Fall on us and hide us from the face of Him who sits on the throne and from the wrath of the Lamb!" Nevertheless, even as they scramble for the mountain caves, "every island fled away, and the mountains were not found." With nowhere to hide, the prayers of the wicked for the rocks to fall on them receive an immediate and positive response. Rev. 6:16; 16:20.

The Day of the Lord—terrible to scoffers

"And great hail from heaven fell upon men, each hailstone about the weight of a talent. Men blasphemed God because of the plague of the hail, since that plague was exceedingly great." Rev. 16 21. This last plague destroys everything that has survived the massive earthquake and *tsunamis*, and is still intact on the face of the earth. At last, the Day of the Lord, long predicted by the prophets, has arrived. This is how some of the prophets have portrayed the climactic day of Jesus' second coming.

> Howl ye; for the day of the LORD is at hand; it shall come as a destruction from the Almighty . . . Behold, the day of the LORD cometh, cruel both with wrath and fierce anger, to lay the land desolate: and he shall destroy the sinners thereof out of it. Is. 13:6, 9.

> Let all the inhabitants of the land tremble; for the day of the LORD is coming, for it is at hand: a day of darkness and gloominess, a day of clouds and thick darkness, like the morning clouds spread over the mountains. The LORD gives voice before His army, . . . for His camp is very great; for strong is the One who executes His word. For the day of the LORD is great and very terrible; who can endure it? Joel 2:1, 2, 11.

> The great day of the LORD is near, it is near, and hastens quickly, even the voice of the day of the LORD: the mighty man shall cry there bitterly. Zeph. 1:14.

> But the day of the Lord will come as a thief in the night; in the which the heavens shall pass away with a great noise, and

the elements shall melt with fervent heat, the earth also and the
works that are therein shall be burned up. 2 Pet 3:10.

Need we add more? For the unrepentant sinner, who has spurned the
proffered hand of Christ, and "who has trampled the Son of God underfoot,
counted the blood of the covenant by which he was sanctified a common
thing, and insulted the Spirit of grace," the Day of the Lord will be most
terrifying experience of his life. It will also be the last for the wicked in
this present age (Heb 10:29). The mountains flee from the presence of
their Creator and His brilliance, and the result is destruction so total that
no man-made structure will remain intact. However, what happens to the
elect during this mayhem?

First resurrection and relief to the elect

At the sound of the final trumpet, and the call of the King of kings, the
graves, which have long interred the bones of the saints of God, open up,
and the inmates thereof wake up and walk out. The joy of the resurrected
saints is unimaginable as they feel their spirit bodies for the first time. They
look down at the hole in the ground and have the final laugh: "O Death,
where is your sting? O Hades, where is your victory?" 1 Cor. 15:55. They
mock death as they rise into the air to meet their Savior.

The most dreadful day to the cursed, is at once the most glorious to
the saints of God who have withstood the last great onslaught of evil in
the final hours of the earth. They shall stand outside the crumbled jails
and caves, and on the mountainsides and valleys. With indescribable joy
on their fatigue-lined faces, they shall gaze up to the eastern sky and shout
"Behold, this *is* our God; we have waited for Him, and He will save us.
This *is* the LORD; we have waited for Him; we will be glad and rejoice in
His salvation." Is. 25:9.

Soon after the dead saints have risen and ascended to meet the Lord, the remnant who have survived the time of trouble "shall all be changed, in a moment, in the twinkling of an eye, . . . (they) shall be changed. For this corruptible must put on incorruption, and this mortal must put on immortality." 1 Cor. 15:51-53. In their new spirit bodies, the saints defy the law of gravity that has fastened them to the planet of sin for ages, as they rise into the air to meet their Savior.

The apostle Paul describes these end time events with concise skill.

> For the Lord Himself will descend from heaven with a shout, with the voice of an archangel, and with the trumpet of God. And the dead in Christ will rise first. Then we who are alive and remain shall be caught up together with them in the clouds to meet the Lord in the air. And thus we shall always be with the Lord. 1 Thess. 4:16, 17.

CHAPTER 16

From Milenium Into Eternity

Satan arrested

You may be wondering where the originator of sin will be at this time.

> Then I saw an angel coming down from heaven, having the key
> to the bottomless pit and a great chain in his hand. He laid hold
> of the dragon, that serpent of old, who is the Devil and Satan,
> and bound him for a thousand years; and he cast him into the
> bottomless pit, and shut him up, and set a seal on him, so that he
> should deceive the nations no more till the thousand years were
> finished. But after these things he must be released for a little
> while." Rev. 20:1-3.

What is the *bottomless pit* that is to be Satan's prison for a thousand
years? 'Abussos' is the original Greek word which means a dark, desolate
waste; a state of chaos. It is the same word that was used to describe the
earth's condition before the creation of Genesis 1. This will be the devil's
prison house for a thousand years. There will be no humans to tempt; just

plenty of time to reminisce over the destruction brought on the planet by his ego.

We must be very clear in our minds what conditions will prevail on earth at end of the Second Advent:

1. The unrepentant sinners who were living at the end lie dead and unburied.

2. The unrepentant sinners who have died since creation remain dead and buried.

3. The saints who died since Eden have risen and ascended to meet Christ.

4. The saints who were alive at the coming of Christ have been transformed and have ascended to meet Christ.

5. Darkness once more envelopes the desolated planet; it is formless, and un-inhabitable.

6. Satan is confined to the bottomless pit for 1000 years.

In which group will you be, dear reader? The choices you are making today, even as you read this page, will determine where you will stand on the Day of the Lord, and whether or not you defy the law of gravity, and rise into the sky to meet Christ.

The millennium

As Moses organized ancient Israel on the journey to Canaan, so the angels organize the saints as they embark on the long trip to Heaven. Where will they live?

> In My Father's house are many mansions; if it were not so, I would have told you. I go to prepare a place for you. And if I go

and prepare a place for you, I will come again and receive you to Myself; that where I am, there you may be also. John 14:2, 3.

How will they be occupied?

And I saw thrones, and they sat on them, and judgment was committed to them. Then *I saw* the souls of those who had been beheaded for their witness to Jesus and for the word of God, who had not worshiped the beast or his image, and had not received *his* mark on their foreheads or on their hands. And they lived and reigned with Christ for a thousand years. Rev. 20:4.

The saints will assist in the judgment of the wicked angels and men. "Do you not know that the saints will judge the world? And if the world will be judged by you, are you unworthy to judge the smallest matters? Do you not know that we shall judge angels? 1 Cor. 6:2, 3.

Will conditions there be any different from the present?

And God will wipe away every tear from their eyes; there shall be no more death, nor sorrow, nor crying. There shall be no more pain, for the former things have passed away. Rev. 21:4.

The second resurrection

What happens to the dead sinners at the end of the Millennium? While the saints are ruling with Christ in Heaven, "the rest of the dead did not live again until the thousand years were finished." Rev. 20:5, first part. This text clearly suggests that at the end of the thousand years, the wicked will live again. The idea of a second resurrection is in line with what we have already studied in an earlier chapter.

How will Satan fare at that time? "Now when the thousand years have expired, Satan will be released from his prison and will go out to deceive the nations which are in the four corners of the earth." (vv. 7, 8). In other words, Satan is free once again to mingle with the resurrected multitudes of wicked humanity.

The new Jerusalem

What about the saints?

> Now I saw a new heaven and a new earth, for the first heaven and the first earth had passed away. Also there was no more sea. Then I, John, saw the holy city, New Jerusalem, coming down out of heaven from God, prepared as a bride adorned for her husband. And I heard a loud voice from heaven saying, "Behold, the tabernacle of God is with men, and He will dwell with them, and they shall be His people. God Himself will be with them and be their God. Rev. 21:1-3.

Christ and the saints will descend back to planet earth encamped within the capital city of the universe—the New Jerusalem! Heaven will come down to its final resting place—of all destinations, planet Earth! The power of God transports the city an entire body to settle upon Earth at the present location of the Mount of Olives, from where the Ascension took place.

> And in that day His feet will stand on the Mount of Olives, which faces Jerusalem on the east. And the Mount of Olives shall be split in two, from east to west, Making a very large valley; half of the mountain shall move toward the north and half of it toward the south. Zech. 14:4.

"As the New Jerusalem, in its dazzling splendor, comes down out of Heaven, it rests upon the place purified and made ready to receive it. (E. G. White 1911, 663). Let us take a closer look at this brilliant City.

> And he carried me away in the Spirit to a great and high mountain, and showed me the great city, the holy Jerusalem, descending out of heaven from God. (Rev21:10.

It is not possible for words in any human vocabulary to describe the splendor of this city. The revelator struggles to provide earthly parallels to convey beauty so exquisite no human mind can conceive or dream of it.

> The construction of its wall was of jasper; and the city was pure gold, like clear glass . . . The foundations of the wall of the city were adorned with all kinds of precious stones: the first foundation was jasper, the second sapphire, the third chalcedony, the fourth emerald; . . . But I saw no temple in it, for the Lord God Almighty and the Lamb are its temple. (vv. 18, 19, 22.)

The purpose of the temple in heaven was for the salvation of mankind. Now that those who would be saved have been saved, the Sanctuary building is no more.

> The city had no need of the sun or of the moon to shine in it, for the glory of God illuminated it. The Lamb *is* its light. And the nations of those who are saved shall walk in its light, and the kings of the earth bring their glory and honor into it. Its gates shall not be shut at all by day (there shall be no night there). (vv. 23-25)

Any attempt to add to this description would only distort this imperfect picture of perfection. Dear reader, would you not be happy in this city? Your place has been prepared. It is up to you to take it up by making the right choices today.

The great white throne judgment: destruction of sin

The resurrected sinners have seen the descending city and are filled with envy. Theirs is a broken up dwelling; and as they view the indescribable glory of the new capital of the saints, they experience a deep sense of regret. Far from repentance, jealousy prompts this feeling. They are wondering and planning how they can take the city by force when once again, Satan is set free to interact with them.

> Now when the thousand years have expired, Satan will be released from his prison and will go out to deceive the nations which are in the four corners of the earth, Gog and Magog, to gather them together to battle, whose number *is* as the sand of the sea. Rev. 20:7, 8.

One more time, Satan rallies men to battle against the Most High. Once again, men allow the enemy of God to deceive them. If he could not ascend "upon the mount of the congregation" by mentally overcoming the saints a thousand years ago, he would do so now by force, for right before him, stands the true congregation of God, the church triumphant.

There is massive conscription as politicians, and mighty men of war from all generations past, led by Satan, organize the world into a mighty army. They are preparing the masses for the final battle to overthrow the government of God. They believe it possible because they far outnumber the occupants of the city.

When all the risen sinners surround the New Jerusalem, the moment arrives for the first and last time when all human beings who have ever lived on earth shall be alive at once. They shall stand then before God all together, with the ungodly outside the walls and the saints within. There will only be two sides—those awaiting final judgment and destruction on the one hand, and those about to commence the glorious journey into eternity, on the other. Look forward, dear reader. Which side do you *want* to be at the end? Which side *are* you likely to be, knowing yourself the way you do? You should make the choice today, before the great final judgment day described in the texts below.

> Then I saw a great white throne and Him who sat on it, from whose face the earth and the heaven fled away. And there was found no place for them. And I saw the dead, small and great, standing before God, and books were opened. And another book was opened, which is the Book of Life. And the dead were judged according to their works, by the things which were written in the books. The sea gave up the dead who were in it, and Death and Hades delivered up the dead who were in them. And they were judged, each one according to his works. Then Death and Hades were cast into the lake of fire. Rev. 20:11-15.

As the books of remembrance are opened, all the events of one's life are recollected. The choices made against God's overtures to save are brought back to memory. It becomes plain to the lost that they have always made choices against the strenuous efforts of God's Spirit to save them. They realize that the judgment is about one's own life choices. They stand condemned by their own works, just as the inmates of New Jerusalem stand justified by theirs.

At each turn of everyday life, there have always been before men two possible courses open to follow. It becomes plain to the cursed that they have made deliberate choices that militated against the precepts of God. The strongmen of this world realize their pitiful frailty in comparison to the King of kings. The wise men for the first time realize that their greatest wisdom has always been foolishness before God. The truth of the depth of God's love, culminating in the sacrifice on the hill of Calvary sinks in. The masses acknowledge the justice of God, yet true to character, in a final act of defiance and stupidity,

> they went up on the breadth of the earth and surrounded the camp of the saints and the beloved city. And fire came down from God out of heaven and devoured them. The devil, who deceived them, was cast into the lake of fire and brimstone where the beast and the false prophet *are*. And they will be tormented day and night forever and ever. (vv. 9,10)

The wicked are destroyed at last by fire that rains upon them and *consumes* them. Note that the sinners are destroyed—*"devoured"!*

> And this shall be the plague with which the LORD will strike all the people who fought against Jerusalem: their flesh shall dissolve while they stand on their feet, their eyes shall dissolve in their sockets, and their tongues shall dissolve in their mouths . . . And at that day the slain of the LORD shall be from one end of the earth even to the other end of the earth. They shall not be lamented, or gathered, or buried; they shall become refuse on the ground. Zech. 14:12; Jer. 25:33.

Earth cleansed

In Noah's day, when sin had reached unprecedented levels, God covered the planet in a flood of water that destroyed all life. Jesus Christ drew a parallel between the destruction of Noah's time with that of the world at the very end. God never assured Noah He would never destroy the earth again; He simply gave the assurance He would not do so with floodwaters. Gen 9:11. This time around the earth will be cleansed by fire, when

> the Lord Jesus is revealed from heaven with His mighty angels, in flaming fire taking vengeance on those who do not know God, and on those who do not obey the gospel of our Lord Jesus Christ. These shall be punished with everlasting destruction from the presence of the Lord and from the glory of His power. 2 Thes 1:7-9.

Other texts support this view:

> "For behold, the day is coming, burning like an oven, and all the proud, yes, all who do wickedly will be stubble. And the day which is coming shall burn them up," says the LORD of hosts, "That will leave them neither root nor branch . . . You shall trample the wicked, for they shall be ashes under the soles of your feet" Mal 4:1, 3.

The apostle Peter also confirms the cleansing of the earth by fire: "But the day of the Lord will come . . . in which . . . the elements will melt with fervent heat; both the earth and the works that are in it will be burned up." 2 Pet 3:10. The entire earth is under fierce flames, and becomes what the Bible terms the "lake of fire," then Death and Hades were cast into the lake of fire. This is the second death. And anyone not found written in the Book of Life was cast into the lake of fire. Rev. 20:14, 15.

At last, the originator of sin and all the angels and men who chose to follow him, have perished. The quiet victory won from the foundation of the earth and confirmed by the events on Calvary and the empty tomb, is finally confirmed openly to the entire universe.

Just as Noah and his family, sheltered inside the ark, were safe from the raging destruction outside, so the saved will be safe from the intense heat that melts everything on earth, outside the New Jerusalem, their ark. Just as Noah waited for the waters to subside, and for signs of new life to show outside the ark before stepping out, so now the saints wait for the fires to die down, and for God to create a new planet.

The new and eternal

When Noah's family stepped out of the ark, it was into a regenerated earth, with grasses, herbs, and trees beginning to bud anew. Likewise, when the saints step out of their capital city, it will be into a completely recreated planet. This stepping out onto a re-created earth is the living hope of all men and women who have lived their lives in obedience to God. Peter aptly summarizes it for us: "Nevertheless we, according to His promise, look for new heavens and a new earth in which righteousness dwells." 2 Pet. 3:13. He who is Alpha and Omega assures the revelator: "Behold, I make all things new." Rev. 21:5. The revelator then sees "a new heaven and a new earth, for the first heaven and the first earth had passed away. Also there was no more sea." Rev. 21:1.

The new dispensation will offer relief beyond present human imagination.

Behold, the tabernacle of God is with men, and He will dwell with them, and they shall be His people. God Himself will be with them and be their God. And God will wipe away every tear from their eyes; there shall be no more death, nor sorrow, nor crying. There shall be no more pain, for the former things have passed away. Rev. 21:3, 4.

We must unbundle the full significance of Revelation 21:3. The Creator intended the present location of Heaven to be temporary right from the foundation of creation. Earth, the planet chosen for revealing the full meaning of sin to the watching universe, has also always been the final destination and permanent home of God, and headquarters of the entire universe.

While it may seem unfair that God should for six thousand years use the occupants of planet earth to fight what is essentially a war between Himself and Satan, yet the reward for those who stand firm on His side in all the battles of life is beyond human appreciation. Imagine living in a mansion next-door to God! Imagine calling God your neighbor! Imagine meeting Him as a matter of course—forever and ever! Talk about rubbing shoulders with royalty!

Dear friend, what, in this present world, could possibly be so pleasant, so fulfilling, so satisfying that you would miss life in the new heaven and earth for it? Could it be your social status? Could it be what you term your wealth? Could it be money, or the lack of it? Is it the power you wield over other earthlings, that holds you back? Is your position in what you call "my church" going to hold you rooted to this cursed earth until final destruction; or are you going to free yourself, cross the line and join the saints—"those who keep the commandments of God and the faith of Jesus."? Rev. 14:12.

Think back to the smoker, who is engaged in a fatal habit while possessing all the facts and knowledge of the associated hazards. Remember, we saw that the smoker's paradoxical nature is alive in each one of us in other areas of life, including religion. How sad it would be, that you should read and understand what we have discussed so far, obtain a full appreciation of the fate awaiting the disobedient, gain a firm conviction of the reality of eternity, then, for the sake of some ego soothing excuse, continue along the path of doom. Make your choice, before probation closes!

Sin eradicated forevermore

The saved of the earth, as well as the inhabitants of the un-fallen worlds who have been watching the unfolding drama on our planet, will gain a full knowledge of sin and its result. Never more will they want to see its ugly head raised! None would ever again question the justice and authority of the God, as Lucifer had done. By free choice, the universe pledges undying allegiance to the Creator. Now a truly sinless eternal life can commence, as we learn to follow the Ten Commandments, based on true love for God and fellow men. It was to this time that God referred, when He said trough the prophet,

> Behold, the days are coming, says the LORD, when I will make
> a new covenant with the house of Israel and with the house of
> Judah . . . I will put My law in their minds, and write it on their
> hearts; and I will be their God, and they shall be My people. Jer.
> 31:31, 33.

Peace, perfect peace

There will be perfect peace at last, not only between human families, societies, and nations, but between animals!

> The wolf also shall dwell with the lamb,
> The leopard shall lie down with the young goat,
> The calf and the young lion and the fatling together;
> And a little child shall lead them. Is 11:6.

In another place, the same prophet summarizes life in the new earth for us:

> They shall build houses and inhabit *them;*
> They shall plant vineyards and eat their fruit.
> They shall not build and another inhabit;
> They shall not plant and another eat;
> For as the days of a tree, *so shall be* the days of My people,
> And My elect shall long enjoy the work of their hands.
> They shall not labor in vain,
> Nor bring forth children for trouble;
> For they *shall be* the descendants of the blessed of the LORD,
> And their offspring with them.
> It shall come to pass
> That before they call, I will answer;
> And while they are still speaking, I will hear. Is. 65:21-24.

Need we say more?

CHAPTER 17

A People on A Mission (The Remnant)

Emerging from the maze

Words synonymous with 'maze' are 'labyrinth', 'tangle', 'web', and 'muddle'. A maze is a structure of numerous interconnecting tunnels that all look similar. Once you have entered a maze it may well be impossible to return to the original opening or come out of it. Experiments with rats placed in a maze show that they soon lose their sense of direction, and go round in circles until fatigue overtakes them and they die within its tunnels.

When one faces myriad possibilities and is required to make just one choice, we can describe him as being in a maze. The probability of making the correct choice at each fork in the tunnel is extremely small, and one cannot leave the selection to chance, if one is to emerge out of the maze. The easiest—if not the only—way to enter a maze and come out again, is to carry a ball of string, which you pay out as you move through the maze. To follow the correct path back, all you have to do is follow the string back to the point of origin.

You, dear reader, have now read and understood some major doctrines based on God's word alone. You may have come to the realization that what you call "my church" has been teaching you some doctrines based on human tradition and philosophy, rather than Scripture. You may now be in the process of making one of the most profound decisions you have ever made—to leave your current congregation! But you also realize you cannot walk out of your church into a vacuum. You must now find and identify yourself with the true Church of God.

The term 'Church of God' is not used here to denote the legally registered name of any denomination on earth. The 'Church of God' and the 'Church of Christ' are not necessarily the true Church of God by virtue of being so named by their human founders. We will soon define the Church of God from the Scriptures; but for now let us return to your perplexing circumstance. You are faced with literally a thousand different *Christian* denominations, all of them claiming to worship the one God, through the same Christ. The problem is, each one is teaching a doctrine differing from the rest. For example one teaches of a 'rapture', in which a few chosen will start disappearing to heaven soon, while another teaches that the dead go to heaven immediately on dying, while yet another may teach that one dies only to be born later as someone—or something—else. The list of conflicting doctrines is endless. So, which one is the true Church of God?

It is inconceivable that God should allow the religious world to become such a baffling maze, without leaving a string along the correct path, to lead back those wishing to rediscover true worship. To come out of this maze, we ought to find this string, and follow it all the way back to the origin, Eden! While we must define what the true Church is, we should first state categorically what it is not.

What the universal church of God is not

The universal Church of God, the one to emerge triumphant in the end, is not a geographically isolated group of men and women who have constituted themselves under any name, under some human leader, no matter what miracles he has performed. A denomination with branches throughout the world is not by mere virtue of this extensive distribution *the* Church of God.

A church so popular that its membership is half the population of the Christendom cannot become the universal Church of God simply because it is named the Catholic (meaning Universal) Church. In short, no single group or grouping of congregations can claim to be the church of the living God, to the exclusion of all other churches, or persons who have not joined them. No group on earth is going to exclude any person from the Church of God by the simple expedient of not including him in its register. No church register can ever exclude a candidate of the Church Triumphant by striking his name off its pages. The true Church of God is not built upon men and women of miracles, or charisma—it is founded on Christ the Rock; it transcends all petty human walls built from the bricks and mortar of pride and prejudice.

The blind, stiff-necked loyalty of individuals to the world's thousands of churches has its roots in the secular world. Ever since the earliest communities of men, political systems have demanded and inculcated within citizens a deep sense of patriotism to the institution, group or nation. The constitution, the flag, and the anthem have become the focal points upon which the entire nation is by force of law required to place allegiance. The principle of democracy, where the thinking of the majority is legally adopted as the correct, forces the minority who disagreed in the vote to accept the decision passed. By not participating in the implementation of the decision of the majority, the minority risk being labeled and ostracized as traitors. The measure of a man lies in how far he is prepared to defend the national flag under all circumstances. Behind the secular system is always a President, Prime Minister, or King who, like the flag, demands loyalty and honour and adulation.

Satan has subtly transferred the same secular values into the religious denominations of the world. A member aspiring to join a particular denomination is required to memorize, not the Bible, but the catechism of the church. In some instances, this book of creeds makes scant reference to the Bible, while in yet others it may even oppose Scriptural doctrines.

Because attractions other than the true Word of God draw many to churches, they readily make a pledge to abide by the creed of their new church. Once they have taken the vows, the sense of patriotism to the institution that we have identified above takes firm root. The member now defends his chosen denomination as "my church." He now assesses any new doctrine against church doctrine, and rejects it if it opposes the creed. Instead of using the Bible as the infallible guide, the commandments of men, as enshrined in the catechism, become the anchor of faith. The member may discover errors within the church creed, or truths outside of it, but because the mind has been conditioned from secular politics to flow with the majority and stick with the institution, he finds it easy to ignore plain truth and stay on.

Attracting most members and holding them fast to *their* church, is of course a man or woman titled Reverend, Pastor, Bishop, Cardinal, Pope, Prophet, or Apostle. The leader is in most cases a man or woman of immense charisma and talent. In the mainstream protestant churches the icon is one of the great reformers of old, such as John Calvin and Martin Luther. Just as in secular matters citizens pledge loyalty to their national leader, so in the world's church denomination members place all their trust in the head of the church, yet the psalmist sang, "It is better to trust in the LORD than to put confidence in man." Ps.118:8.

Another bond holding members to their churches '*in truth and in error, till death do us part*' are circles of deeply entrenched friendships and fellowship, which give one a sense of heaven on earth. Yet others are firmly held to their current churches by the deep roots of position held in the church, which give a sense of power and influence to the member. For most, their church is the only place where they have ever risen to a position of any authority. Some become blinded to truth by financial benefits derived either honestly or otherwise by virtue of their positions in the church. Think seriously about your membership to your church. Could it be remotely possible that you fall into any one of these categories?

This final chapter is about to deal with a very serious subject. It is about choice and decision. You, dear friend have read through this book, and probably agreed with a lot that has been said, having checked the Scriptures for yourself. You could now be feeling the need for making a change. However as you read on, you may find the biggest obstacle in the questions: *Whom does the author think he is to tell me which church to join? What right has he to condemn all other churches?* You may even begin to convince yourself that all the things you have read in this book are fallacies meant to lead you to a particular church, or denomination.

If this is beginning to happen, I urge you to take a break. Sit back and reflect once more on the first chapter of this book. Read it again if need be. Remember that it is only more natural for a human being who has been conned, to choose to remain so, than to admit it publicly and make a fresh start. The ego avoids bruises. If you put away all prejudices and loyalties, and follow the path taken by God's remnant from Eden as we shall trace its progress to this day, you might well feel a spontaneous urge to join them.

What the church of god is

We must emphasize from the onset "that there is one body and one Spirit, just as you were called in one hope of your calling; one Lord, one faith, one baptism; one God and Father of all, who is above all, and through all, and in you all." Eph. 4:4-6. The authority of this single movement derives solely from Christ, "for no other foundation can anyone lay than that which is laid, which is Jesus Christ." 1 Cor. 3:11.

The word *church* derives from the Greek ekklesia. "The sacred writers use the word derived from the Greek *'ekklesia'* to denote an organized community acknowledging the Lord Jesus Christ as their supreme ruler, and meeting statedly, or as opportunities offered for religious worship." (Davis 1944) The Greek word is itself a translation from the Hebrew *'qahal'* meaning 'gathering', 'assembly' or 'congregation'. In the New Testament we find a broadening of the meaning of the word 'church'. Scripture uses the word to mean, progressively:

- Believers assembled for worship in a specific place (1 Cor. 11:18; 14:19, 28)
- Believers living in a certain locality (1 Cor. 16:1; Gal. 1:2; 1 Thess. 2:14)
- A group of believers in the home of an individual (1 Cor. 16:19; Col. 4:15; Philemon 2)
- A group of congregations in a given geographical area (Acts 9:31)
- The whole body of believers throughout the world (Matt. 16:18; 1 Cor. 10:32; 12:28)
- The entire faithful creation in heaven and on earth (Eph. 1:20-22; Phil. 2:9-11).

All the foregoing descriptions of the church fall under the church visible or church invisible.

The church visible

The visible church is the community of believers who confess Jesus Christ as Lord and Savior. They have responded to the call to come out of the world and join for worship, fellowship, instruction in the Word, celebration of the Lord's Supper, and for service to mankind. This service includes proclamation of the gospel, the good news of salvation into the Kingdom through Jesus Christ alone. It is the duty of the present-day church to warn the world of judgment, and of the soon coming of the Lord Jesus.

The visible church started as a family church in the days of Adam, Seth, Enoch, Noah, Shem, and Abraham. It transformed into the congregation that was the nation Israel; and finally to the missionary movement that it is today, where "there is neither Jew nor Greek, there is neither slave nor free, there is neither male nor female; for you are all one in Christ Jesus." Gal. 3:28. The mandate of the church is to 'make disciples of all nations'.

The Bible uses several metaphors to depict the church. In Colossians 1:18 the church is compared to a body whose head is Christ. It likens the many members of the church to the many parts of the human body, which all have different but important functions. First Corinthians 3:9-11 depicts the church as a building whose foundation is Christ. Paul presents the church as the bride of Christ, a chaste virgin, in 2 Corinthians 11:2. The church is likened to an army fighting the forces of darkness on earth in Ephesians 6, and its members are encouraged to "take unto you the whole armour", which is faith, in this war (v.13).

A small core of disciples formed the nucleus of the church at its inception. The rapid growth of the church soon revealed the necessity for some form of organization. In Jerusalem, newly appointed deacons took over administrative duties, thus releasing the apostles to concentrate on the missionary work unimpeded. It soon became necessary to organize all the local churches in the same manner. Soon it became necessary to have a central body of administrators to co-ordinate the activities of all the geographically scattered churches. The church had to create an infrastructure. It was this original infrastructure of the church, which un-repented pagans infiltrated and corrupted, to create the papacy, and the numerous other denominations of today. Although Satan, through the agency of men took over the structures of the original visible church, the church invisible persisted, uncorrupted and pure. It continued in the same manner it would have done had the apostles lived on to this day.

The church invisible

The church invisible is the universal church of God. It includes the people of God throughout the world; those in the visible church and many who have followed all the light that Christ has revealed along their path, but do not belong to any church organization. Some have never had the opportunity to learn the truth about Jesus Christ, but because they responded positively to the Holy Spirit, their lives have reflected, "by nature the things contained in the law" of God. Rom. 2:14. Through the Holy Spirit, God leads His people from the invisible church to the visible: "And other sheep I have which are not of this fold; them also I must bring, and they will hear My voice; and there will be one flock and one shepherd." John 10:16.

The church in the 'wilderness', hiding in the times of persecution past and future, is included under the term 'church invisible,' as it possesses no visible structures or systems. The invisible church includes also the united church in heaven and on earth. "But you have come to Mount Zion and to the city of the living God, the heavenly Jerusalem, to an innumerable company of angels." Heb. 12:22. The angels, and all other intelligent un-fallen existence, are members of the universal church of God, together with the visible and invisible components of the earthly church.

Now that we have defined what the church of God is, in its diverse forms, we must find out in what visible form it exists on earth today. Revelation foretold current affairs. The term used in this book of to describe the church in these last days is 'remnant'. If we are to find the church of God, we must therefore trace the footsteps of this remnant from the beginning of earth's history, to the Second Advent.

Defining the remnant of god

We must define the word remnant in its daily usage before we can gain an appreciation of its meaning as it applies to the Church in Revelation. 'Remnant' has the same meaning as 'remainder', 'remains', 'residue', 'vestige' and 'left-over'. Supposing a bag contains ten similar balls, and you are required to pick out eight at random. The two that remain in the bag are the remainder, the remnant. They will look the same as any one of the eight balls picked out first. A bolt of cloth is unrolled and sold to many customers until the last metre is left. This piece is no different—merely because of being the remnant—from the very first metre cut off from the same roll.

Likewise, the remnant as applied to the people of God is a reference to groups of people—whether in one geographical location or diverse—that have been present on earth at any one time, keeping the precepts of God as orally relayed by God, or as written in the Scriptures. Their doctrine has not changed over the millennia. They have kept the original Sabbath as instituted in Eden. They have been—and will be—the custodians of God's unchanging truth, undiluted and uncompromised by the traditions of men.

If any of the Apostles should visit the remnant of today, he would neither be surprised at the content of the sermons preached, nor be alarmed by the doctrines taught. He should easily fall into the seven-day cycle, with Preparation day on Friday and Sabbath on Saturday. This is what the word remnant means. We should all study the doctrines and practices of our current denominations with a view to establishing what features would shock Paul, or Peter, should he visit today.

The remnant of God in all generations has always had a dual purpose on earth, namely:

- to act as custodians of truth
- to broadcast God's message of the time to the world

The remnant: from Eden to the Flood

When, through Cain, Satan eliminated Abel, his aim had been to thwart God's plan to provide the seed of man that would bruise his head as pronounced in the sentence passed upon him by God in Eden. However, another son, Seth, was born to the first couple. "And as for Seth, to him also a son was born; and he named him Enosh. Then men began to call on the name of the LORD." Gen. 4:26.

The line of Seth produced Enoch who "walked with God," and was the great grandfather of Noah. By Noah's time, the world had become so evil that God regretted creating mankind. The Creator decided to destroy humanity from the face of the planet, "But Noah found grace in the eyes of the LORD." Gen. 6:8. God preserved righteous Noah and his family as a remnant, to replenish the earth in a fresh start. Before the execution of the judgment, Noah's family—the remnant—had a message for the world to repent, for the judgment was nigh! Inside the ark, the remnant kept track of the Sabbaths by continuing to count the days in cycles of seven. One of the first things Noah did upon emerging from the ark was to build an altar, and make an offering to the Lord. Thus, the Sabbath and the right form of worship were preserved by the remnant of the time, and passed on to the post-diluvian world.

The remnant: from the flood to the Messiah

Noah had three sons, Shem, Ham, and Japheth. Genesis 11 reveals the genealogy from Shem to Abram, whose name God changed to Abraham. Abraham was the only righteous man found suitable for the honour of founding patriarch of the nation Israel, which God would create. Abraham bore Isaac who in turn fathered Jacob whom God renamed Israel.

Israel became the father of the twelve tribes jointly known as Israel. We met the nation Israel and its intended purpose in an earlier chapter. The baton for preserving true worship and the law of God passed from individual and small family remnants to an entire nation, which focused on the sanctuary, as the congregation of God. We have already seen how the Lord intended for Israel to be the world's torchbearer, leading pagans to the true God. We also saw how Israel failed in this noble calling. While the outcome of Israel's *corporate* mission may be summed up in the one word, '*failure*', it is important to note that there existed at all times a remnant, within Israel and Judah, which remained loyal to God and preserved true worship, the Ten Commandments, including Sabbath-keeping, to be passed on to the next generation.

At the height of institutionalized apostasy under Ahab and Jezebel, Israel was rotten to the core. To the prophet Elijah, it appeared as if there was not a single person left on God's side. Nevertheless, even under these circumstances, God could tell the prophet, "Yet I have reserved seven thousand in Israel, all whose knees have not bowed to Baal, and every mouth that has not kissed him." 1 Kings 19:18. That seven thousand was the remnant of the time.

When God pronounced punishment on Judah for continual transgression and idolatry, He promised to keep a remnant through the difficult times ahead. "I send My four severe judgments on Jerusalem . . . Yet behold, there shall be left in it a remnant who will be brought out, *both* sons and daughters." Ez. 14:21. Even when Israel and Judah were conquered, plundered, and scattered over the face of the earth, a remnant was still present.

> Then the remnant of Jacob shall be in the midst of many peoples,
> like dew from the LORD, like showers on the grass, that tarry
> for no man nor wait for the sons of men. And the remnant of
> Jacob shall be among the Gentiles, in the midst of many peoples.
> Micah 5:7, 8.

It was this remnant, geographically scattered throughout the world, which was responsible for keeping God's truth alive. It kept all the Ten Commandments of God, including the seventh-day Sabbath. Many returned to Palestine after the decree to rebuild Jerusalem. Many remained among other tribes and nations. The presence of this God-fearing people saved that ancient world from utter destruction. The prophet Isaiah reminds us of this fact, "Unless the LORD of hosts had left to us a very small remnant, we would have become like Sodom, we would have been made like Gomorrah." Is.1:9.

At the time of the first advent of Christ, there existed a remnant that was eagerly awaiting the coming of the Messiah. Although other peoples formed part of this group, it comprised mainly the tribe of Judah. These had read and correctly interpreted the Scriptures, and knew the time was ripe. This ability to interpret the written prophecies to the world has always been a distinguishing mark of the remnant as well as one of its key result areas in all generations.

The non-Jewish men who visited baby Jesus from the east were among God's remnant that was on the lookout for signs of fulfillment of prophecy in the birth of the Messiah. John the Baptist summed up the message of the remnant at the time of Jesus' birth "and saying, 'Repent, for the kingdom of heaven is at hand!'" Matt.3:2. Those who were first to heed John's call and be baptized were the remnant, who had been eagerly awaiting the coming Kingdom.

The readiness of those called to be disciples by Jesus Christ to abandon all and follow Him is suggestive of people who had been waiting expectantly. Philip confirms this view, and summarizes the thinking of the disciples on being called up: "We have found Him of whom Moses in the law, and also the prophets, wrote—Jesus of Nazareth, the son of Joseph." John 1:45.

Many people followed the Lord during His three-and-a-half-year ministry. They believed He was the Messiah from the miracles He performed, and from the authority of His message. They believed Jesus Christ would ultimately lead them in a military campaign to liberate the Jews from Roman bondage. In their time, He would become king in the mold of David.

Multitudes cheered Him when He made His last entry into Jerusalem on the back of a colt. A few days later, as He hung pitifully on the cross of Calvary, the same crowd mocked Him as an impostor. During His sham of a trial and intense persecution, His closest disciples deserted Him. When He died, the disillusioned disciples abandoned the ministry and returned to their former occupations. "Simon Peter said to them, 'I am going fishing.' They said to him, 'We are going with you also.' They went out and immediately got into the boat" John 21:3.

The resurrection of their master brought a new lease of life to the eleven disciples. Amidst an entire population that had condemned its Messiah as a fraud, the eleven formed the core of the remnant that would set the world ablaze with the gospel of repentance unto everlasting life through Christ. Comparing that period to the time of the prophet Elijah of old, the apostle Paul had this to say:

> But what does the divine response say to him? "I have reserved for Myself seven thousand men who have not bowed the knee to Baal." Even so then, at this present time there is a remnant according to the election of grace. Rom. 11:4, 5.

This confirms the view that there will be a remnant present in the world at all times.

The remnant of revelation chapter twelve

Revelation 12 describes a mighty conflict between God and Satan. Because Satan fights God through His people on earth, we would do well to study the details of this war. If we are able to identify the human targets of Satan's wrath in history, it may turn out to be a study of the history of the remnant. Let us follow the texts carefully.

> Now a great sign appeared in heaven: a woman clothed with the sun, with the moon under her feet, and on her head a garland of twelve stars. (v. 1)

We have already seen in earlier studies that a virtuous woman is the true congregation or Church of the living God. The Church is seen clothed with the sun, which is the robe of Christ's righteousness. The moon under her feet is the written Word of God that reflects the light from Christ. The twelve stars are the pillars of the Church—the twelve tribes of Israel in the Old Testament congregation, and the twelve apostles in the New Testament congregation. Thus, the woman is representing the true Church in all the ages.

> Then being with child, she cried out in labor and in pain to give birth. . . . She bore a male Child who was to rule all nations with a rod of iron. And her Child was caught up to God and His throne. (vv. 2, 5)

There is only one man child who went up to Heaven, to sit beside God and who will rule all nations from God's throne—Jesus Christ, the Son of Man. These texts are therefore describing the remnant, which was yearning for the coming of the Messiah at the time of Jesus' birth.

> And the dragon stood before the woman who was ready to give birth, to devour her Child as soon as it was born. (v. 4, last part).

Doesn't that sound familiar? The dragon, we know by now, is Satan. He employed the agency of the pagan Roman government, and more specifically Herod, who was king over the Jews, in his attempt to "devour" the Christ. To the wise men who were searching for the infant Jesus Herod said, "Go and search carefully for the young Child, and when you have found Him, bring back word to me, that I may come and worship Him also." Matt. 2:8. His intention was of course to kill the baby. Divine-inspired flight to Egypt saved the infant.

> Now when the dragon saw that he had been cast to the earth, he persecuted the woman who gave birth to the male Child. (v. 13)

Having failed to kill Jesus in infancy or derail His sacrificial mission in adulthood, the devil was effectively stripped of his claim to the throne of the planet earth. No longer could he enter the heavenly courts on behalf of mankind as in the days of Job. Satan next turned his furious attention upon the Church that Jesus had come to establish. Thus began the persecution of the early Church.

The first phase of persecution was at the hands of pagan Rome and spanned the first three centuries of the life of the Christian Church. This era ended around a.d.320 when Emperor Constantine was baptized into the Church of Rome; then began the great falling that led to the creation of a pagan institution veiled under the name of Christianity. We saw already how the Bishop of Rome merged religious and political power to give birth to the papacy in A. D. 538. In that year the persecution of the true Church resumed, this time at the hands of papal Rome in the Dark Ages. In this period, fifty million true saints were martyred for refusing to give up their hold on the scriptures as the only guide. It is important to note that the persecutors identified their victims through their stubborn persistence in the original worship of the apostolic era, especially seventh-day Sabbath keeping.

> But the woman was given two wings of a great eagle, that she might fly into the wilderness to her place, where she is nourished for a time and times and half a time, from the presence of the serpent. So the serpent spewed water out of his mouth like a flood after the woman, that he might cause her to be carried away by the flood. But the earth helped the woman, and the earth opened its mouth and swallowed up the flood which the dragon had spewed out of his mouth. (v. 14-16).

The remnant that survived the great persecution did so by seeking refuge in the mountains, caves, and forests, which constituted the "wilderness." Chief among those who disappeared from public view were the Waldenses.

They carried on the work of preserving true worship, hiding in the Alpine mountains and valleys of Europe. In this way, the earth opened its mouth to swallow the waters of the flood of persecution. The earth opened its mouth in yet another way, to swallow the flood. The opening up of the American continent provided an alternative destination for true Christians escaping persecution to exercise their right to religious liberty. By these means, a remnant survived which would re-ignite the fire of the true gospel at the end of the persecution in 1798. That year marked the end of the "time, and times, and half a time," the 1260 years[27] of papal persecution foretold also in Daniel 12:7.

And the dragon was enraged with the woman, and he went to make war with the rest of her offspring, *who keep the commandments of God and have the testimony of Jesus Christ."* Rev. 12:17, emphasis supplied.

Satan's aim in fighting Christianity was that no man should remain faithful to God. His failure to achieve this, initially through the persecution of pagan Rome, and finally through papal apostasy, was largely due to a small number of believers who were prepared to die for truth. In fury, he set out on his final onslaught against the few remaining children of God, the *remnant* of the Church, which bore the following characteristics:

- They are a remnant of the original Church whose foundation is the twelve tribes of Israel and the twelve Apostles. They maintain the original doctrine and keep the same Sabbath in the same manner as the Apostles.
- They keep all the (ten) commandments of God rather than the traditions of men, and
- They have the testimony of Jesus (which is the spirit of prophecy (Rev. 19:10)). They are able to read, interpret and simplify the gospel of Christ and unravel the prophecies.

Revelation mentions the remnant bearing similar characteristics, in another part of the book:

> Here is the patience of the saints; here are those *who keep the commandments of God and the faith of Jesus.* Rev. 14:12

Note the close association between the remnant and the keeping of the commandments. Observe further that they have the faith *of* Jesus, not just faith *in* Jesus. Keep these characteristics in mind as we continue.

Unlocking Revelation chapter ten

The 'wound' inflicted on the papacy in 1798 resulted in the remnant of God emerging from the wilderness into the open. It was the turn of the papal system to enter its own wilderness. The truth that Satan had suppressed for over a thousand years immediately exploded in a worldwide blossom of Christian revival! The Great Missionary Awakening and the Bible Society Movement started during this great revival. There was an accompanying interest in the prophecies of the Bible, which led to the Great Second Advent Awakening, an aroused interest in the second coming of Christ.

In Revelation 10, therefore, we meet the remnant in the eighteenth century, a relatively recent setting. Only a short piece of string is left before we emerge out of the maze. Let us follow scripture and history to trace this group to the present day. The revelator foretells their story in Revelation 10.

> I saw still another mighty angel coming down from heaven, clothed with a cloud. And a rainbow was on his head, his face was like the sun, and his feet like pillars of fire. He had a *little*

book open in his hand. And he set his right foot on the sea and his
left foot on the land. Rev. 10:1, 2, emphasis supplied.

What is the identity of this bright angel? What is the little book in
his hand? Why is the book open? Scripture never leaves us with unsolved
mysteries. The wording used to describe the vision of Revelation 10 is so
similar to that of Daniel 12 it is obvious the Spirit is drawing the reader to
connect the two texts, "here a little, there a little." Setting them side by side
solves the mystery of the open book of Revelation 10. The table below[28]
reveals the parallels between the two prophecies. Please read the whole of
Daniel 12 and Revelation 10 before returning to the table.

(Table adapted from: *'Instruction Manual for the New "Pictorial Aid"*
by Frank Braeden. Study Guide No. 43. Page 175.)

DANIEL 12	REVELATION 10
"the man clothed in linen" (v. 6)	"(an) angel clothed with a cloud" (v. 1)
"was upon the waters" (vv. 6,7)	"he set his right foot upon the sea" (v. 2)
"held up his right hand . . . unto heaven, and sware by him that liveth for ever" (v. 7)	"lifted up his hand to heaven, and sware by him that liveth for ever and ever.." (vv. 5, 6)
"How long shall it be to the end?" (v. 6, 8)	"there should be time no longer" (v. 6)
"these things shall be finished" (v. 7)	"the mystery . . . should be finished" (v 7)
"shut up the words, and *seal the book*, even to the time of the end" (v. 4, emphasis supplied)	"in his hand a *little book open*" (v. 2, emphasis supplied)

Notice that Revelation 10 is an answer to Daniel 12. The texts clearly show that the book of Daniel, sealed back then, is the very same book now held open at the time indicated in Revelation 10. The revelator sees a "little" book because by the time of its "opening," the book of Daniel would only be a small fraction of what would become the Bible. The angel Gabriel told Daniel not to worry about the interpretation of the visions he had seen: "Go your way, Daniel, for the words are closed up and sealed till the time of the end." Dan. 12:9. The Spirit would reveal the meaning of the book of Daniel only to the generations living in the end times. At that right time, Bible students would begin to understand the meaning of the apocalyptic prophecies. History confirms that the understanding of the book of Daniel dawned on the remnant, which was searching for truth, at the end of the 18th and beginning of the 19th centuries.

The remnant of Revelation ten

The discovery of the keys to understanding the prophecies of Daniel generated a widespread interest in prophecy. When truth seekers used these keys, they found that the actual dates of the birth and death of the Messiah agreed exactly with those obtained from calculations based on the Daniel prophecies. This heightened the interest in the prophetic book throughout the Christian world.

One text that came under scrutiny was Daniel 8:14:

> Unto two thousand and three hundred days; then shall the sanctuary be cleansed. (KJV)

The angel Gabriel told Daniel the 2300 'days' were to be reckoned from the decree to rebuild Jerusalem. This decree went out in 457 B. C., the seventh year of Persian king Artaxerxes. By the time of the Advent Awakening, all other events predicted in the 2300-year period had happened at the exact time prophesied. The 2300 years were still not finished. The cleansing of the sanctuary was yet in the future. Calculations revealed that 1844 would mark the end of the 2300 years. Therefore, according to bible scholars, in October of 1844, the cleansing of the sanctuary would take place.

A study of the Mosaic sanctuary proceedings revealed that the cleansing of the sanctuary happened on the Day of Atonement, when the sanctuary was relieved of the sins accumulated in the past year. The High Priest then piled all sins upon their originator, Satan, represented by the goat Azazil. The remnant concluded that "the cleansing of the sanctuary" was the cleansing of this sinful planet by fire. Scriptures quoted earlier in this book reveal that the destruction of the present earth would occur at the Second Advent of Christ. The remnant, reading the same texts, reached the conclusion, which settled into solid conviction, that Christ was coming in October 1844 to cleanse the earth with fire and take the righteous away to heaven.

The sweet-bitter experience

This interpretation was responsible for giving momentum to the Second Advent Awakening throughout the Christian world. The word 'advent' means 'coming on'; 'arrival'; 'dawn' or 'beginning'. In this context, it means the Second Coming of Jesus Christ. A sense of excitement and sweet anticipation spread among the flock. Many flocked to those churches that were heralding the advent. In America, these people initially became known as *Millerites*, after William Miller. This man was among the first in America to preach the gospel of the imminent coming of the Lord. He sold his worldly possessions and began an extensive evangelistic campaign, alerting the world that Jesus Christ was to return shortly. His calculation pinpointed 22 October 1844 as the day Christ would come again.

Many from the protestant churches flocked to listen to William Miller and others, who were preaching this message with clear references to the book of Daniel. These people felt a thirst for more truth than their churches offered at the pulpit. A great number were struck off their church registers for accepting the message of the Second Coming. They began to congregate where they could preach and receive this message freely. These people, by and by, became known as *Adventists*, because of their strong belief in the imminent coming of their Lord Jesus. So strong was their conviction and anticipation of the Second Coming that many Adventists sold their worldly possessions, and waited for 22 October.

The day came. The day passed. Nothing happened. Nothing happened on the next day either, nor on the next after it. As days turned to weeks, it became obvious that Christ was not coming after all! To say the Adventists were disappointed would be to make the greatest understatement ever. The sweet anticipation turned overnight to bitter disappointment and disillusionment. Many scoffers who had doubted from the onset felt vindicated and scoffed even more. Many, who had joined the Adventists for fear of judgment, turned and walked away. Only a few remained—the remnant of the remnant. Because of their small number compared to the rest, Christendom wrote them off as a minority cult. The great disappointment of 1844 remains one of the reasons for the continued perception, in some quarters, of the Adventists as an alarmist, extremist cult. Nevertheless, the remnant remained convinced their calculation of the date was correct. Why then had Christ not come? They returned to the scriptures with tears of humility in their eyes, and this time the Holy Spirit led them to the book of Revelation.

Self discovery of the Adventists

> Then the voice which I heard from heaven spoke to me again
> and said, "Go, take the little book which is open in the hand of
> the angel who stands on the sea and on the earth." Rev. 10:8.

Adventists interpreted the open book to be the revealed book of Daniel, as we have seen above.

> So I went to the angel and said to him, "Give me the little book."
> And he said to me, "Take and eat it; and it will make your
> stomach bitter, but it will be as sweet as honey in your mouth."
> Then I took the little book out of the angel's hand and ate it, and
> it was as sweet as honey in my mouth. But when I had eaten it,
> my stomach became bitter. (vv. 9, 10.)

"Eating" the book meant studying it. The sweetness in the mouth referred to their experience of sweet anticipation of the second coming of Christ. The bitterness in the stomach was the bitter disappointment experienced by the Adventists when Christ did not materialize as expected.

> You must prophesy again about many peoples, nations, tongues,
> and kings. (v. 11)

They took this as an extension of the great commission of Matthew 28:19. Despite the great disappointment, they should persevere, because there was yet a message to preach to the world. They were greatly encouraged and sustained by other scriptures.

> Do not cast away your confidence, which has great reward. For
> you have need of endurance, so that after you have done the

will of God, you may receive the promise: For yet a little while, And He who is coming will come and will not tarry. Now the just shall live by faith; but if anyone draws back, My soul has no pleasure in him. Heb. 10:35-38.

A small number of believers had remained, seeking for truth, when the majority turned back and mocked them, as they "renounced their faith . . . and ascribed to human or satanic agencies the powerful influence of the Holy Spirit which had attended the Advent movement." (E. G. White 1911, 431-432.) It was a trying period for the truth seekers people.

The passing of time in 1844 was followed by a period of great trial for those who still held the Advent faith. Their only relief, so far as ascertaining their true position was concerned, was the light which directed their minds to the sanctuary above. (Ibid. 431)

The Holy Spirit led them to discover their error, and hence, uncover the truth. Those who had arrived at the 1844 date had done a tremendous work. However, in interpreting the present location of the sanctuary, they had erred by taking for granted the popular theology of the time, that the entire earth had become the sanctuary after the destruction of the one in Jerusalem. This had led them to conclude it was the earth due for cleansing in 1844. Nevertheless, like all great pioneers, they let their failure become a lesson from the past, and revisited the holy pages. The Holy Spirit was at hand to assist in this renewed quest for truth.

And there was given me a reed like unto a rod: and the angel stood, saying, Rise, and measure the temple of God, and the altar, and them that worship therein. But the court which is without the temple leave out, and measure it not. Rev. 11:1, 2.

They now directed their efforts to a thorough study of the Mosaic sanctuary the proceedings thereof. They focused on the sanctuary and the sanctuary alone, in interpreting the prophecy, and left out all other presuppositions and existing interpretations. Suddenly, the truth was plain before them. They marveled that it had eluded them before. The only sanctuary standing in 1844 was the one in heaven. Any proceedings in the sanctuary in this age have to be in the *heavenly*. In the spring of 1844 therefore, Christ entered the Most Holy place of the temple in heaven, to begin the process of cleansing the sanctuary, and commence the judgment.

The error of the Adventists was not in the calculation, but in the nature of the event to take place on that day. It marked the beginning of the second phase of Christ's ministry in heaven: the judgment phase, since the Day of Atonement had been a day of judgment in the earthly proceedings.

The disappointment of the Adventist movement turned into the most exhilarating experience of their lives. Through the bitter experience, they had discovered themselves in the pages of prophecy as the remnant of the time! New hope filled their hearts as they set out to prophecy once again to the world, "for the testimony of Jesus is the spirit of prophecy." Rev. 19:10. This time, their message was that of the three angels of Revelation 14, which we have met already. Since 1844, they have carried the messages: *Worship God for judgment is in progress; Babylon is fallen and Come out of Babylon!* Added to these is the message of Exodus 20:8—"Remember the Sabbath, to keep it holy."

Seventh-day Adventism

The people of prophesy, as identified in the preceding paragraphs, became known as Seventh-Day Adventists, a name they chose in honour

of the biblical Sabbath, combined with an expression of their strong hope
in the second advent of Jesus Christ. Adventism is a missionary movement
that spans the entire continent. Scriptures have so far led us to believe that
this group is the current custodian of God's truth.

Our study of the meaning of the church of the living God has shown
the error of assuming that all Adventists belong to the universal church of
God by virtue of appearing on the earthly Adventist church register. It is
equally erroneous to assume that exclusion from the Adventist church is
automatic exclusion from the church of God, the church invisible.

The Seventh-day Adventist church holds today the place that Israel
held in the Old Testament world. That nation was the custodian of the
Ten Commandment law, and the Sanctuary ceremonies. This corporate
custodial status never rendered holiness to all individual Israelites. Even
some of the Priests and leaders of the church were sinful in the eyes of God
and men. However, the presence of sinners in the visible congregation
of God does not reduce the fact of the congregation's divine mission.
Jesus likened the church to a field, in one parable. In Mathew 13:24-30,
He taught that we are not to judge the character of the church by the
yardstick of corrupt individuals, lest we abandon the congregation for the
sake of weeds planted by the enemy. The task of weeding out impostors
is His alone,

> lest while you gather up the tares you also uproot the wheat with
> them. Let both grow together until the harvest, and at the time
> of harvest I will say to the reapers, "First gather together the tares
> and bind them in bundles to burn them, but gather the wheat
> into my barn." Matt. 13:29, 30.

Final call

Paul invites you today to be,

> no more strangers and sojourners, but fellow citizens with the saints, and of the household of God; . . . built upon the foundation of the apostles and prophets, Jesus Christ himself being the chief cornerstone; in whom all the building fitly framed together grows unto a holy temple in the Lord; in whom you are built together for a habitation of God through the Spirit. Eph. 2:19-22.

Let not ego stand in the way. Allow the database of truth that we have now built to become the basis for all decisions. After coming this far, will you be like the smoker, who for the sake of his generated feelings, chooses sooner to die than heed the warning clearly emblazoned on his packet of cigarettes? Just as the warnings of cancer and death on the packet of cigarettes are for real, so the warnings in the Bible threatening the loss of eternal life are for real. They apply to you and me, and have no respect for social class, education, race, gender, or age. Every single decision we make in our lives is either for God or for the devil, with no votes in between.

> The Lord is soon coming. The watchmen on the wall of Zion are called to awaken to their God-given responsibilities. God calls for watchmen who, in the power of the Spirit, will give the world the last warning message; who will proclaim the time of night. He calls for watchmen who will arouse men and women from their lethargy, lest they sleep the sleep of death. (E. G. White, *Testimonies for the Church* 1948, 304.)

The time has come to stop belonging to a denomination or congregation merely because it feels good. It is time now to "work out your own salvation with fear and trembling." Philip. 2:12. There is a cosmic war raging for supremacy over your mind and soul. In the end, of course, God will prove victorious. He and His people will assert the victory soon. Are you going to be like the ant, frantically scrambling for tiny breadcrumbs, yet unable to recognize the big loaf from which the crumbs fall; mistaking the source of sustenance for a huge obstacle in its way? The possessions, positions, joys, and satisfaction we derive from our positions in society and churches are nothing compared to the splendor of eternity in heaven. Remember, Satan's ambition is to sit "upon the mount of the congregation."

APPENDIX I

Steps to The One World Order

The following is a brief chronological outline of the progression of the One World Order agenda (Cyberpatriot 2010). The author's source is the website: http://www.geocities.com/CapitolHill/Lobby/1887/secondessay.htm (all emphasis is supplied)

1. 1773—Mayer Amschel Rothschild assembles twelve of his most influential friends and convinces them that if they all pool their resources together, *they can rule the world.* This meeting takes place in Frankfurt, Germany. Rothschild also informs his friends that he has found the perfect candidate, an individual of incredible intellect and ingenuity, to lead the organization he has planned—Adam Weishaupt.

2. May 1, 1776—Adam Weishaupt (code named Spartacus) establishes a secret society called the Order of the Illuminati. Weishaupt is the Professor of Canon Law at the University of Ingolstadt in Bavaria, part of Germany. [This date, May Day, is to become highly significant to the Soviet Communists. They held festive military

parades on this day.] The Illuminati seek to establish a New World Order. Their objectives are as follows:

- Abolition of all ordered governments
- Abolition of private property
- Abolition of inheritance
- Abolition of patriotism
- Abolition of the family
- Abolition of religion
- Creation of a world government

3. July 1782—The Order of the Illuminati joins forces with *Freemasonry* at the Congress of Wilhelmsbad . . ."

4. 1848—Moses Mordecai Marx Levy, alias Karl Marx, writes "The Communist Manifesto." Marx is a member of an Illuminati front organization called the League of the Just. He not only advocates economic and political changes; he advocates moral and spiritual changes as well. He believes the family should be abolished and that all children should be raised by a central authority. He expresses his attitude toward God by saying: *"We must war against all prevailing ideas of religion, of the state, of country, of patriotism. The idea of God is the keynote of a perverted civilization. It must be destroyed."*

5. 1875—Russian occultist Helena Petrovna Blavatsky founds the Theosophical Society. Madame Blavatsky claims that Tibetan holy men in the Himilayas, whom she refers to as the Masters of Wisdom, communicated with her in London by telepathy. She insists that the Christians have it all backwards—that Satan is good and God is evil. She writes: "The Christians and scientists must be made to respect their Indian betters. The Wisdom of India, her philosophy and achievement, must be made known in Europe and America."

6. 1890-1896—Cecil Rhodes, an enthusiastic student of John Ruskin, is Prime Minister of South Africa, a British colony at the time. He is able to exploit and control the gold and diamond wealth of South Africa. He works *to bring all the habitable portions of the world under the domination of a ruling elite.* To that end, he uses a portion of his vast wealth to establish the famous Rhodes Scholarships.

7. 1893—The Theosophical Society sponsors a Parliament of World Religions held in Chicago. The purpose of the convention is *to introduce Hindu and Buddhist concepts, such as belief in reincarnation, to the West.*

8. 1909-1913—Lord Alfred Milner organizes . . . . various Round Table Groups in the British dependencies and the United States.

9. 1913—President Woodrow Wilson publishes "The New Freedom" in which he reveals: "Since I entered politics, I have chiefly had men's views confided to me privately. Some of the biggest men in the U.S., in the field of commerce and manufacturing, are afraid of somebody, are afraid of something. They know that there is *a power somewhere so organized, so subtle, so watchful, so interlocked, so complete, so pervasive,* that they had better not speak above their breath when they speak in condemnation of it."

10. Dec. 23, 1913—The Federal Reserve [neither federal nor a reserve—it's a privately owned institution] is created. It was planned at a secret meeting in 1910 on Jekyl Island, Georgia, by a group of bankers and politicians, including Col. House. This transfers the power to create money from the American government to a private group of bankers. The Federal Reserve Act is hastily passed just before the Christmas break. Plank #5 of "The Communist Manifesto" had called for just such a central bank. [It is probably the largest generator of debt in the world.] Congressman Charles

A. Lindbergh Sr. (father of the famed aviator) warns: "This act establishes the most gigantic trust on earth. When the President signs this act the invisible government by the money power, proven to exist by the Money Trust investigation, will be legalized. The money power overawes the legislative and executive forces of the Nation and of the States. I have seen these forces exerted during the different stages of this bill."

11. 1916—Three years after signing the Federal Reserve Act into law, President Woodrow Wilson observes: "I am a most unhappy man. I have unwittingly ruined my country. A great industrial nation is controlled by its system of credit. Our system of credit is concentrated. The growth of the nation, therefore, and all our activities are in *the hands of a few men*. We have come to be one of the worst ruled, one of the most completely *controlled and dominated* governments in the civilized world. No longer a government by free opinion, no longer a government by conviction and the vote of the majority, but a government by the opinion and duress of *a small group of dominant men*."

12. 1916—Italian Socialist Antonio Gramsci states: "Socialism is precisely the religion that must overwhelm Christianity. Socialism is religion in the sense that it too is a faith with its mystics and rituals; religion, because *it has substituted for the consciousness of the transcendental God of the Christians, the faith in man and in his great strengths as a unique spiritual reality.*"

13. 1921—Col. House reorganizes the American branch of the Institute of International Affairs into the Council on Foreign Relations (CFR). [For the past 60 years, 80% of the top positions in every administration—whether Democrat or Republican—have been occupied by members of this organization. During that time, only two Presidents have not been directly affiliated with the CFR—John

Kennedy and Ronald Reagan. Kennedy was assassinated and an attempt was made on Reagan's life!]

14. December 15, 1922—The CFR endorses World Government in its magazine "Foreign Affairs." Author Philip Kerr states: "Obviously there is going to be *no peace or prosperity for mankind as long as the earth remains divided into 50 or 60 independent states,* until some kind of international system is created. The real problem today is that of world government."

15. 1932—"Plan for Peace" by American Birth Control League founder Margaret Sanger is published. She calls for coercive sterilization, mandatory segregation, and rehabilitative concentration camps for all "dysgenic stocks," including Blacks, Hispanics, American Indians and Catholics. [The American Birth Control League eventually becomes Planned Parenthood—the nation's foremost promoter and provider of abortion services. Many today are not aware of the racist origins of Planned Parenthood.]

16. 1933—"The Shape of Things to Come" by H. G. Wells is published. *Wells predicts a second world war around 1940, originating from a German-Polish dispute.* After 1945 there would be an increasing lack of public safety in "criminally infected" areas. *The plan for the "Modern World State" would succeed on its third attempt, and come out of something that occurred in Basra, Iraq.* The book also states: "Although world government had been plainly coming for some years, although it had been endlessly feared and murmured against, it found no opposition anywhere."

17. 1934—"The Externalization of the Hierarchy" by Alice Bailey29 is published. Bailey is an occultist, taking over from Annie Besant as head of the Theosophical Society. Bailey's works are channeled from a spirit guide, the Tibetan Master [demon spirit] Djwahl Kuhl. [Her teachings form the foundation for the current New

Age movement.] She writes: "The hour for the ancient mysteries has arrived. These Ancient Mysteries were hidden in numbers, in ritual, in words, and in symbology; these veil the secret. There is no question therefore that the work to be done in familiarizing the general public with the nature of the Mysteries is of paramount importance at this time. These Mysteries will be restored to outer expression through the medium of the Church and the Masonic Fraternity." She further states: "Out of the spoliation of all existing culture and civilization, the new world order must be built." [The book is published by the *Lucis Trust, incorporated originally in New York as the Lucifer Publishing Company.* Lucis Trust is a United Nations NGO (Non-Governmental Organization) and has been a major player at the recent UN summits. Later, Assistant Secretary General of the U.N. Robert Muller would credit the creation of his World Core Curriculum for education to the underlying teachings of Djwahl Kuhl, via Alice Bailey's writings on the subject.]

18. March 1942—An article in "TIME" magazine chronicles the Federal Council of Churches [which later becomes the National Council of Churches, a part of *the World Council of Churches]* lending its weight to efforts to establish a global authority. A meeting of the top officials of the council comes out in favor of: 1) a world government of delegated powers; 2) strong immediate limitations on national sovereignty; 3) international control of all armies and navies. Representatives (375 of them) of 30-some denominations assert that "a new order of economic life is both imminent and imperative"—a new order that is sure to come either "through voluntary cooperation within the framework of democracy or through explosive revolution."

19. October 24, 1945—The United Nations Charter becomes effective. Also on October 24, Senator Glen Taylor (D-Idaho)

introduces Senate Resolution 183, calling upon the U.S. Senate to go on record as favoring creation of a world republic, including an international police force.

20. 1948—The preliminary draft of a "World Constitution" is published by U.S. educators, advocating regional federation on the way toward world federation. It provides for a "World Council" with a "Chamber of Guardians" to enforce world law, as well as a call for nations to surrender their arms to the world government, and the right of this "Federal Republic of the World" to seize private property for its use.

21. Feb. 7, 1950—International financier and CFR member James Warburg tells a Senate Foreign Relations Subcommittee: "We shall have world government whether or not you like it—*by conquest or consent.*"

22. 1959—Nikita Khrushchev, ruthless dictator of the Soviet Union, states: "We can't expect the American people to jump from Capitalism to Communism, but we can assist their elected leaders in giving them small doses of Socialism until they awaken one day to find they have Communism."

23. Nov. 25, 1959—Council on Foreign Relations Study Number 7 calls for a " . . . new international order which must be responsive to world aspirations for *peace, for social and economic change* . . . an international order . . . including states labeling themselves as 'socialist' [communist]."

24. 1959—The World Constitution and Parliament Association is founded, which develops a "Diagram of World Government Under the Constitution for the Federation of Earth."

25. 1959—"The Mid-Century Challenge to U.S. Foreign Policy" is published, sponsored by the Rockefeller Brothers' Fund. It explains that the U.S. "cannot escape, and indeed should welcome . . . the

task which *history has imposed upon us.* This is the task of helping *to shape a new world order in all its dimensions—spiritual, economic, political, social."*

26. Nov. 13, 1963—It is alleged that just ten days prior to his assassination, President John F. Kennedy tells a Columbia University audience: "The high office of President has been used to foment a plot to destroy the Americans' freedom, and before I leave office I must inform the citizens of this plight."

27. May 18, 1972—In speaking of the coming world government, Roy M. Ash, Director of the Office of Management and Budget, declares that: " . . . within two decades the institutional framework for a world economic community will be in place . . . and aspects of individual sovereignty will be given over to a supernational authority."

28. 1973—International banker and staunch member of the subversive Council on Foreign Relations, David Rockefeller founds a new organization called the Trilateral Commission. He invites future President Jimmy Carter to become one of the founding members. Zbigniew Brzezinski is the organization's first director.

29. 1973—"Humanist Manifesto II" is published: "The next century can be and should be the humanistic century . . . we stand at the dawn of a new age . . . a secular society on a planetary scale . . . as non-theists we begin with humans not God, nature not deity . . . we deplore the division of humankind on nationalistic grounds . . . Thus we look to the development of a system of world law and a world order based based upon trans-national federal government . . . The true revolution is occurring."

30. 1973—The Club of Rome, a U.N. operative, issues a report entitled "Regionalized and Adaptive Model of the Global World System." This report divides the entire world into ten kingdoms.

31. Fall 1976—Radio operators all over the world begin receiving peculiar electronic pulses which they dub the "woodpecker." [It is learned that the source of the woodpecker is the Soviet Union. Soviet weather engineers are sending out the most powerful man-made radio beams ever created—many times more powerful than anything even planned before that—*in efforts to alter the earth's weather*.] [The "woodpecker" is a 1 megawatt CW tube that can now be purchased commercially from *Svetlana of St. Petersberg Russia*—the peripatetic Ed.]

32. April 1978—The *U.S. Department of the Army* adds in its *"Chaplain's Handbook* of Religious Requirements" new religions which had become federally recognized and which could be legally practiced on all military bases throughout the world. These "new" religions are *Satanism, witchcraft and other occult religions.*

33. April 25, 1982—A full-page ad appears in major newspapers around the world proclaiming: "THE CHRIST IS NOW HERE." The advertising campaign coincides with the beginning of a speaking tour by one Benjamin Creme, a British theosophist. In various interviews and speeches, Creme explains that in speaking of "the Christ," *he does not mean Jesus Christ* but *Lord Maitreya*, the World Teacher. According to Creme, Jesus, Buddha, Krishna, and others are merely disciples of Maitreya. These Ascended Masters comprise an enlightened Spiritual Hierarchy which has guided humanity's evolution throughout history. He maintains that Lord Maitreya fulfills the expectations of all peoples. Maitreya is the Christ awaited by the Christians; to the Jews he is the Messiah, to the Moslems he is the Imam Mahdi, to the Buddhists he is the Fifth Buddha, to the Hindus he is Krishna. In the past, Creme tells us, these Ascended Masters have usually worked through disciples, but now they're among us and ready to help our world take its

next step. [Benjamin Creme's publication "Share International" is now produced in association with the U.N.'s Department of Public Information.]

34. July 8, 1987—The "Arizona Republic" reports: "For reasons unknown even to weather experts, the *temperature at Greensberg, Kansas, jumped 20 degrees in ten minutes.*" Bill Ellis, an observer for the National Weather Service, says: "I've never seen anything like it, and I don't know anybody that ever has." [A secret experiment in weather modification?]

35. Aug. 11, 1987—The U.S. Patent Office grants Patent Number 4,686,605 to Dr. Bernard Eastlund, a physicist who is a consultant for the Atlantic Richfield Company. Dr. Eastlund also does work for the Defense Department's ARPA (Advanced Research Projects Agency). The *patent* is for a technology to *"change the weather by redirecting the very high wind patterns."* By bombarding the jet stream with high-intensity electromagnetic waves, Dr. Eastlund is able to divert it and alter the weather patterns in a particular area.

36. June 1988—*Lord Maitreya* mysteriously appears before an audience in *Nairobi, Kenya.* [Maitreya has appeared to several groups in different parts of the world since that time. When Maitreya appears, it is claimed that water in the area is "charged"—that it takes on miraculous healing powers. Benjamin Creme's attitude toward those who refuse to accept this figure as the *world's Messiah* is seen in this statement: "When men see Maitreya they will know that *the time has come to choose; to go forward with Him into a future dazzling in its promise—or to cease to be.*"]

37. 1990—In his book "The Keys of This Blood," Catholic priest Malachi Martin quotes *Pope John Paul II* as saying: "By the *end of this decade* we will live under *the first One World Government* that has ever existed in the society of nations . . . a government with

absolute authority to decide the basic issues of survival. One world government is *inevitable.*"

38. Sept. 11, 1990—In an address to Congress entitled "Toward a New World Order," George Bush says: "The *crisis* in the Persian Gulf offers a *rare opportunity* to move toward an historic period of *cooperation.* Out of these troubled times a *new world order can emerge.* We are now in sight of a United Nations that performs as envisioned by its founders." [But who were the founders of the U.N. and what exactly were their intentions? At least 43 members of the U.S. delegation to the founding conference in San Francisco were also members of the CFR. The Secretary General at the U.N. founding conference in 1945 was a U.S. State Department official named Alger Hiss. It was later determined that Alger Hiss was a Soviet spy. He was convicted of perjury for lying about his pro-Soviet activities. And Hiss was not just an aberration. The U.N. has always chosen socialist one-worlders for leaders.]

39. 1991—President Bush praises the New World Order in a State of the Union Message: "What is at stake is more than one small country, it is a big idea—a new world order . . . to achieve the universal aspirations of mankind . . . based on shared principles and the rule of law . . . The illumination of a thousand points of light . . . The winds of change are with us now." [Theosophist Alice Bailey used that very same expression—"points of light"—in describing the process of occult enlightenment.]

40. 1991—On the *eve of the Gulf War,* General Brent Scowcroft, President Bush's National Security Advisor, proclaims: "A colossal event is upon us, the *birth of a New World Order.*"

41. July 1991—On a CNN program, former CIA Director Stansfield Turner (CFR), when asked about Iraq, responds: "We have a much bigger objective. We've got to look at the long run here.

This is an example—the situation between the United Nations and Iraq—where the *United Nations is deliberately intruding* into the sovereignty of a sovereign nation . . . Now this is a *marvelous precedent* to be *used in all countries of the world . . .*"

42. Aug. 1991—We are told that hard-liners in the Soviet Union have mounted a coup and that Mikhail Gorbachev has been arrested. The coup attempt fails, and this results in the apparent demise of the Soviet system and the installation of Boris Yeltsin. [It has since been learned that the "coup" was a sham designed to convince the West that Communism had fallen when in reality it had not. Mikhail Gorbachev had actually planned the staged coup three weeks before it happened. All the leaders of the coup have been pardoned and released.]

43. May 21, 1992—In an address to the Bilderberger organization meeting in Evian, France, former Secretary of State Henry Kissinger declares: "Today Americans would be outraged if U.N. troops entered Los Angeles to restore order; tomorrow they will be grateful! This is especially true if they were told there was an outside threat from beyond, whether real or promulgated, that threatened our very existence. It is then that all peoples of the world will plead with world leaders to deliver them from this evil. The one thing every man fears is the unknown. When presented with this scenario, individual rights will be willingly relinquished for the guarantee of their well being granted to them by their world government."

44. 1993—A second Parliament of World Religions is held in Chicago on the 100th anniversary of the first. Like the first convention, this one seeks *to join all the religions of the world* into "one harmonious whole," but it wants to make them "merge back into their original element." Traditional beliefs of monotheistic religions

such as *Christianity are considered incompatible* with individual "enlightenment" and *must be drastically altered.*

45. Sept. 23, 1994—The globalists realize that as more and more people begin to wake up to what's going on, they have only a limited amount of time in which to implement their policies. Speaking at the United Nations Ambassadors' dinner, David Rockefeller remarks: "This present window of opportunity, during which a truly peaceful and interdependent world order might be built, will not be open for too long." [Notice that he did not question if world order would come—only whether it would arrive peacefully.] He believes: "We are on the verge of a global transformation. All we need is the right major crisis and the nations will accept the New World Order."

46. June 1996—*Episcopal Bishop William Swing* moves to bring *all religions of the world into a single organization* called the UR (United Religions). The UR would be the *spiritual counterpart of the UN.* Swing plans to create a UR charter by June 1997 and to establish its headquarters in San Francisco by the year 2000. Christian denominations that say one can *only come to God through Jesus* Christ are considered *"intolerant"* and must be *forced to acknowledge* that there are *other* paths to God.

47. March 1997—In Benjamin Creme's "The Emergence" newsletter, readers are *alerted* that the coming of *Lord Maitreya*, the supposed New Age Christ, is at hand: *"Stand ready to see the Great Lord,* for the time of His emergence is nigh. Respond quickly to His call. End forever the hatred and intolerance of men."

48. June 17, 1998—The Transportation Department's National Highway Traffic Safety Administration issues a directive to implement driver's license-ID provisions passed by Congress. This directive contemplates requiring all states to submit certificates of

compliance to the Department of Transportation by September 30, 2000. The directive also "urges states to adopt as many security features as possible," including biometric devices—like fingerprints and retina-scan data. Rep. Ron Paul (R-TX) elaborates on this heavy-handed state of affairs: "Under the current state of the law, the citizens of states which have driver's licenses that do not conform to the federal standards by October 1, 2000, will find themselves essentially stripped of their ability to participate in life as we know it. On that date, Americans *will not be able to get a job, open a bank account, apply for Social Security or Medicare, exercise their Second Amendment rights, or even take an airplane flight, unless they can produce a state-issued ID that conforms to the federal specifications.*" [Many reasons have been advanced as justification for a national ID system—assurance of health care, tracking deadbeat dads, fighting illegal immigration. But no matter how noble or politically attractive the cause, no federal law or regulation is justifiable on moral or other grounds if it is unconstitutional in the first place. Americans ignore at their peril the promulgation of national IDs. A national ID has always been a cornerstone of totalitarianism. *The relentless push for a national ID brings us ever closer to the day when "no man might buy or sell, except that he had the mark of the beast."* (Rev. 13:17)]

FIG 2. MAP

APPENDIX II

Map of Proposed One World Order

(Presents_of_God_Ministry 2006)
Link: *www.RemnantofGod.org*

The Ten Kingdoms of the New World Government

Kingdom 1: Canada and the United States of America

Kingdom 2: European Union - Western Europe

Kingdom 3: Japan

Kingdom 4: Australia, New Zealand, South Africa, Israel and Pacific Islands

Kingdom 5: Eastern Europe

Kingdom 6: Latin America - Mexico, Central and South America

Kingdom 7: North Africa and the Middle East *(Moslems)*

Kingdom 8: Central Africa

Kingdom 9: South and Southeast Asia

Kingdom 10: Central Asia

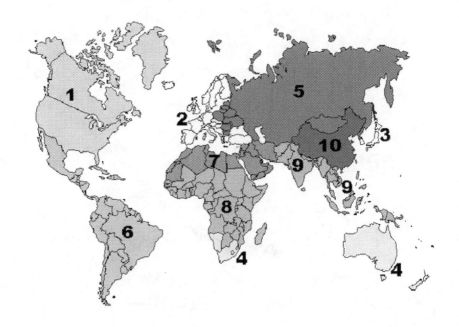

Adaptive Model of the Global World System

"The Club [of Rome] had its beginnings in April of 1968, when leaders from ten different countries gathered in Rome...**The organization claims to have the solutions for world peace and prosperity.**..The Club of Rome has been charged with the task of overseeing the regionalization and **unification of the entire world** . . .

"The Club's findings and recommendations are published from time to time in special, highly confidential reports, which are sent to the power-elite to be implemented. On 17 September 1973 the Club released one such report, entitled *Regionalized and Adaptive Model of the Global World System* . . . The document reveals that the Club has divided the world into *ten* **political/ economic regions, which it refers to as** *'kingdoms.'*"

FIG 3.

APPENDIX III

Nebuchadnnazer's Dream.

THE IMAGE AND DANIEL'S INTERPRETATION
(SOURCE: DANIEL CHAPTER 2)

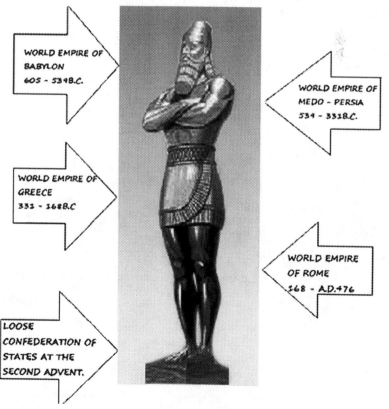

WORLD EMPIRE OF
BABYLON
605 - 539 B.C.

WORLD EMPIRE OF
MEDO - PERSIA
539 - 331 B.C.

WORLD EMPIRE OF
GREECE
331 - 168 B.C

WORLD EMPIRE
OF ROME
168 - A.D.476

LOOSE
CONFEDERATION OF
STATES AT THE
SECOND ADVENT.

APPENDIX IV

Claims of the Roman Catholic Church

POPE IS GOD ON EARTH

1. "The Pope is of so great dignity and so exalted that he is not a mere man, but as it were God, and the Vicar of God. The Pope is of such lofty and supreme dignity that properly speaking, he has not been established in any rank of dignity, but rather has been placed upon the very summit of all ranks of dignities . . . He is likewise the divine monarch and supreme emperor and king of kings. Hence the Pope is crowned with a triple crown, as King of Heaven and of Earth and of the Lower Regions."—Lucius Ferraris, *Prompta Bibliotheca*, vol. 6, pp. 438, 442.

2. "For thou art the shepherd, thou art the physician, thou art the husbandman; finally, thou art another God on earth."—Christopher Marcellus's Oration in the Fifth Lateran Council, 4th session. J. D. Mansi, *Sacrorum Councilliorum . . . Collectio*, volume 32, col. 761, translated.

3. "The Pope is supreme judge of the law of the land . . . He is the vicegerent of Christ, who is not only a Priest forever, but also King

of kings and Lord of lords."—*La Civilta Cattolica*, March 18, 1871, quoted in Leonard Woolsey Bacon, *An Inside View of the Vatican Council,* American Tract Society, p. 229.

4. "The Pope is not only the representative of Jesus Christ, but he is Jesus Christ, hidden under a veil of flesh."—*The Catholic National,* July 1895.

5. "We hold upon this earth the place of God Almighty." *Pope Leo XIII, in an Encyclical Letter, dated June 20, 1894.*

SUNDAY: PAPAL MARK OF AUTHORITY

6. "Prove to me from the Bible alone that I am bound to keep Sunday holy. There is no such law in the Bible. It is the law of the holy Catholic Church alone. The Bible says "Remember the Sabbath day to keep it holy." The Catholic Church says, No. By my divine power I abolish the Sabbath day and command you to keep holy the first day of the week. And lo! The entire civilized world bows down in reverend obedience to the command of the Holy Catholic Church."—Thomas Enright, CSSR, President, Redemptorist College (Roman Catholic), Kansas City, MO., February 18, 1884.

7. "The observance of Sunday by the Protestants is an homage they pay, in spite of themselves, to the authority of the (Catholic) church."—Monsignor Louis Segur, *Plain talk About the Protestantism of Today,* (1868), p. 213.

8. "If Protestants would follow the Bible, they should worship God on the Sabbath Day (Saturday). In keeping Sunday, they are following a law of the Catholic Church."—Albert Smith, Chancellor of the Archdiocese of Baltimore, replying for the Cardinal in a letter of February 10, 1920.

9. "The State, in passing laws for the due sanctification of Sunday, is unwittingly acknowledging the authority of the Catholic Church, and carrying out more or less faithfully its prescriptions."

10. "The Sunday, as a day of the week set apart for the obligatory public worship of Almighty God, to be sanctified by suspension of all servile labour, trade, and worldly avocations and by exercises of devotion, is purely a creation of the Catholic Church."—*The American catholic Quarterly Review,* January, 1883, pp. 152, 139.

11. "Protestants . . . accept Sunday rather that Saturday as the day for public worship after the Catholic Church made the change . . . But the Protestant mind does not seem to realize that . . . in observing the Sunday, they are accepting the authority of the spokesman for the church, the Pope."—*Our Sunday Visitor*, February 5, 1950.

12. "It is well to remind the Presbyterians, Baptists, Methodists and all other Christians, that the Bible does not support them anywhere in their observance of Sunday. Sunday is an institution of the Catholic Church, and those who observe the day observe a commandment of the Catholic Church."—Priest Brady, in an address, reported in the *Elizabeth*, N.J. "News," March 18, 1903.

BIBLIOGRAPHY

Catholic Baltimore Cathechism No. 3.

Cyberpatriot. "Geocities.com." *The Architecture of Modern Political Power.* 2010. http://www.geocities.com/CapitolHill/Lobby/1887/secondessay.htm (accessed 2009).

Davis, John D et al. *Westminster Dictionary of the Bible.* Edited by Henry Snyder Gehman. London & New York: The Westminster Press, 1944.

Der Spiegel. 1997.

Encyclopedia Britannica. www.britannica.com (accessed November 11, 2010).

Ferraris, Lucius. *Prompta Bibliotheca.* Vol. 6.

Hill, Jenny. "Ancient Egypt on Line." *Religion in Ancient Egypt: Bull Cults.* 2010. http://www.ancientegyptonline.co.uk/bullcult.html (accessed June 16, 2011).

http://www.jeremiahproject.com/prophecy/ecumen01.html. (accessed May 7, 2011).

Hyslop, Alexander. "The Two Babylons." *Philologos.org.* April 1901. http://philologos.org/__eb-ttb/ (accessed June 4, 2011).

Icke, David. *The Biggest Secret.* Scottsdale: Bridge of Love Publications, 1999.

Marcussen, Jan A. *National Sunday Law.* Thompsonville, Illinois: Amazing Truth Publcations, 2004.

New World Encyclopedia—Organizing knowledge for happiness, prosperity, and world peace. June 2, 2008. http://www.newworldencyclopedia.org/entry/Osiris (accessed May 7, 2011).

Paulien Ph.D., Jon. *What is Armageddon? Investigating "Armageddon".* 2010 © Jon Paulien. 2010. http://www.thebattleofarmageddon.com/article-2.html#_ftnref1 (accessed May 14, 2011).

Presents_of_God_Ministry. *Globalization: Sooner rather then Later.* June 2006. http://www.remnantofgod.org/ (accessed December 21, 2010).

Reninger, Elizabeth. *Maitreya.info—emergence of THE WORLD TEACHER.* November 15, 2006. http://www.maitreya.info/media/return-christ.html (accessed May 7, 2011).

Report, Roundtable. *Preparation for The Reappearance of the World Spiritual Teacher—The Work of the United Nations and the World-Wide Esoteric Communi.* April 7, 2001. http://www.aquaac.org/meetings/RT2001Report.html.

Segur, Monsignor. *Plain Talk About the Protestantism of Today.*

"The American Heritage Dictionary of the English Language." *The American Heritage Dictionary of the English Language.* 4th. Houghton Mifflin Company, 2009.

The Catholic Record. Septermber 1, 1923.

Weber, Gudrun S. "Diamond Light." *Newsletter of the Aquarian Age Community.* Aquarian Age Community. 2005. http://www.aquaac.org/dl/05nl1art2.html (accessed June 16, 2011).

White, Ellen G. *Fundamentals of Christian Education.* Nashville, Tennessee: Southern Publishing Association, 1923.

—. *Testimonies for the Church.* Vol. 8. 9 vols. Mountain View, CA: Pacific Press Publishing Association, 1948.

White, Ellen G. *The Great Controversy Between Christ and Satan.* Vol. 1. 8 vols. Mountain View, CA: Pacific Press Publishing Association, 1911.

Whitham, A R. *The History of the Christian Church to the Separation of East and West.* Fouth. London: Rivingstons, 1957.

Wikipedia. *Illuminati.* May 9, 2011. http://en.wikipedia.org/wiki/The_Illuminati (accessed May 15, 2011).

—. *Louis-Alexandre Berthier.* May 11, 2011. http://en.wikipedia.org/wiki/General_Berthier (accessed May 15, 2011).

—. *Radio-frequency Identification.* May 10, 2011. http://en.wikipedia.org/wiki/Radio-frequency_identification#Human_implants (accessed May 13, 2011).

NOTES

Introduction

1. The Reformation was the response of true Christians to the apostasy of Rome. John Wycliffe, John Calvin, Martin Luther, John Huss, and others are some of the best known names in this movement to restore truth where the enemy had sown error. It is also known as the Protestant Movement. Read *The Great Controversy* by Ellen G. White (see bibliography) for a fuller coverage of this phase of church history.

2. Quoted from *The Great Controversy*, Harvestine Books edition, Atlamont, U.S.A. 1998. Supplement to chapter 3, Forty-eight steps down, pp. 78-79.

Chapter 4

3. Secret Society - Any of various oath-bound societies devoted to brotherhood (or sisterhood), moral discipline, and mutual assistance. Such societies usually conduct rituals of initiation to instruct new

members in the rules of the group (see rite of passage). Greek and Roman mystery religions had their secular counterparts in clandestine social clubs, some of which served as platforms for political dissent. In West Africa secret societies such as Poro (for men) and Sande (for women) serve to translate slight advantages of wealth and prestige into political authority. In parts of New Guinea secret men's societies serve as repositories of tribal knowledge. Fraternal orders such as the Freemasons (see Freemasonry) may be considered secret societies, as may criminal groups such as the Mafia and the Chinese Triads and hate groups such as the Ku Klux Klan. (Encyclopedia Britannica n.d.)

Chapter 5

4. Read Ezra 4:6 and Numbers. 14:34.
5. Read the books Daniel Revels the Future and Revelation of Things to Come, both by Robert J Wieland, published by Stanborough Press Ltd.
6. A heretic was effectively any person whose beliefs and opinions contrary to the doctrine of the Roman Catholic Church.
7. See Appendix IV: Claims of the Catholic Church.
8. The church visible and invisible are discussed in chapter 16.
9. Pope John Paul II issued a series of apologies between 1992 and 2001. They can be found at many web sites by searching for "apologies of Pope John Paul II." Examples are http://en.wikipedia.org/wiki/Apologies_by_Pope_John_Paul_II and http://www.religioustolerance.org/pope_apo.htm.

Chapter 6

10. The Illuminati (plural of Latin illuminatus, "enlightened") is a name given to several groups, both historical and modern, and both real

and fictitious. Historically, the name refers specifically to the Bavarian Illuminati, an Enlightenment-era secret society founded on May 1, 1776. In modern times it is also used to refer to a purported conspiratorial organization which acts as a shadowy "power behind the throne", allegedly controlling world affairs through present day governments and corporations, usually as a modern incarnation or continuation of the Bavarian Illuminati. In this context, the Illuminati are believed to be the masterminds behind events that will lead to the establishment of a New World Order. (Wikipedia 2011, The Illuminati)

11. "Ecumenism," is defined as *the organized attempt to bring about the cooperation and unity of all believers in Christ."* . . . We saw the beginning of institutional ecumenism in the 1960's, with The World Council of Churches. . . . Today, however, that spirit of compromise has invaded Evangelicalism. . . . What we're seeing instead is a broadening of the gospel, a redefining of what it means to be a Christian, and a growing emphasis on inclusion and tolerance. Ecumenism has come to mean "reducing all elements of faith to the lowest common denominator" . . . and sound doctrine and correction are despised as "divisive" and "unloving." (http://www.jeremiahproject.com/prophecy/ecumen01.html n.d.)

12. The World-Wide Esoteric Community—"The great task before the world-wide esoteric community is to unite spirit and matter in consciousness without falling into separation." ((Weber 2005)

Chapter 12

13. Amnesia—loss of memory (Oxford)

14. The most famous of the bull cults is undoubtedly that of the Apis bull (also known as the Hapis Bull or "Hapi-ankh"). The bull was the incarnation of a god, but unlike the other animal totems (who only provided a link

to the god) the Apis was thought to host the god himself. The Apis bull was originally viewed as the manifestation of Ptah. However, the Apis was soon linked to Osiris when Ptah and Osiris merged and so Plutarch described the Apis as the "fair and beautiful image of the soul of Osiris". According to one myth the Apis was the living embodiment of Ptah while he lived and Osiris when he died. (Hill 2010)

15. Wikipedia. (http://en.wikipedia.org/wiki/Week-day_names)

Chapter 14

16. This calculation is intended only to convey the idea that Satan has many more lieutenants that living men. It should be considered qualitatively, rather than quantitatively.

17. 'Ngozi' is the name given to the (supposed) spirit of a murdered person, which has returned to exact vengeance on the murderer and his family.

18. Please note, the terms 'dead man', 'prophet', 'man of God', 'holy water' and 'holy spirit' are used without qualifying, in order to portray what I believed at the time.

19. A bira is an all-night dance ceremony where traditional sorghum beer is consumed in honour of ancestral spirits.

20. The terms 'prophet', 'man of God', 'holy water' and 'holy spirit' are used without qualifying, in order to portray what I believed at the time.

21. *Sangoma* (*pl. zangoma*) is a word understood by many, in the Southern African region, to mean witchdoctor.

Chapter 15

22. **Osiris** (whose name is a Greek transliteration of the Egyptian *Asar*) is the Egyptian god of life, death, fertility, and the underworld. His extreme antiquity is attested to by his inclusion in pyramid texts dated

to 2400 b.c.E., when his cult was already well established. In addition to the god's primary mythic and religious affiliation with the land of the dead, Osiris was also seen as the underworld agency that granted all life, including sprouting vegetation and the fertile flooding of the Nile River. (New World Encyclopedia - Organizing knowledge for happiness, prosperity, and world peace 2008)

23. See Appendix III for a picture of the image and Daniel's interpretation.

24. *The Catholic Record*, London, Ontario, September 1, 1923.

25. **Radio-frequency identification (RFID)** is a technology that uses communication through the use of radio waves to exchange data between a reader and an electronic tag attached to an object, for the purpose of identification and tracking . . . It is possible in the near future, RFID technology will continue to proliferate in our daily lives the way that bar code technology did over the forty years leading up to the turn of the 21st century bringing unobtrusive but remarkable changes when it was new . . . RFID makes it possible to give each product in a grocery store its own unique identifying number, to provide assets, people, work in process, medical devices etc. all with individual unique identifiers - like the license plate on a car but for every item in the world . . . In October 2004, the FDA approved USA's first RFID chips that can be implanted in humans. The 134 kHz RFID chips, from VeriChip Corp. can incorporate personal medical information and could save lives and limit injuries from errors in medical treatments, according to the company . . . Implantable RFID chips designed for animal tagging are now being used in humans. An early experiment with RFID implants was conducted by British professor of cybernetics Kevin Warwick, who implanted a chip in his arm in 1998. In 2004 Conrad Chase offered implanted chips in his night clubs in Barcelona[69]

and Rotterdam to identify their VIP customers, who in turn use it to pay for drinks. (Wikipedia 2011. http://en.wikipedia.org/wiki/Radio-frequency_identification#Human_implants)

26. Tsunami (Tsunamis) A very large ocean wave caused by an underwater earthquake or volcanic eruption.

Chapter 17

27. Time = 1 year = **360** days; times = 2 years = **720** days; and half a time = 6 months = **180** days; total =**1260** days. 1 day = 1 prophetic year; therefore period of persecution = **1260** years.

28. Table adapted from 'Instruction Manual for the New "Pictorial Aid" by Frank Braeden. Study Guide No. 43. Page 175.'

Appendix I

29. British neo-Theosophical occultist Alice Bailey, one of the founders of the so-called New Age movement, prophesied in 1940 the eventual victory of the Allies of World War II over the Axis powers (which occurred in 1945) and the establishment by the Allies of a political and religious New World Order. She saw a federal world government . . . guided by the Masters of the Ancient Wisdom, intent on preparing humanity for the mystical second coming of Christ, and the dawning of the Age of Aquarius. According to Bailey, a group of ascended masters called the Great White Brotherhood works on the "inner planes" to oversee the transition to the New World Order but, for now, the members of this Spiritual Hierarchy are only known to a few occult scientists, with whom they communicate telepathically, but as the need

for their personal involvement in the plan increases, there will be an "Externalization of the Hierarchy" and everyone will know of their presence on Earth. (*New World Order (Conspiracy Theory)*, Accessed from www.wikipedia.com, Dec. 22, 2010.)